ANTI-POVERTY PROGRAMMES IN RURAL INDIA

ANTI-POVERTY PROGRAMMES IN RURAL INDIA

DR. NEERAJ SHARMA

DEEP & DEEP PUBLICATIONS PVT. LTD.
F-159, Rajouri Garden, New Delhi - 110 027

ANTI-POVERTY PROGRAMMES IN RURAL INDIA

ISBN 978-81-8450-278-7

Printed in India at MAYUR ENTERPRISES
WZ Plot No. 3, Gujjar Market, Tihar Village, New Delhi - 110 018

Published by DEEP & DEEP PUBLICATIONS PVT. LTD.,
F-159, Rajouri Garden, New Delhi - 110 027 • Phones : 25435369, 25440916
E-mail : ddpubs@gmail.com • ddpbooks@yahoo.co.in
Showroom :
2/13, Ansari Road, Daryaganj, New Delhi - 110 002 • Telefax : 23245122

Dedicated to

My Loving Children

Aditya & Apoorva

Contents

Preface

Poverty is an acute problem in many Third World countries. It remains the biggest challenge in the developmental efforts to bring about a perceptible change in the quality of life of teeming millions in these countries. It has been one of the vexed issues of politics, economics and international relations of the second half of twentieth century. The developing nations are caught in the vicious circle of poverty on account of capital deficiency and are passing through very critical times. Poverty arises mainly due to occupational concentration of population in agriculture, traditional methods of farming and therefore, low labour productivity and lack of employment opportunities outside agriculture. Poverty is a complex problem. It is an outgrowth of the impact of political process and policy development. It perpetuates despite the consistent efforts being made through the planned development process. At the beginning of the new millennium 260 million people in India did not have incomes to access a consumption basket which defines the poverty line. Of these 75 per cent were in the rural areas. India is a home to 22 per cent of the world poor. Such a high incidence of poverty is a matter of concern in view of the fact that poverty eradication has been one of the major objectives of the development planning process.

Since Rural Development is aimed at alleviating poverty, it must be clearly planned and designed to increase production and raise productivity not only of the country in general but of the rural poor in particular. National objectives of rural development should also recognize that the improved food supplies and nutrition, along with other basic services such as health and education, are not only necessary for direct improvement of the well-being and better quality of life of the rural poor, but also are essentially required to play an important role to enhance their productivity and their ability to contribute to the nation's economy. The operative objectives of rural development are rather complex in nature and extend beyond any particular sector. Besides increasing the national income and productivity to attain a satisfactory Gross Domestic Product (GDP), they should include improved productivity and thus higher income for the target groups of rural poor simultaneously as well as a minimum acceptable level of food, shelter, education and health services. Fulfilment of these complex nature objectives causes an expansion of goods and services available in the country, with particular reference to the rural poor to benefit fully from the whole range of economic and social services, so that the development process can be made self-sustainable. In order to ensure growth with social justice it is necessary that the target groups be properly identified and encouraged to actively participate in the organization and implementation of the programmes.

Objectives of rural development programmes must be clearly spelled out for organising, planning and implementation of the programme involving adequate local planning, strong co-ordination at all levels of administration, including the operational level, creation of effective local level organizations and active participation of the village people including the rural poor in both planning and implementing process.

In order to help the rural poor to increase their production and income, it is necessary to assist them to improve their existing resources and also encourage them to acquire new assets. Hence asset development and asset availability are two important objectives in any programme for alleviating rural poverty.

The present study on the impact of poverty alleviation programmes on the socio-economic conditions of weaker sections in rural areas of Haryana is composed of nine Chapters.

Chapter I deals with the general introduction of poverty, various poverty alleviation programmes and an overview of the region under study. The review of the related studies has been presented in *Chapter II*. The definition of concepts and the methods of analysis have been dealt with in *Chapter III*. *Chapter IV* deals with the demographic and socio-economic profile of the sample households. The distribution pattern of household assets and household income among the sample households has been presented in *Chapter V*. The pattern of human labour time utilization as well as the extent of unemployment among the sample households has been presented in *Chapter VI*. *Chapter VII* deals with the pattern of household consumption expenditure and the value of poverty index among the sample households both before and after the implementation of poverty alleviation programmes. The nature and extent of savings, indebtedness and the impact of anti-poverty programmes on the assets, income, employment and consumption have been dealt with in *Chapter VIII*, whereas, *Chapter IX* deals with the summary and conclusions of the present study.

NEERAJ SHARMA

Acknowledgements

It is my proud privilege to thank all those who helped me directly or indirectly in the completion of this research work.

I am extremely grateful to Prof. Dalip Singh Thakur, Department of Economics, Himachal Pradesh University, Shimla whose able guidance, sustained encouragement, constructive criticism and valuable suggestions enabled me to complete this research work. This work is a reward of his blessings.

I am thankful to all the faculty members of the Department of Economics, Himachal Pradesh University, Shimla for their moral support during the course of this study.

I owe very special debt of gratitude to Prof. R.K. Gupta, Department of Correspondence Courses who helped and encouraged me at every stage of this work with his inestimable suggestions.

I am thankful to Sh. Ranvir Gupta, Economic and Statistical Advisor to Government of Haryana and District Statistical Officers for the cooperation extended to me in making available useful materials and documents for this research work.

I am highly grateful to Sh. Vijayendra Kumar, IAS, Deputy Commissioner, Yamunanagar, Sh. Brijender Singh, IAS, Additional Deputy Commissioner, Yamunanagar; Sh. Hukam Singh Rana, Assistant Project Officer, District Rural Development Agency, Yamunanagar and Sh. Raj Pal Singh,

Economic Officer, Planning Commission, Government of India for providing me relevant material and information in time for the present work.

I acknowledge my indebtedness to all the sample households of the study area who supplied the relevant information at the time of data collection to me. I am also thankful to the Block Development Officers of district Yamunanagar and the staff for providing me the lists of beneficiaries under different poverty alleviation programmes.

I am thankful to the Department of Rural Development, Haryana, Department of Census Operations, Haryana; Department of Agriculture, Haryana; Planning Commission, Government of India for extending the required facilities to me whenever needed.

With pleasure I put on record my gratitude and appreciation for the staff of Panjab University Library, Chandigarh; Himachal Pradesh University Library, Shimla; Libraries of Political Science and Economics Departments of Panjab University, Chandigarh.

I owe a sense of admiration to Prof. Suman Sharma, Dr. Rakbir Kaur, Sh. Ranvir Parashar from the Department of Evening Studies, Panjab University for their constant encouragement during the course of this research work.

I find no words to express my gratitude to my parents whose love and moral support keeps me always enthusiastic and never allows the fountain of hope dry up in me. I feel indebted to my brothers Sanjay, Ajay and sister Meenakshi, my nieces Ritu and Priyanka for their cooperation and encouragement in this pursuit.

I have no words to express my deep heartfelt thanks and appreciation to my loving and understanding son Aditya and daughter Apoorva who cooperated with me by foregoing their right for claims on my time and attention during the pursuit of my work. Without their patience and forbearance the realization of this work would not have been possible.

Perhaps, above all, much more than the usual debt of gratitude must be expressed to my closest friend and husband 'Raj', who is an eternal source of motivation, encouragement and heartily devotion in ways more than I can enumerate and acknowledge in completion of this research work. He not only provided me a congenial atmosphere for studies at home, but also relieved me from a number of family responsibilities and even more, at times, directly helped me in my work.

I extend my special thanks to Sh. J. Gandhi for his diligent and efficient typing of this work during the shortest possible time.

NEERAJ SHARMA

1

Introduction

Securing rapid economic growth and expansion of employment, reduction of inequalities in income and wealth and prevention of concentration of economic power and creation of the values and attitudes of a free and equal society have been among the objectives of all our Five Year Plans. One of the most striking experiences of planned efforts in India is that economically backward and socially oppressed people in the underdeveloped regions have gained little. Benefits of successive Five Year Plans have passed more to the already developed regions, and even within sub-regions, benefits accrued proportionately more to the already rich and socially privileged sections of the society, perpetuating social inequalities and disparities of wealth and income distribution. The benefits of planning accruing only to a selected region and selected people are undesirable from the point of view of balanced regional development and distributive Justice.[1]

The prosperity of an economy depends on the standard of living of its inhabitants. Therefore, the primary objective of development policies in an economy is to achieve growth with 'Social Justice'. Economic development of an economy means higher per capita real income, accompanied by an increase both in production and productivity, reduction in the inequalities of income and asset distribution and removal of poverty and unemployment.

The co-existence of relatively developed and economically depressed States and regions within each State is known as regional inequality. There exist wide regional variations in terms of per capita income, the proportion of population living below the normative minimum, working population in agriculture, the per centage of urban population to total population, the per cent age of workers in manufacturing industries etc. in India.[2]

Regional imbalances may be natural or man-made. Natural imbalances arise due to unequal natural endowments. Man-made imbalances are caused by the neglect of some regions and preference for others for investment and developmental activities. Regional imbalances may be inter-state or intra-state; they may be total or sectoral.[3] Economic backwardness of a region is indicated by factors like high pressure of population on land resulting in low productivity and large scale disguised unemployment, low level of industrialisation, absence of large scale urbanisation, absence of social and economic infrastructural facilities, etc.

The inequalities are natural as well as man-made. The natural inequalities occur mainly due to different geographical conditions prevailing in different regions, climatic differences, different topography and differences in soils, while the man-made disparities are caused by inequitable distribution of means of production, economic concentration, poverty, tax evasion, capital-intensive technology, low productivity per unit of labour, unemployment and under development, population growth, lack of irrigation, employment opportunities in the industrial sector, transportation, power, education and health facilities.

Removal of regional inequalities has now become a cherished objective of all regions.[4] Therefore, serious attempts are being made by the governments to simultaneously develop all sectors of their economies on account of the awakening as well as the main objective of social equity in the field of economic development. The concept implicitly argues a case for economic equality in resource allocation to develop various economic activities so as to reduce economic distances within as well as between different regions.

During the decade of 1950s and 1960s exclusive emphasis was laid on raising the aggregate rate of growth of domestic product. This tendency was reinforced by international aid agencies, which, set growth targets and devised 'performance' indicators on the basis of which assistance was allocated. This focus on aggregate rates of growth was prompted by the belief that the rapid industrialisation and structural transformation would spread the benefits of growth throughout the various strata of society eventually by the 'Trickle Down Process.' It was assumed that 'reduction of poverty could be tackled only after a certain level of Gross National Product (GNP) had been reached. First the cake had to be produced and made bigger before it could be equally distributed. Equitable income distribution, while acknowledged as a desirable objective, was traded for the immediate goal of maximizing the GNP. In the idioms of the period there was no point in becoming concerned about distribution when there was practically nothing to distribute. Once higher income levels were attained, distribution was supposed to exert its leveling effect with greater ease through the 'Trickle Down Process'. Hence greater inequality in the earlier stages followed as a necessary precondition for rapid growth in some leading growth models. This initial trade-off between the objectives of growth and distribution was viewed as a transitional cost of successful development before their eventual complimentarity was established.[5]

For many years, economic theories, which depicted growth as a function of increase in capital stock dominated which wrongly believed in the automatic trickle down effect to alleviate rural poverty once the GNP of the country improves. The concept of growth with equity was not thought of and target-oriented development was unknown. Although the target-oriented approach has been accepted since India's Fourth Five Year Plan and has covered the entire country in the Sixth Five Year Plan, it is not progressing as expected.[6] The absolute number of the poor especially in the developing countries is increasing. The basic problem of tackling poverty is equitable distribution of food stuffs and means to acquire such basic ingredients which allow the poor to have an active and healthy living. Although economic theory explains the phenomenon of poverty, yet it fails to provide any solution. It is observed that economic theory during the last two hundred years has been mainly concerned with those who were already rich, through control of capital and land to become further rich while the distribution dimension has been given minimum attention. There is a need to develop a new economic theory which should show greater sensitivity to questions concerning the distribution of opportunity and wealth, both between and within nations.[7]

In the context of national economy of our country, it has been observed that growth in GNP has not been able to reduce the widespread poverty marked by technological backwardness of agricultural sector. Further, the incapacity of even technologically advanced sectors such as industry to absorb the fast growing labour force as a result of population growth resulted in increased unemployment. Again due to rise in population the expansion of the education and health care, vital for human resource development were restricted. Population pressure in the country also forced to go in for foreign aid, thus generating economic dependency.[8]

The ultimate aim of economic growth must be the betterment of living conditions of the poor. Economic growth that does not lead to sharp and sustained reductions in poverty may create more problems than it solves. Similarly, if rapid economic growth can be achieved only at the expense of worsening the distribution of resources, such growth would ultimately become unsustainable as it would create social tensions. It is indeed possible to imagine a situation in which economic growth leads to such worse economic inequality that poverty actually rises.[9]

Dandekar and Rath (1971)[10] stated that : "the problem of poverty in India is a problem of low national income and its unequal distribution, of slow pace of development and inequitable distribution of the small gains of development."

Mansoor Ali (1979)[11] rightly remarked that, it can not be definitely said that economic welfare has increased even if real national income and real per capita income has risen, until and unless the resultant distribution of income is also considered. Even the growth theory according to which rapid industrialisation and structural transformations would spread the benefits of growth among the various strata of society eventually by 'trickle-down process' has failed to reduce the social and economic inequalities in the Indian situation. In addition to growth aspect emphasis should also be laid on the redistributional aspect through the spread of education, wage creation, and asset transfer policies so that the benefits of development can reach directly to each and every down-trodden category of the society.

Kurian (1978)[12] stated that mass poverty and chronic under-utilization of the vast human potential are widely recognized as our most pressing problems. Poverty, for instance, is no abstract drawback of the economy. It is a concrete fact that all over the country there are men, women and children who do not have drinking water within their reach. It is the fact of the farm workers in Uttar Pradesh who have no land of their own to cultivate and can not find enough work on other peoples' land. It is the problem of the thronging millions in Calcutta and Bombay who do not have a roof over their heads, if such is the nature of poverty, its eradication can also be only in terms of such common everyday categories; food for the hungry, work for the jobless, shelter for the homeless and cloth for the naked. Thus the term poverty may be defined as the socio-economic phenomenon whereby the resources available to a society are used to satisfy the wants of the few while the many do not have even their basic needs met.

The *Publication of United Nations ESCAP (1985)*[13] *states:* "The rural poor may not be all starving but more often they are malnourished and frequently suffer from diseases. These rural poor are mostly illiterate or not much educated. They are insufficiently clothed, mostly bare footed and often live in temporary houses roofed with grass and located in unsanitary conditions. This section of the poor further lacks sufficient resources to purchase food and other necessities of life and is forbidden to enjoy the living conditions which are customary in their societies. Their purchasing power is very low as a result of which they are excluded from normal living pattern, customs and other activities.

In India some factors responsible for poverty are internal to a person such as low calorie intake, malnutrition, sickness, low mental and physical capabilities and hence low productive capacity. Whereas, some other factors causing poverty are external to the poor person like absence of proper socio-economic infrastructure viz. rural roads, safe drinking water, schools and hospitals or lack of opportunity to bear a proper means of livelihood. It is a combination of both internal and external forces which causes poverty. Besides, the above factors, the magnitude of poverty that the Indian society is confronted with is the result of many other factors such as faulty distribution system and natural calamity. Whereas, one part of the country faces draught another part faces flood simultaneously.[14]

Mass poverty in India is also the result of the low resources base of the poor who own a very small portion of the total assets in the form of land, capital, house, property, etc. The low resource-base of the poor inhibits them from providing education and training to their children. As a result, the children of the poor are, by and large, either engaged in unskilled occupations or some semi-skilled occupations. This enables them to earn a very low and meagre wages and thus perpetuates poverty. Poverty in India is also a consequence of obsolete methods of production and the exploitative social structure.

P.D. Ojha (1970)[15] rightly remarked that "the phenomenon of relative poverty is found to exist even in affluent societies such as the United States of America; the relative status is largely a subjective matter. The absolute level of poverty is a question of fact and it is not based on any subjective judgment. The estimates of people below such a 'poverty line' refer to those who are unable to earn a physical sustenance, let alone other minimum comforts."

Thus there are two concepts of poverty viz.; relative and absolute poverty. While relative poverty is measured in terms of inequality in the distribution of income, absolute poverty is reckoned in terms of same kind of notion of subsistence considered appropriate to the circumstances of the country concerned. In a developing country like India where incomes are low, absolute poverty is generally reflected mainly in inadequacy of food-intake and the consequent under-nourishment on a mass scale, though the definition of subsistence appropriate to such countries might (in fact should) also include other essential minimum needs such as clothing, housing, fuel, light, education and health, etc.[16]

Poverty as a concept is closely related to inequality. Given the average income level, a higher level of inequality (reflected by the usual measures) will tend to be associated with a higher level of poverty. Furthermore, the so-called 'poverty line' may sometimes be drawn in the light of socially accepted 'minimal' standard of living, and the latter can be influenced by the average income level, so that poverty measures, thus defined may catch an aspect of 'relative' inequality as well.[17] Poverty has been identified not merely with inequality but also with unemployment. Dandekar and Rath have defined it as "an adequate level of employment . . . in terms of its capacity to provide minimum living to the population".[18] In his four-fold classification of unemployment Raj Krishna, identifies this approach to unemployment as 'the income criterion'.[19]

There are, however, two major problems involved in defining the concept of poverty. The first relates to the problem of identifying the 'poor' and the second is the problem of 'measurement'. The terms such as 'poor' 'disadvantaged', 'economically weak' and 'less privileged' are used interchangeably. But the specific groups to which these descriptions are applied differ from study to study; the reference is to either socially backward groups pursuing economic activities which do not provide reasonable levels of living. The differences in the nomenclatures and their application to specific sections of the population notwithstanding the basic underlying characteristics of the groups described as poor or weak or disadvantaged or miserably low levels of income and the palpably small productive resources at their command. A considerable body of evidences exists to show that the bulk of the low-income population is concentrated in households engaged in cultivation on small holdings and agricultural labour; these households typically combine other low income rural occupations such as non-agricultural labour, traditional rural arts and crafts, and low grade professions such as barbers, cobblers, tailor, weavers and potter, etc. Consideration of these two categories of households as the low-income sections would, therefore, be adequate. Secondly, small landholders and labourers belong overwhelmingly to low social strata composed of relatively low

Hindu castes, scheduled castes and scheduled tribes and in some case religious minorities.[20]

The magnitude of poverty can be measured both in relative as well as absolute terms. Bhatty (1974)[21] stated that both absolute and relative poverty are closely aligned to inequality in income distribution. Relative poverty arises entirely as a consequence of an unequal distribution of income irrespective of what the income level or the corresponding state of deprivation, of the people at the bottom end of the income scale might be. Absolute poverty, on the other hand, expresses a collective view as deprivation in its somewhat physical manifestation. Thus, wherever be the line any society chooses to draw to separate deprivation from relative comfort, those on the wrong side of the line are defined as poor irrespective of how comfortable or affluent the others may be. The fact that the sense of deprivation among the poor may also depend on how wide the gap between their income and the income of those who are not poor, is not a consideration relevant to the notion of absolute poverty, though it very much is to the notion of relative poverty.

The magnitude of relative poverty is usually measured with the help of Head Count ratio, Lorenz Curve, Gini-coefficient, Sen's Index of Poverty, etc., whereas the extent of absolute poverty is measured with the help of 'normative measures' wherein comparison between actual levels of aggregate utility and the level of total utility if income were equally divided and the 'equally distributed equivalent income' of a given distribution of a total income, are based on the value of utility of each person which is quite a subjective and arbitrary approach based on the judgment of individuals. The minimum nutrient requirement norms fixed by the specialised agencies are comparatively more valid and is mostly used in measuring the extent of poverty since 1960s in India. The nutritional approach to the problem provides a little more than an index of poverty. It enables us to gain some very necessary insight into the structure of poverty and, by implication, the policy requirements of any poverty-eradication programme.[22]

On the basis of minimum nutrients required norms 'poverty line' can be determined in terms of the value of consumption basket of food and non-food items which provides a minimum subsistence for a family as a whole or for each member of the family separately. The minimum subsistence level of food-items is determined in terms of the value of calorie-intake and the value of subsistence of non-food items such as clothing, fuel, light, health and education, etc. is determined on the basis of minimum human needs and other relevant factors within the society. The value equivalent of such a consumption basket (food and non-food items) of household on per capita basis is considered as a dividing line, where those who earn and/or spend less than this value are 'poor' and those who earn and/or spend more than this figure are 'not poor'. This is termed as 'Critical Poverty Point'. There is no consensus on the minimum per capita requirement of calories for a population and naturally so, since a number of variables like age, sex, body weight, nature of occupation, topography and climatic conditions, etc., affect the energy expenditure. The Planning Commission on the recommendation of nutrition experts has defined poverty line on the basis of the value of 2400 calories per person per day for rural areas and 2100 calories per person per day for urban areas. In case of non-food items there is an even greater degree of arbitrariness, because the minimum needs norms and the other factors like topography, climatic conditions, nature and intensity of economic activities carried out by the people, vary from region to region within a country and/or a State.

Since independence and in all our plans special attention has been paid to the weaker sections and there have been many policy measures directed specifically towards their welfare in response to the constitutional provisions that "the state shall promote with special care the educational and economic interests of the weaker sections of the people, and in particular of the scheduled caste and scheduled tribes, and shall protect them from social injustice and all forms of exploitation.[23]

In the draft of First Five Year Plan it has been stated, "The central objective of planning in India is to raise the standard of living of the people and to open to them opportunities for a richer and more varied life. Planning must, therefore, aim both at utilising more effectively, the resources, human and material available to the community so as to obtain from them a larger output of goods and services, and also at reducing inequalities of income, wealth and opportunity. A programme aiming only at raising output might result in most of the increased wealth flowing into the hands of a few, leaving the masses of the people in the present state of poverty."[24]

The main objective of the First Five Year Plan (1951-56) was to initiate a process of all round balanced development which would ensure a rising national income and a steady improvement in living standard over a period. During this Plan Community Development Programme (CDP) and National Extension Service in 1953 were introduced. The Programme laid emphasis on all round development of the whole of the country with special emphasis on weaker and under privileged sections through the area development. The Community Development Programme could not bring expected improvement in conditions of rural areas nor could much success be achieved in the area of agricultural development. This culminated in the adoption of Intensive Agricultural District Programme (IADP).[25] Second Five Year Plan (1956-61) aimed at setting up of a "socialist pattern of society" or development along socialist lines. Indian planners visualised the establishment of a socialist society in which everyone would be equal and would have equal opportunities in the matter of education, occupation, etc.[26] During the Third Five Year Plan (1961-66) the basic objective was to provide the masses of India the opportunity to lead a good life by combating the course of poverty with all the ills that it produces and it was recognised that this could only be done through socio-economic advance so as to build up a technologically mature society and a social order which offers 'equal opportunities' to all citizens.[27] The Fourth Five Year Plan (1969-74) aimed at ensuring better standard of living for the people by enlarging the income, supplies of food articles, agricultural raw materials, agricultural production, reducing the growth rate of population and the development of human resources by providing substantial additional facilities in the social service sector, especially for the rural areas.[28]

The Fifth Five Year Plan (1974-79) attempted to coordinate various sectors of the economy in terms of the new slogan 'Garibi Hatao'. In the Fifth Five Year Plan it was stated that "at present over 220 million are estimated to be living below poverty level". The clear expression of the diagnosis of poverty was made in the Fifth Five Year Plan when it stated, "Unemployment, underemployment and low resource base of a multitude of procedures, particularly in agriculture, are the principal causes of poverty..... the elimination of the abject poverty will not be attained as a corollary to certain acceleration in the rate of growth of the economy alone. In the Fifth Plan it will be necessary to launch a direct attack on the problems of unemployment, underemployment and massive low-end poverty". Integrated Rural Development Programme was introduced during 1978-79. Its main objective was the alleviation of poverty through creation or improvement of productive assets and skills.[29]

The Sixth Five Year Plan defined poverty line on the basis of the recommended requirements of 2400 calories per person per day for rural areas and 2100 calories per person per day for urban areas.[30] Poverty reduction through full employment of human resources was the major objective of the Sixth Five Year Plan (1980-85).[31] By using the norms of calorie consumption, the Plan projected the per centage population below the poverty line at 48 per cent.[32]

During the Sixth Five Year Plan the goal of poverty alleviation was sought to be achieved by using two main instruments: (i) a set of self-employment schemes for the poor, i.e. Integrated Rural Development Programme and its two sub-programmes: (a) Training of Rural Youth for Self-Employment (TRYSEM), (b) Development of Women and Children in Rural Areas (DWCRA), launched in 1982-83, (ii) Wage Employment Programme namely National Rural Employment Programme (NREP) which was introduced in 1980 and Rural Landless Employment Guarantee Programme (RLEGP) which was launched in 1983. These two programmes were later on merged in Jawahar Rozgar Yojana in 1989.[33]

Training of Rural Youth for Self-Employment (TRYSEM) aimed at to provide technical skills to rural youth in the age group of 18-35 years from families below poverty line to enable them to take up gainful employment as well as wage employment in any of the economic activity. However, the scheme was not free from certain inherent weaknesses, such as lack of confidence of the trainee for self-employment venture; wrong identification of beneficiaries; training by untrained teachers; lack of adequate training centres etc. Development of Women and Children in Rural Areas (DWCRA) was designed exclusively for the women members of rural households below the poverty line to provide income generation according to their skills and local conditions. This programme was also not free from certain flaws. The qualitative standards of the working of these groups was uneven. There was no up-gradation of skills and technology among group members.

National Rural Employment Programme (NREP) was designed to generate additional gainful employment for unemployed and under employed persons in the rural areas. But the target of generation of gainful employment under the programme was not achieved fully. The selection of beneficiaries was not proper. The wage rate paid was very low and hence the scheme was not attractive to wage earning class. Rural Landless Employment Guarantee Programme (RLEGP) was launched to improve and expand employment opportunities to guarantee employment to at least one member of every rural landless labourer household upto 100 days in a year. Like National Rural Employment Programme, this programme too suffered from certain pitfalls. It was not mentioned in the programme, what weightage should be given to skilled and unskilled labourers. Only skilled labourers were employed for completing the projects, therefore, a major part of landless labourers remained unbenefitted from this programme. Thus, both National Rural Employment Programme and Rural Landless Employment Guarantee Programme remained ineffective in their purpose and were merged into a new programme called Jawahar Rozgar Yojana in 1989.

While discussing the 'tasks ahead' the Seventh Five Year Plan (1985-90) document, recognized that the government had still to play a major role in the development process in order to promote the interests of the poor, reduce disparities in income and wealth, curb regional inequalities in the level of development, etc., as these matters could not be left to the free play of market forces.[34]

Elimination of poverty was one of the major objectives of Eighth Five Year Plan (1992-97). The expansion of employment opportunities and augmentation of productivity and income levels of both the underemployed and unemployed poor were made the principle instruments for achieving the goal. During the Eighth Five Year Plan employment was provided to underemployed and unemployed through various employment programmes namely Integrated Rural Development Programme (IRDP), Jawahar Rozgar Yojana (JRY) and Nehru Rozgar Yojana (NRY). In the Plan document, it was stated that, "It must be recognised that while these programmes meet the short-term objective of providing temporary work to unemployed they must contribute to the creation of productive capacity of areas or/and individuals. This would be better achieved by a greater integration of the existing special employment programmes with other sectoral programmes, which in turn would generate larger and more sustainable employment."[35]

In the Ninth Five Year Plan (1997-2002) also the poverty eradication remained one of the major objectives. The Plan laid emphasis on primary health facilities, safe drinking water, nutrition to school and pre-school children, shelter for poor and public distribution system with a focus on poor. The Plan mentioned the causes of poverty as: (i) lack of income and purchasing power attributable to lack of productive employment and considerable underemployment and not to lack of unemployment per cent; (ii) a continuous increase in the price of food, especially food grains which accounts for 70-80 per cent of the consumption basket; and (iii) inadequacy of social infrastructure, affecting the quality of life of the people and their employability.[36]

The Integrated Rural Development Programme (IRDP), introduced in selected blocks in 1978-79 and universalised from 2 October 1980 has provided assistance to the rural poor in the form of subsidy and bank credit for productive employment opportunities through successive Plan periods. Subsequently, Training of Rural Youth for Self Employment (TRYSEM), Development of Women and Children in Rural Areas (DWCRA), Supply of Improved Tool Kits to Rural Artisans (SITRA) and Ganga Kalyan Yojana (GKY) were introduced as sub-programmes of Integrated Rural Development Programme to take care of the specific needs of the rural population. These schemes were however implemented as 'stand alone programmes', an approach which substantially detracted from their effectiveness. The mid-term appraisal of Ninth Five Year

Plan had indicated that these sub-programmes "presented a matrix of multiple programmes without desired linkages". The programme suffered from sub critical investments, lack of bank credit, over-crowding in certain projects and lack of market linkages. The programme was basically subsidy driven and ignored the processes of social intermediation necessary for the success of self-employment programmes. A one-time provision of credit without follow-up action and lack of a continuing relationship between borrowers and lenders also undermined the programmes objectives. The marginal impact of self-employment programmes led to the constitution of a Committee by the Planning Commission in 1997 to review self-employment and wage employment programmes. The Committee recommended the merger of all self-employment programmes for the rural poor and a shift from individual beneficiary approach to a group-based approach. It emphasized the identification of activity clusters in specific areas and strong training and marketing linkages. The Committee's recommendations were accepted by the Government.[37]

At present special beneficiary-oriented, wage employment programmes are being implemented for the purpose of poverty alleviation. The Government of India has launched a scheme known as Sampooran Grameen Rojgar Yojana (SGRY) from September 2001. The basic aim of the scheme is the generation of wage employment, creation of durable economic infrastructure in rural areas and provision of food and nutrition security to the poor. The works taken up under the programme are labour-intensive and the workers are paid the minimum wages notified by the States. Payment of wages is done partly in kind—5 Kg. of food grains and the balance in cash. The Centre and the States share the cost of the cash component of the scheme in the ratio of 75:25.[38]

Indira Awas Yojana (IAY) initiated in 1985-86, the Indira Awas Yojana is the core programme for providing free housing to Below Poverty Line families in rural areas and targets scheduled caste/scheduled tribe households and free bonded labourers. It was first merged with the Jawahar Rozgar Yojana in 1989 and then spun off into a separate housing scheme for the rural poor in 1996.[39]

On 1 April 1999, the IRDP and other programmes including Million Wells Schemes (MWS), were merged into a single programme known as Swaran Jayanti Gram Swarozgar Yojana (SGSY). The Swaran Jayanti Gram Swarozgar Yojana is conceived as a holistic programme of micro-enterprise development in rural areas with emphasis on organizing the rural poor into self-help groups, capacity buildings, planning of activity clusters, infrastructure support, technology credit and marketing linkages. It seeks to provide a network of agencies, namely, the District Rural Development Agency (DRDA), line departments of state Governments, Banks, Non-Governmental Organizations and Panchayati Raj Institutions (PRIs) for implementation of the Programme. The Swaran Jayanti Gram Swarozgar Yojana recognises the need to focus on key activities and the importance of activity clusters. The programme has in-built safeguards for the weaker sections. It insists that 50 per cent of the self-help groups must be formed exclusively by women and that 50 per cent of the benefits should flow to scheduled castes and scheduled tribes. There has also been a provision for disabled beneficiaries. The programme is credit driven and subsidy is back ended. The credit and subsidy ratio is pegged at 3:1. Funds under the scheme are shared between the Centre and States Governments in the ratio of 75:25.[40]

The Government of India from the year 2000-01 introduced Pradhan Mantri Gramodya Yojana (*Gramin Awas*) to provide shelter to the rural poor. The scheme is generally based on the pattern of Indira Awas Yojana. The objective of this scheme is to supplement the efforts being made to provide housing facilities to the poor people in the rural areas. The target groups under this scheme are the families living below the poverty line. The selection of the beneficiaries is required to be made by the Gram Sabha of the concerned village. The beneficiaries have the complete freedom to construct the houses as per their requirements. The ceiling of construction assistance was Rs. 20,000 per unit for plain areas and Rs. 22,000 per unit for hilly/difficult areas. The entire funds were provided by the Government of India to the State Government so that the funds could be utilised as per felt needs of the rural areas.[41]

According to the Tenth Five Year Plan (2002-07), "Effective implementation of Anti-Poverty Programmes would be central to achieving the planned reduction in poverty. The challenge before the state is to provide employment opportunities which provide enhanced incomes. This becomes more important in view of the fact that substantial additions to labour force are expected to take place during the next five years. Enlargement of self and wage employment programmes and their effective delivery becomes an imperative in such scenario."[42]

During 2004-07 the Government launched some new programmes and schemes for the welfare of weaker sections in the country.

A. PROGRAMMES FOR THE IMPROVEMENT IN THE LEVELS OF LIVING OF THE PEOPLE

Cooked Mid-Day Meal

In order to improve enrolment, attendance and health of school-going children, the Government launched the National Cooked Mid-Day Meal Programme for Government-run and Government aided primary schools countrywide. The programme covers around 12 crore children in over 9½ lakh schools and is the world's largest school feeding programme. Earlier, states were only provided free uncooked food grains. Provision has also been made for mid-day meals during summers in drought-affected areas. The Programme was revised in June 2006 to provide cooked mid-day meal containing nutritional value of minimum 450 calories and 12 grams of protein, as against earlier provision of minimum 300 calories and 8-12 gram of protein. To this end, states were advised to include minimum quantity of 100 gram of wheat/ rice, 20 gram of pulses, 5 gram of oil and fats, and iodised salt, condiments, micronutrient supplementation and de-worming as required. Mid-day meal plan outlay was increased more than five-fold to Rs. 7,324 crore in 2007-08.

Food Security

Food security is being addressed through the National Rural Employment Guarantee Scheme, expanded outlays under the Sampooran Grameen Rozgar Yojana, expanded Antyodya Anna Yojana and the revised scheme of village grain banks. Antyodya Anna Yojana was expanded to cover additional one crore households. The scheme of village grain banks was revised, giving it wider coverage and making it more comprehensive, as a safeguard against starvation during periods of natural calamities and the lean season. Earlier, the scheme covered only persons belonging to the Scheduled Tribes and persons from among the Schedule Castes in tribal areas The scheme now covers all willing families living below the poverty line in drought prone areas, desert areas and inaccessible hilly areas in food scarce parts of the country.

National Tribal Policy

The Government has formulated a draft National Tribal Policy covering all important issues that concern tribal people, such as alienation of tribal land, tribal-forest interface, resettlement and rehabilitation, primitive tribal groups, empowerment, enlisting support of NGOs, tribal culture, traditional knowledge, development and administration of tribal areas, scheduling and de-scheduling of tribes, etc.

Education

Constitution has been amended to facilitate greater access to education for students belonging to the Scheduled Castes and Tribes and the socially and educationally backward classes. The Government has extended scholarships to students belonging to these categories and has initiated the legislation enacted for widened access to higher education for the OBCs. To prepare candidates from among the SCs and the STs for selection to academic positions and for doctoral studies, the Rajiv Gandhi National Fellowship Scheme has been launched for funding 2,000 fellowships annually.

Rehabilitation of Manual Scavengers

To rehabilitate scavengers and empower the most deprived among the Scheduled Castes in alternative occupations, the Government has launched a new Self Employment Scheme for Rehabilitation of Manual Scavengers that provides assistance to them and their dependants in the form of credit-linked subsidy and loans at concessionary rates of interest for undertaking self-employment ventures as well as training up to one year for skill development. The aim is to eradicate the practice of manual scavenging within two years.

Institutional Focus

The Committee of Ministers on Dalit Affairs has been set-up to bring greater focus on Dalit affairs. Separate National Commission has been set-up for Scheduled Castes and Scheduled Tribes. A Commission has also been set-up on denotified tribes.

Developing Lands of SCs and STs

The National Rural Employment Guarantee Scheme provides for improvement of fields of farmers belonging to the Scheduled castes and the Scheduled tribes. A National Project for the Repair, Renovation and Restoration of Water Bodies used by farmers, especially in dry land, remote and tribal areas, has been launched on pilot basis to augment the storage capacity of water bodies and restore their lost or wasted irrigation potential. This gives priority to SC/ST farmlands.

Outlays for the Scheduled Castes and Tribes

The allocation for Scheduled castes and the Scheduled tribes has been substantially enhanced each year. The allocation for schemes benefiting them was increased to Rs. 17,691 crore in 2007-08 from Rs. 12,592 crore in 2006-07.

Senior Citizens

Pension under the National Old Age Pension Scheme has been increased from Rs. 75 to Rs. 200 per beneficiary per month for destitute persons of the age of 65 years and above, to extend support for managing their livelihoods. An exclusive health insurance scheme for senior citizens has been launched. The Maintenance and Welfare of Parents and Senior Citizens Bill, 2007 was introduced in Parliament to provide for more effective provisions for maintenance and welfare of parents and senior citizens. It proposes to cast an obligation on the persons who inherit the property of aged relatives to maintain such aged relatives and also proposes to make provisions for setting up old age homes for providing maintenance to indigent holder persons. It further proposes to provide better medical facilities to senior citizens and make provision for protecting their lives and property.

B. PROGRAMMES FOR INCREASING EMPLOYMENT OPPORTUNITIES

Rural Employment Guarantee

A major step has been taken towards provision of social security to labour in the unorganized sector in rural areas though enactment of the National Rural Employment Guarantee Act.

Aam Admi Bima Yojana

To extend death and disability insurance cover through the Life Insurance Corporation of India to an estimated 1.5 crore rural landless households, a new scheme called Aam Admi Bima Yojana has been announced. To begin with, 70 lakh households will be covered through existing schemes of the LIC with the support of some state governments and the social security fund with the LIC. Under the new scheme, the Government will cover such rural landless households that do not enjoy any cover currently. The Government will bear half the cost of the premium and the state governments will be urged to bear the other half.

National Commission on Enterprises in the Unorganized Sector

The National Commission on Enterprises in the Unorganized Sector has been set-up to act as an advisory body and a watchdog and to submit periodic reports to the Government. Its terms of reference cover broadly the entire gamut of issues relating to unorganized sector and it has done significant work on relevant legislation through wide-ranging consultations with stakeholders, particularly state governments with the objective of providing a social security net, including health insurance and other schemes for these workers. The Commission has also undertaken a review of labour laws in India for improving productivity and ensuring greater competitiveness and employment generation in various sectors like textiles, IT and SEZs, consistent with labour rights. Cluster-based growth poles, skill formation through public-private partnership, provision of micro-finance have been identified as priority areas. Measures are also being identified for protecting and promoting livelihoods for self-employed workers, through provision of credit, right to common property and natural resources, and use of public space to engage in economic activity. The report of the National Commission for Enterprises in the Unorganised Sector is near finalization.

Conditions of Work and Livelihood Promotion

The Unorganised Sector Workers (Conditions of Work and Livelihood Promotion) Bill to provide for conditions of work and measures for protection and promotion of livelihoods is being finalised.

Setting up a National Fund

The modalities for setting up a National Fund for providing technical, marketing and credit support to enterprises in the informal sector are being worked out.

Agro and Rural Industries

The Khadi and Village Industries Commission has been revamped. The Mahatma Gandhi Institute for Rural Industries has been set-up at Wardha by revamping the Jamnalal Bajaj Central Research Institute to build capacity and upgrade technology in Khadi and Village Industries. The Government has launched the Scheme of Fund for Regeneration of Traditional Industries (SFURTI), under which 104 clusters of khadi, village and coir industry have been approved for comprehensive development over five years. A new scheme, 'Rejuvenation of Coir Sector and Modernisation Programme for Coir Industry', is being introduced under the Eleventh Plan.

C. PROGRAMMES OF RURAL DEVELOPMENT

Bharat Nirman

Bharat Nirman is a four-year programme (2005-09) for achieving identified goals in six selected areas of rural infrastructure—irrigations, drinking water, housing, roads, telephony and electrification. In four of these areas the aim is to have universal coverage, where every village will have telecom services and electricity, and every habitation will have access to safe drinking water and—for a population of at least one thousand, or 500 in hilly/tribal areas—access to all weather roads.

One crore hectare under assured irrigation will be achieved through completion of ongoing major and medium irrigation projects (42 lakh hectare), minor irrigation schemes (28 lakh hectare), enhanced utilization of completed projects (20 lakh hectare), and ground water development in areas with unutilized ground water potential (10 lakh hectare). The Government has initiated steps for putting in place a mechanism for large-scale investment in irrigation. The goal for drinking water is to ensure that estimated 55,000 habitations without safe source of drinking water, estimated 2.8 lakh habitations that have slipped back from full coverage, and estimated 2.17 lakh habitations that have problems of water quality are provided access to safe drinking water. 66,802 habitations will be connected to a road aimed over the period 2005-09 though construction of 1.46 lakh km of roads and upgrading of 1.94 lakh km of existing roads at an investment of approximately Rs. 48,000 crore. Simultaneously, more than 50 million rural connections are targeted for rollout and, thereafter, a connection will be available on demand. Over 100,000 villages do not have electricity. To remedy this, the Government has initiated Rajiv Gandhi Grameen Vidyutikaran Yojana. Not only will electricity be reached to the remaining villages, but also electricity connections will be offered to an estimated 2.3 crore households. Most of the yearly targets have been met for projects undertaken through Bharat Nirman, except in a few states. Programmes for rural roads, rural electrification, rural telephony, rural housing and rural drinking water supply are on track. 9,481 habitations had been connected by January 2007, with over 30,000 km length of new roads and nearly 29,000 km length of upgraded roads. Over 23 lakh houses had been constructed. 1.5 lakh habitations had been provided safe drinking water as per norms. Over 37,000 non-electrified villages and 6.25 lakh rural households had been provided electricity, besides augmentation of power infrastructure in rural areas.

Rural Employment

The National Rural Employment Guarantee Act (NREGA) has been passed. For the first time, it recognizes the right to work as a fundamental legal right and entitles the rural poor to guaranteed employment for hundred days. Over 1.4 crore households have benefited under the Rural Employment Guarantee Scheme under the Act made operational in 200 districts initially with expansion to another 130 districts during 2007. Over 500,000 works are under operation under the Act in different parts of the country, of which over half are in the area of water conservation and drought-proofing, contributing to rebuilding of the natural resource-base. A social safety net of this dimension has not been undertaken ever before anywhere in the world. The law commits the Government to expand the Rural Employment Guarantee Scheme throughout the country within five years.

Agriculture and Cooperation

(a) Irrigation

Besides one crore hectare of fresh capacity over the period 2005-09 under Bharat Nirman, micro-irrigation through drip and sprinkler irrigation is being promoted through drip irrigation and sprinkler irrigation. Rural Infrastructure Development Fund (RIDF) was revived in 2004-05 and its corpus has been progressively enhanced to Rs. 12,000 crore in 2007-08.

(b) National Rainfed Area Authority

The Government has established a National Rainfed Area Authority as an integrating and coordinating mechanism to look into all dimensions of managing water resources in the rain-fed areas and provide scientific and intellectual support to Panchayati Raj institutions. It will foster harvesting, conservation and sustainable and equitable use of rainwater for strengthening health, nutrition and livelihood security of rural communities, and will help ensure security and productivity of crop and animal husbandry, forestry and fisheries. It will be a professional body, whose recommendations and action plans will be characterized by high scientific content and economic credibility and will be guided by principles of ecology, economics, equity and generation of employment.

(c) Credit

The disbursement of credit to agriculture and allied activities has expanded rapidly in volume as well as reach, while also making it more affordable. In June 2004, the Government announced a comprehensive policy envisaging the doubling of credit delivery to agriculture over the next three years.

Equal attention has been paid to increasing the reach of credit through the formal credit structure as well as micro-finance. Public sector banks, Regional Rural Banks and cooperative banks together added over two crore new farmers to their portfolio of borrowers over three years and a further 50 lakh are targeted for 2007-08. A Committee on Financial Inclusion has given its interim report on a plan for delivering credit to every household and the Government has decided to implement immediately two recommendations. The first is to establish a Financial Inclusion Fund with the NABARD for meeting the cost of developmental and promotional interventions. The second is to establish a Financial Inclusion Technology Fund to meet the costs of technology adoption. Each fund will have an overall corpus of Rs. 500 crore, with initial funding to be contributed by the Central Government, the RBI and the NABARD. Regional Rural Banks have been asked to undertake an aggressive branch expansion programme and, during 2007-08, open at least one branch in the 80 uncovered districts of the country.

The Micro Financial Sector (Development and Regulation) Bill, 2007 was introduced in Parliament to provide for promotion, development and orderly growth of the micro-finance sector to help ensure universal access to integrated financial services, especially to women and certain disadvantaged sections of society as well as to regulate hitherto unregulated micro-finance organizations. The Bill proposes to entrust the functions of development Council to advise it, and to constitute the Micro Finance Development and regulation to the NABARD, with a Micro Finance Development Council to advise it, and to constitute the Micro Finance Development and Equity

Fund to provide loans, refinance, grant, seed capital or other financial assistance to micro-finance organizations for training and capacity building, investment in equity, research experimentation, study, as well as design, promotion and propagation of practices conducive to growth. It also proposes appointment of ombudsmen.

(d) Package for Suicide-prone Districts

A special package, amounting to more than Rs. 16,000 crore, is being implemented in 31 districts worst affected by farmers suicides. The interventions cover short-term as well as long-term measures and address issues of credit, irrigation, agriculture inputs and alternative sources of income. A special package for livestock and fisheries for these districts has also been approved. This covers induction of high milk-yield animals, calf-rearing, breeding services, animal healthcare, milk chilling units, feed and fodder supply, and enhanced subsidy for fisheries.

(e) Horticulture

The National Horticulture Mission has been launched to promote holistic development of horticulture with backward and forward linkages through technology-driven cluster approach and regionally differentiated strategies. Most states have formulated and obtained approval for annual action plans.

(f) Cotton

Development of market yards, modernization of ginning and pressing factories and other measures taken under the Technology Mission on Cotton has begun yielding results in terms of increase in cotton production and reduction in cotton imports.

(g) Bamboo

A National Bamboo Mission has been launched across 28 states to promote holistic growth of the bamboo sector with interventions for research, plantation development, post-felling management and marketing. The Mission is to undertake activities on the basis of properly identified compact areas to facilitate development of requisite infrastructure and intensive management. This will result in plantation over 1.76 lakh hectare and generation of over 5.5 crore many-days over a five-year period, resulting in production of over three million tonnes of bamboo annually from the fourth year and improvement in productivity from the existing level of two to three tonnes per hectare to 18 tonnes per hectare.

(h) Crop Insurance

With a view to cover the risks involved in agricultural operations, the scope and coverage of the National Agricultural Insurance Scheme has been expanded. The Government has asked the Agricultural Insurance Corporation to start a weather-based crop insurance scheme on pilot basis in two or three states as an alternative to the existing scheme.

(i) Livestock Insurance

The Livestock Insurance Scheme has been launched in 100 selected districts across all states except Goa for providing insurance cover for crossbred and high-yielding cattle and buffaloes. The Government is providing 50% subsidy on insurance premium.

(j) Fisheries

The Government has approved the setting up of a National Fisheries Development Board. Its activities include intensive freshwater aquaculture, reservoir fisheries, brackish water coastal aquaculture, deep-sea fishing and tuna processing, mariculture, sea ranching, seaweed cultivation, infrastructure for post-harvest programmes, fish-dressing centres and solar drying of fish, and domestic marketing. Expected increase in annual production of fish will be 3.9 million tonnes at the end of a six-year period in 2012, which may be compared to the present production level of 3.4 to 3.5 million tonnes. A comprehensive Marine Fishing Policy, 2004 has been adopted to have sustainable and responsible fisheries and exploit deep-sea fishery resources in the Exclusive Economic Zone of India.

(k) Storage and Marketing

In October 2004, the revised Grameen Bhandaran Yojana scheme was launched with wide eligibility for accessing capital subsidy to construct rural godowns. A new scheme, linked with reform of APMC Acts, was launched in 2005 to provide capital subsidy for development of infrastructure for marketing, grading and standardization. A new component has been added to the National Horticulture Mission for funding modern terminal market projects for horticulture commodities in public-partnership mode.

(l) Research

Budget allocation for agricultural research has been substantially enhanced. The National Fund for Strategic Research in Agriculture has been set-up. The National Agricultural Innovation Project has been initiated with an outlay of over Rs. 1,200 crore with the objective of transferring research-based knowledge to the field. Establishment of Krishi Vigyan Kendras in all 589 rural districts was taken up. 541 Kendras were established by the end of 2006.

(m) Education

The Government has launched a scheme for strengthening and developing agricultural education with total assistance to the tune of Rs. 804 crore. Its main elements are development and strengthening of 34 state agricultural universities, five deemed universities and three Central universities, rural awareness work experience programme, a number of incentive schemes, establishment of Sher-e-Kashmir University of Agricultural Science and Technology at Jammu, etc. Special grant of Rs. 100 crore has been provided for the Punjab Agricultural University, and grant of Rs. 50 crore each to the Gobind Ballabh Pant University of Agriculture and Technology at Pantnagar and the Tamil Nadu Agricultural University at Coimbatore has been announced.

(n) Extension

Under the Scheme for Support to State Extension Programmes for Extension Reforms, state level HRD institutions have been identified, Agricultural Technology Management Agencies constituted, State Extension Work Plans approved, and public-private partnership initiatives pilot tested across 252 districts. Establishment of Agriculture Technology Management Agencies in additional 300 districts is targeted during 2007-08.

(o) Cooperatives

The Government has introduced a Constitution amendment bill on cooperative societies in Parliament. The bill seeks to make the management of cooperative societies accountable to members, restrict interference by the State, prevent misuse of powers by the management and bring about greater transparency in the functioning of cooperative societies as democratic societies.

Water Management

(a) Water Conservation

A substantial proportion of funds under the schemes mandated by the National Rural Employment Guarantee Act is earmarked for water conservation works. A National project for Repair, Renovation and Restoration of Water Bodies used by farmers has been launched on pilot basis. The DPAP and IWDP, the two programmes for watershed development, have been brought under a common guideline. States have been asked to direct municipal bodies to make rainwater-harvesting part of design approvals by local bodies. A number of states have done work on rainwater harvesting and/or taken steps to amend municipal or building laws.

(b) Desalination plants

Approval from the foreign investment and environmental angles have been accorded for setting up of a desalination plant of 100 million litre per day capacity at Chennai in public-private partnership at a cost of the order of Rs. 500 crore. Provision exists under the guidelines for the Jawaharlal Nehru National Urban Renewal Mission and the Urban Infrastructure Development Scheme for Small and Medium Town. The Government has developed a unique technology of low temperature thermal desalination for conversion of cold deep-sea water into warm surface water. The first such plant has been successfully running with a capacity of one lakh litre per day in Lakhshadweep and other eight such plants are being installed there, besides one such one million litre per day capacity plant off the coast of Chennai.[43]

In India the planning process began in 1951 with the launching of the First Five Year Plan and we are now in the Eleventh Five Year Plan. The planning endeavor in India has already covered more than five and a half decades, and failure of these Five Year Plans to yield tangible results in terms of visible improvement in the standards of living of the people belonging to the lower strata has understandably bred some amount of skepticism among the articulate sections. No one denies that planning has provided special thrust to development in every area of economic activity. India has achieved a high degree of sophistication in many areas like the manufacture of engineering goods, electronic goods and computers, increasing the area under irrigation, introduction of high yielding varieties of seeds, increased supply of inputs like fertilizers and a more liberal development of industrial credit.

What causes concern to all enthusiasts of planned development is the failure of Indian planners to achieve, during the planning period, certain long-term goals like the eradication of poverty through the provision of minimum needs to all people and the containment of unemployment and inequalities within prudent limits. The percentage of population below poverty line was 54.88 per cent during 1973-74.[44] It reduced to 48.3 per cent in 1977-78 and 44.48 per cent in 1983. The per centage of population below poverty line further reduced to 35.97 per cent during 1993-94.[45] About 26.10 per cent of population in India was estimated to be below poverty line, as per report of the Planning Commission in 1999-2000.[46]

The Planning Commission in its Approach to the Eleventh Five Year Plan stated, "Using the methodology of the Expert Group on Estimation of Proportion and Number of Poor 1993, the per centage of population below the poverty line is provisionally estimated at 27.8 per cent in 2004-05. Thus the average decline in per centage of population below the poverty line over the period 1993 to 2004 is 0.74 per centage points per year, much less than implied by the official 1999-2000 data. Because of the slower pace of reduction in the per centage of the poor, the estimated number of poor is estimated to be approximately 300 million in 2004-05, larger than the official estimate of 1999-2000."[47]

The state level data presents a mixed picture. A number of states exhibited an increase in the poverty ratio whereas some other indicated considerable reduction in the poverty ratio between 1973-74 and 2004-05. Table 1.1 shows that during 1973-74, 54.88 per cent of population (56.44 per cent in rural areas and 49.01 per cent in urban areas) was below poverty line. The poverty ratio was the highest in Orissa whereas West Bengal, Bihar, Madhya Pradesh, Kerala, Uttar Pradesh and Tamil Nadu had poverty ratio above the national average of 54.88 per cent. (See Table 1.1)

TABLE 1.1
Incidence of Poverty in 1973-74

Sl. No.	*State*	*Rural*		*Urban*		*Total*	
		No. of Poor (Lakhs)	*Poverty Ratio (%)*	*No. of Poor (Lakhs)*	*Poverty Ratio (%)*	*No. of Poor (Lakhs)*	*Poverty Ratio (%)*
1.	Andhra Pradesh	178.21	48.41	47.48	50.61	225.69	48.86
2.	Assam	76.37	52.67	5.46	36.92	81.83	51.21
3.	Bihar	336.52	62.99	34.05	52.96	370.57	61.91
4.	Gujarat	94.61	46.35	43.81	52.57	136.42	48.15
5.	Haryana	30.08	34.23	8.24	40.18	38.32	35.36
6.	Himachal Pradesh	9.38	27.42	0.35	13.17	9.73	26.39
7.	Karnataka	128.40	55.14	42.27	52.53	170.67	54.47
8.	Kerala	111.36	59.19	24.16	62.74	135.52	59.79
9.	Madhya Pradesh	231.21	62.66	45.09	57.65	276.30	61.78
10.	Maharashtra	210.84	57.71	76.58	43.87	287.42	53.24
11.	Orissa	142.24	67.28	12.23	55.62	154.47	66.18
12.	Punjab	30.47	28.21	10.02	27.96	40.49	28.15
13.	Rajasthan	101.41	44.76	27.10	52.13	128.51	46.14
14.	Tamil Nadu	172.60	57.43	66.92	49.40	239.52	54.94
15.	Uttar Pradesh	449.99	56.53	85.74	60.09	535.73	57.07
16.	West Bengal	257.96	73.16	41.34	34.67	299.30	63.43
17.	All India	2612.90	56.44	600.46	49.01	3213.36	54.88

Note : Report of the Expert Group on Estimation of Proportion and Number of Poor (1993).

Source : Planning Commission, Government of India.

During 1983, 44.48 per cent of population (45.65 per cent in the rural area and 40.79 per cent in the urban area) was below poverty line. Table 1.2 clearly indicates that poverty ratio was the highest in case of Orissa whereas it was above the national average, i.e. 44.48 per cent in Bihar, West Bengal, Madhya Pradesh and Uttar Pradesh. (See Table 1.2)

Table 1.3 depicts that during 1993-94, 35.97 per cent of population (37.27 per cent in rural areas and 32.36 per cent in urban areas) were below poverty line. Poverty ratio was above the national average of 35.97 per cent in Bihar, Orissa, Madhya Pradesh, Sikkim, Assam, Uttar Pradesh, Arunachal Pradesh, Tripura, Meghalaya, Nagaland and Maharashtra. (See Table 1.3)

During 1999-2000, the states with poverty ratio above the national average of 26.10 per cent included Orissa, Bihar, Madhya Pradesh, Sikkim, Assam, Tripura, Meghalaya, Nagaland, Uttar Pradesh, Manipur and West Bengal. During this period 27.09 per cent of the total population in the rural areas and 23.62 per cent in the urban areas was below poverty line. (See Table 1.4)

Planning Commission's 2004-05 Estimates of Poverty were based on the data collected on uniform recall period (URP) consumption using 30 days for all items. The data was also available using 365 days for five frequently purchased non-food items namely, clothing, footwear, durable goods, education and institutional medical expenses and 30 days recall period for the remaining items, known as mixed recall period (MRP), the Planning Commission, using the expert group methodology had estimated poverty in 2004-05 using both the distributions.

Poverty estimates based on URP showed 28.3 per cent of rural population and 25.7 per cent of urban population was below the poverty line. For the country as a whole, 27.5 per cent of total population was below poverty line in 2004-05. Table 1.5 indicates that the lowest poverty ratio was 5.40 per cent for Jammu & Kashmir and highest poverty ratio was for Orissa (46.4 per cent). States with poverty ratio of less than the national average of 27.5 per cent included Jammu & Kashmir, Punjab, Haryana, Himachal Pradesh, Delhi, Goa, Kerala, Gujarat, Assam, Rajasthan, Tamil Nadu, West Bengal, Karnataka and Andhra Pradesh. Whereas, states with poverty ratio above the national average were Maharashtra, Uttar Pradesh, Bihar,

TABLE 1.2
Number and Percentage of Population below Poverty Line (1983)

State/UTs	Rural			Urban			Combined	
	No. of Persons (Lakhs)	% of Persons	Poverty Line (Rs.)	No. of Persons (Lakhs)	% of Persons	Poverty Line (Rs.)	No. of Persons (Lakh)	% of Persons
(1)	(2)	(3)	(4)	(5)	(6)	(7)	(8)	(9)
Andhra Pradesh	114.34	26.53	72.66	50.24	36.30	106.43	164.58	28.91
Arunachal Pradesh	2.70	42.60	98.32	0.12	21.73	97.51	2.82	40.88
Assam	73.43	42.60	98.32	4.26	21.73	97.51	77.69	40.47
Bihar	417.70	64.37	97.48	44.35	47.33	111.80	462.05	62.22
Goa	1.16	14.81	88.24	1.07	27.00	126.47	2.23	18.90
Gujarat	72.88	29.80	83.29	45.04	39.14	123.22	117.92	32.79
Haryana	22.03	20.56	88.57	7.57	24.15	103.48	29.60	21.37
Himachal Pradesh	7.07	17.00	88.57	0.34	9.43	102.26	7.41	16.40
Jammu & Kashmir	13.11	26.04	91.75	2.49	17.76	99.62	15.60	24.24
Karnataka	100.50	36.33	83.31	49.31	42.82	120.19	149.81	38.24
Kerala	81.62	39.03	99.35	25.15	45.68	122.64	106.77	40.42
Madhya Pradesh	215.48	48.90	83.59	62.49	53.06	122.82	277.97	49.78
Maharashtra	193.75	45.23	88.24	97.14	40.26	126.47	290.89	43.44
Manipur	4.76	42.60	98.32	0.89	21.73	97.51	5.65	37.02
Meghalaya	5.04	42.60	98.32	0.57	21.73	97.51	5.62	38.81
Mizoram	1.58	42.60	98.32	0.37	21.73	97.51	1.96	36.00
Nagaland	3.19	42.60	98.32	0.31	21.73	97.51	3.50	39.25

(Contd.)

TABLE 1.2 (Contd.)

(1)	(2)	(3)	(4)	(5)	(6)	(7)	(8)	(9)
Orissa	164.65	67.53	106.28	16.66	49.15	124.81	181.31	65.29
Punjab	16.79	13.20	88.57	11.85	23.79	101.03	28.64	16.18
Rajasthan	96.77	33.50	80.24	30.06	37.94	113.55	126.83	34.46
Sikkim	1.24	42.60	98.32	0.10	21.73	97.51	1.35	39.71
Tamil Nadu	181.61	53.99	96.15	78.46	46.96	120.30	260.07	51.66
Tripura	8.35	42.60	98.32	0.60	21.73	97.51	8.95	40.03
Uttar Pradesh	448.03	46.45	83.85	108.71	49.82	110.23	556.74	47.07
West Bengal	268.60	63.05	105.55	50.09	32.32	105.91	318.69	54.85
Andaman Nicobar	0.84	53.99	96.15	0.26	46.96	120.30	1.11	52.13
Chandigarh	0.09	23.79	101.03	1.10	23.79	101.03	1.19	23.79
Dadra & N. Haveli	0.16	14.81	88.24	0.02	27.00	126.47	0.18	15.67
Delhi	0.44	7.66	88.57	17.95	27.89	123.29	18.39	26.22
Lakshadweep	0.09	39.03	99.35	0.10	45.68	122.64	0.19	42.36
Pondicherry	1.56	53.99	96.15	1.72	46.96	120.30	3.28	50.06
All India	2519.57	45.65	89.50	709.40	40.79	115.65	3228.97	44.48

Notes : 1. Poverty Ratio of Assam is used for Sikkim, Arunachal Pradesh, Meghalaya, Mizoram, Manipur, Nagaland and Tripura.
2. Poverty Ratio of Tamil Nadu is used for Pondicherry and Andaman & Nicobar Islands.
3. Poverty Ratio of Kerala is used for Lakshadweep.
4. Poverty Ratio of Goa is used for Dadra & Nagar Haveli, Daman and Diu.
5. Urban Poverty Ratio of Punjab is used for both rural and urban poverty of Chandigarh.
6. Poverty Line of Maharashtra and expenditure distribution of Goa is used to estimate poverty ratio of Goa.
7. Poverty Line is in Rupees per capita per month; 1 Lakh is equivalent to 100,000.

Source : Planning Commission, Government of India.

TABLE 1.3
Number and Percentage of Population below Poverty Line—1993-94

State/UTs	Rural			Urban			Combined	
	No. of Persons (Lakhs)	% of Persons	Poverty Line (Rs.)	No. of Persons (Lakhs)	% of Persons	Poverty Line (Rs.)	No. of Persons (Lakhs)	% of Persons
(1)	(2)	(3)	(4)	(5)	(6)	(7)	(8)	(9)
Andhra Pradesh	79.49	15.92	163.02	74.47	38.33	278.14	153.97	22.19
Arunachal Pradesh	3.62	45.01	232.05	0.11	7.73	212.42	3.73	39.35
Assam	94.33	45.01	232.05	2.03	7.73	212.42	96.36	40.86
Bihar	450.86	58.21	212.16	42.49	34.50	238.49	493.35	54.96
Goa	0.38	5.34	194.94	1.53	27.03	328.56	1.91	14.92
Gujarat	62.16	22.18	202.11	43.02	27.89	297.22	105.91	24.21
Haryana	36.56	28.02	233.79	7.31	16.38	258.23	43.88	25.05
Himachal Pradesh	15.40	30.34	233.79	0.46	9.18	253.61	15.86	28.44
Jammu & Kashmir	19.05	30.34	233.79	1.86	9.18	253.61	20.92	25.17
Karnataka	95.99	29.88	186.63	60.46	40.14	302.89	156.46	33.16
Kerala	55.95	25.76	243.84	20.46	24.55	280.54	76.41	25.43
Madhya Pradesh	216.19	40.64	193.10	82.33	48.38	317.16	298.52	42.52
Maharashtra	193.99	37.93	194.94	111.90	35.15	328.56	305.22	36.86
Manipur	6.33	45.01	232.05	0.47	7.73	212.42	6.80	33.78
Meghalaya	7.09	45.01	232.05	0.29	7.73	212.42	7.38	37.92
Mizoram	1.64	45.01	232.05	0.30	7.73	212.42	1.94	25.66
Nagaland	4.85	45.01	232.05	0.20	7.73	212.42	5.05	37.92
Orissa	140.90	49.72	194.03	19.70	41.64	298.22	160.60	48.56

(Contd.)

TABLE 1.3 (Contd.)

(1)	(2)	(3)	(4)	(5)	(6)	(7)	(8)	(9)
Punjab	17.76	11.95	233.79	7.35	11.35	253.61	25.11	11.77
Rajasthan	94.68	26.46	215.89	33.82	30.49	280.85	128.50	27.41
Sikkim	1.81	45.01	232.05	0.03	7.73	212.42	1.84	41.43
Tamil Nadu	121.70	32.48	196.53	80.40	39.77	296.63	202.10	35.03
Tripura	11.41	45.01	232.05	0.38	7.73	212.42	11.79	39.01
Uttar Pradesh	496.17	42.28	213.01	108.28	35.39	258.65	604.46	40.85
West Bengal	209.90	40.80	220.74	44.66	22.41	247.53	254.56	35.66
Andaman Nicobar	0.73	32.48	196.53	0.33	39.77	296.63	1.06	34.47
Chandigarh	0.07	11.35	253.61	0.73	11.35	253.61	0.80	11.35
Dadra & N. Haveli	0.72	51.95	194.94	0.06	39.93	328.56	0.77	50.84
Daman & Diu	0.03	5.34	194.94	0.15	27.03	328.56	0.18	15.80
Delhi	0.19	1.90	233.79	15.32	16.03	309.48	15.51	14.69
Lakshadweep	0.06	25.76	243.84	0.08	24.55	280.54	0.14	25.04
Pondicherry	0.93	32.48	196.53	2.38	39.77	296.63	3.31	37.40
All India	2440.31	37.27	205.84	763.37	32.36	281.35	3203.68	35.97

Notes : 1. Poverty Ratio of Assam is used for Sikkim, Arunachal Pradesh, Meghalaya, Mizoram, Manipur, Nagaland and Tripura.
2. Poverty Ratio of Tamil Nadu is used for Pondicherry and Andaman & Nicobar Islands.
3. Poverty Ratio of Kerala is used for Lakshadweep.
4. Poverty Ratio of Goa is used for Daman & Diu.
5. Urban Poverty Ratio of Punjab is used for both rural and urban poverty of Chandigarh.
6. Poverty Line of Maharashtra and expenditure distribution of Goa is used to estimate poverty ratio of Goa.
7. Poverty Line of Maharashtra and expenditure distribution of Dadra & Nagar Haveli is used to estimate poverty ratio of Dadra & Nagar Haveli; Poverty ratio of Himachal Pradesh is used for Jammu & Kashmir.
8. Poverty line is in Rupees per capita per month; 1 Lakh is equivalent to 100,000.

Source : Planning Commission, Government of India.

TABLE 1.4

Number and Percentage of Population below Poverty Line—1999-2000

State/UTs	*Rural*			*Urban*			*Combined*	
	No. of Persons (Lakhs)	*% of Persons*	*Poverty Line (Rs.)*	*No. of Persons (Lakhs)*	*% of Persons*	*Poverty Line (Rs.)*	*No. of Persons (Lakhs)*	*% of Persons*
(1)	*(2)*	*(3)*	*(4)*	*(5)*	*(6)*	*(7)*	*(8)*	*(9)*
Andhra Pradesh	58.13	11.05	262.94	60.88	26.63	457.40	119.01	15.77
Arunachal Pradesh	3.80	40.04	365.43	0.18	7.47	343.99	3.98	33.47
Assam	92.17	40.04	365.43	2.38	7.47	343.99	94.55	36.09
Bihar	376.51	44.30	333.07	49.13	32.91	379.78	425.64	42.60
Goa	0.11	1.35	318.63	0.59	7.52	539.71	0.70	4.40
Gujarat	39.80	13.17	318.94	28.09	15.59	474.41	67.89	14.07
Haryana	11.94	8.27	362.81	5.39	9.99	420.20	17.34	8.74
Himachal Pradesh	4.84	7.94	367.45	0.29	4.63	420.20	5.12	7.63
Jammu & Kashmir	2.97	3.97	367.45	0.49	1.98	420.20	3.46	3.48
Karnataka	59.91	17.38	309.59	44.49	25.25	511.44	104.40	20.04
Kerala	20.97	9.38	374.79	20.07	20.27	477.06	41.04	12.72
Madhya Pradesh	217.32	37.06	311.34	81.22	38.44	481.65	298.54	37.43
Maharashtra	125.12	23.72	318.63	102.87	26.81	539.71	227.99	25.02
Manipur	6.53	40.04	365.43	0.66	7.47	343.99	7.19	28.54
Meghalaya	7.89	40.04	365.43	0.34	7.47	343.99	8.23	33.87
Mizoram	1.40	40.04	365.43	0.45	7.47	343.99	1.85	19.47
Nagaland	5.21	40.04	365.43	0.28	7.47	343.99	5.49	32.67
Orissa	143.69	48.01	323.92	25.40	42.83	473.12	169.09	47.15

(Contd.)

TABLE 1.4 (Contd.)

(1)	(2)	(3)	(4)	(5)	(6)	(7)	(8)	(9)
Punjab	10.20	6.35	362.68	4.29	5.75	388.15	14.49	6.16
Rajasthan	55.06	13.74	344.03	26.78	19.85	465.92	81.83	15.28
Sikkim	2.00	40.04	365.43	0.04	7.47	343.99	2.05	36.55
Tamil Nadu	80.51	20.55	307.64	49.97	22.11	475.60	130.48	21.1
Tripura	12.53	40.04	365.43	0.49	7.47	343.99	13.02	34.44
Uttar Pradesh	412.01	31.22	336.88	117.88	30.89	416.29	529.89	31.15
West Bengal	180.11	31.85	350.17	33.38	14.86	409.22	213.49	27.02
Andaman Nicobar	0.58	20.55	307.64	0.24	22.11	475.60	0.82	20.99
Chandigarh	0.06	5.75	388.15	0.45	5.75	388.15	0.51	5.75
Dadra & N. Haveli	0.30	17.57	318.63	0.03	13.52	539.71	0.33	17.14
Daman & Diu	0.01	1.35	318.63	0.05	7.52	539.71	0.06	4.44
Delhi	0.07	0.40	362.68	11.42	9.42	505.45	11.49	8.23
Lakshadweep	0.03	9.38	374.79	0.08	20.27	477.06	0.11	15.60
Pondicherry	0.64	20.55	307.64	1.77	22.11	475.60	2.41	21.67
All India	1932.43	27.09	327.56	670.07	23.62	454.11	2602.50	26.10

Notes : 1 Poverty Ratio of Assam is used for Sikkim, Arunachal Pradesh, Meghalaya, Mizoram, Manipur, Nagaland and Tripura.
2. Poverty Ratio of Tamil Nadu is used for Pondicherry and Andaman & Nicobar Islands.
3. Poverty Ratio of Kerala is used for Lakshadweep: Poverty Ratio of Goa is used for Daman & Diu.
4. Poverty Line of Maharashtra and expenditure distribution of Goa is used to estimate poverty ratio of Goa.
5. Urban Poverty Ratio of Punjab is used for both rural and urban poverty of Chandigarh.
6. Poverty Line of Maharashtra and expenditure distribution of Dadra & Nagar Haveli is used to estimate poverty ratio of Dadra & Nagar Haveli; Poverty Ratio of Himachal Pradesh is used for Jammu & Kashmir.
7. Urban Poverty Ratio of Rajasthan may be treated as tentative.
8. Poverty line is in Rupees per capita per month; 1 Lakh is equivalent to 100,000.

Source : Planning Commission, Government of India.

Table 1.5
Number and Percentage of Population below Poverty Line by States—2004-05 (Based on URP-Consumption)

Sl. No.	State	Rural		Urban		Combined	
		%age of Persons	No. of Persons (Lakhs)	%age of Persons	No. of Persons (Lakhs)	%age of Persons	No. of Persons (Lakhs)
	(1)	(2)	(3)	(4)	(5)	(6)	(7)
1.	Andhra Pradesh	11.2	64.70	28.0	61.40	15.8	126.10
2.	Arunachal Pradesh	22.3	1.94	3.3	0.09	17.6	2.03
3.	Assam	22.3	54.50	3.3	1.28	19.7	55.77
4.	Bihar	42.1	336.72	34.6	32.42	41.4	369.15
5.	Chhattisgarh	40.8	71.50	41.2	19.47	40.9	90.69
6.	Delhi	6.9	0.63	15.2	22.30	14.7	22.93
7.	Goa	5.4	0.36	21.3	1.64	13.8	2.01
8.	Gujarat	19.1	63.49	13.0	27.19	16.8	90.69
9.	Haryana	13.6	21.49	15.1	10.60	14.0	32.10
10.	Himachal Pradesh	10.7	6.14	3.4	0.22	10.0	6.36
11.	Jammu & Kashmir	4.6	3.66	7.9	2.19	5.4	5.85
12.	Jharkhand	46.3	103.19	20.2	13.20	40.3	116.39
13.	Karnataka	20.8	75.05	32.6	63.83	25.0	138.89
14.	Kerala	13.2	32.43	20.2	17.17	15.0	49.60
15.	Madhya Pradesh	36.9	175.65	42.1	74.03	38.3	249.68
16.	Maharashtra	29.6	171.13	32.3	146.25	30.7	317.38
17.	Manipur	22.3	3.76	3.3	0.20	17.3	3.95
18.	Meghalaya	22.3	4.36	3.3	0.16	18.5	4.52
19.	Mizoram	22.3	1.02	3.3	0.16	12.6	1.18
20.	Nagaland	22.3	3.87	3.3	0.12	19.0	3.99
21.	Orissa	46.8	151.75	44.3	26.74	46.4	178.49
22.	Punjab	9.1	15.12	7.1	6.50	8.4	21.63
23.	Rajasthan	18.7	87.38	32.9	47.51	22.1	134.89
24.	Sikkim	22.3	1.12	3.3	0.02	20.1	1.14
25.	Tamil Nadu	22.8	76.50	22.2	69.13	22.5	145.62
26.	Tripura	22.3	6.18	3.3	0.20	18.9	6.38
27.	Uttar Pradesh	33.4	473.00	30.6	117.03	32.8	590.05
28.	Uttarakhand	40.8	27.11	36.5	8.85	39.6	35.96
29.	West Bengal	28.6	173.22	14.8	35.14	24.7	208.36

(Contd.)

TABLE 1.5 (*Contd.*)

(1)	*(2)*	*(3)*	*(4)*	*(5)*	*(6)*	*(7)*
30. A & N Islands	22.9	0.60	22.2	0.32	22.6	0.92
31. Chandigarh	7.1	0.08	7.1	0.67	7.1	0.74
32. Dadra & N. Haveli	39.8	0.68	19.1	0.15	33.2	0.84
33. Daman & Diu	5.4	0.07	21.2	0.14	10.5	0.21
34. Lakshadweep	13.3	0.06	20.2	0.06	16.0	0.11
35. Pondicherry	22.9	0.78	22.2	1.59	22.4	2.37
All-India	28.3	2209.25	25.7	807.96	27.5	3017.20

URP consumption = Uniform Recall Period consumption in which the consumer expenditure data for all the items are collected from 30-day recall period.

Notes : 1. Poverty Ratio of Assam is used for Sikkim, Arunachal Pradesh, Meghalaya, Mizoram, Manipur, Nagaland and Tripura.
2. Poverty Line of Maharashtra and expenditure distribution of Goa is used to estimate poverty ratio of Goa.
3. Poverty Ratio of Tamil Nadu is used for Pondicherry and A & N Island.
4. Urban Poverty Ratio of Punjab used for both rural and urban poverty of Chandigarh.
5. Poverty Line of Maharashtra and expenditure distribution of Dadra and Nagar Haveli is used to estimate poverty ratio of Dadra & Nagar Haveli.
6. Poverty ratio of Goa is used for Daman & Diu.
7. Poverty Ratio of Kerala is used for Lakshadweep.

Source : Planning Commission, Government of India.

Jharkhand, Madhya Pradesh, Chhattisgarh, Uttarakhand and Orissa. (See Table 1.5)

The poverty ratio obtained on the basis of Mixed Recall Period (MRP) indicates that 21.8 per cent of rural population and 21.70 per cent of the urban population was below poverty line. For the country as a whole, 21.80 per cent of the total population was below poverty line in 2004-05. (See Table 1.6)

On the basis of State level data from 1973-74 to 2004-05, it can be concluded that the States which had higher poverty ratio showed a slower rate of decline. The position of Bihar, Orissa and Madhya Pradesh is almost the same in 2004-05 as their position during the year 1973-74. Whereas the States which had the poverty ratio much below the national average like Gujarat, Punjab and Haryana in 1973-74 are still at the bottom end in

TABLE 1.6
Number and Percentage of Population below Poverty Line by States—2004-05 (Based on MRP-Consumption)

Sl. No.	State	Rural		Urban		Combined	
		%age of Persons	No. of Persons (Lakhs)	%age of Persons	No. of Persons (Lakhs)	%age of Persons	No. of Persons (Lakhs)
	(1)	(2)	(3)	(4)	(5)	(6)	(7)
1.	Andhra Pradesh	7.5	43.21	20.7	45.50	11.1	88.71
2.	Arunachal Pradesh	17.0	1.47	2.4	0.07	13.4	1.54
3.	Assam	17.0	41.46	2.4	0.93	15.0	42.39
4.	Bihar	32.9	262.92	28.9	27.09	32.5	290.01
5.	Chhattisgarh	31.2	54.72	34.7	16.39	32.0	71.11
6.	Delhi	0.1	0.01	10.8	15.83	10.2	15.83
7.	Goa	1.9	0.13	20.9	1.62	12.0	1.74
8.	Gujarat	13.9	46.25	10.1	21.18	12.5	67.43
9.	Haryana	9.2	14.57	11.3	7.99	9.9	22.56
10.	Himachal Pradesh	7.2	4.10	2.6	0.17	6.7	4.27
11.	Jammu & Kashmir	2.7	2.20	8.5	2.34	4.2	4.54
12.	Jharkhand	40.2	89.76	16.3	10.63	34.8	100.39
13.	Karnataka	12.0	43.33	27.2	53.28	17.7	96.60
14.	Kerala	9.6	23.59	16.4	13.92	11.4	37.51
15.	Madhya Pradesh	29.8	141.99	39.3	68.97	32.4	210.97
16.	Maharashtra	22.2	128.43	29.0	131.40	25.2	259.83
17.	Manipur	17.0	2.86	2.4	0.14	13.2	3.00
18.	Meghalaya	17.0	3.32	2.4	0.12	14.1	3.43
19.	Mizoram	17.0	0.78	2.4	0.11	9.5	0.89
20.	Nagaland	17.0	2.94	2.4	0.09	14.5	3.03
21.	Orissa	39.8	129.29	40.3	24.30	39.9	153.59
22.	Punjab	5.9	9.78	3.8	3.52	5.2	13.30
23.	Rajasthan	14.3	66.69	28.1	40.50	17.5	107.18
24.	Sikkim	17.0	0.85	2.4	0.02	15.2	0.87
25.	Tamil Nadu	16.9	56.51	18.8	58.59	17.8	115.10
26.	Tripura	17.0	4.70	2.4	0.14	14.4	4.85
27.	Uttar Pradesh	25.3	357.68	26.3	100.47	25.5	458.15
28.	Uttarakhand	31.7	21.11	32.0	7.75	31.8	28.86
29.	West Bengal	24.2	146.59	11.2	26.64	20.6	173.23

(*Contd.*)

TABLE 1.6 (Contd.)

(1)	(2)	(3)	(4)	(5)	(6)	(7)
30. A & N Islands	16.9	0.44	18.8	0.27	17.6	0.71
31. Chandigarh	3.8	0.04	3.8	0.36	3.8	0.40
32. Dadra & N. Haveli	36.0	0.62	19.2	0.16	30.6	0.77
33. Daman & Diu	1.9	0.03	20.8	0.14	8.0	0.16
34. Lakshadweep	9.6	0.04	16.4	0.05	12.3	0.09
35. Pondicherry	16.9	0.58	18.8	1.34	18.2	1.92
All-India	21.8	1702.99	21.7	682.00	21.8	2384.99

MRP consumption = Mixed Recall Period consumption in which the consumer expenditure data for five non-food items, namely, clothing, footwear, durable goods, education and institutional medical expenses are collected from 365-days recall period and the consumption data for the remaining items are collected from 30-day recall period.

Notes : 1. Poverty Ratio of Assam is used for Sikkim, Arunachal Pradesh, Meghalaya, Mizoram, Manipur, Nagaland and Tripura.
2. Poverty Line of Maharashtra and expenditure distribution of Goa is used to estimate poverty ratio of Goa.
3. Poverty Ratio of Tamil Nadu is used for Pondicherry and A & N Island.
4. Urban Poverty Ratio of Punjab used for both rural and urban poverty of Chandigarh.
5. Poverty Line of Maharashtra and expenditure distribution of Dadra and Nagar Haveli is used to estimate poverty ratio of Dadra & Nagar Haveli.
6. Poverty ratio of Goa is used for Daman & Diu.
7. Poverty Ratio of Kerala is used for Lakshadweep.

Source : Planning Commission, Government of India.

terms of poverty ratio of 2004-05. Five states namely Uttar Pradesh, Maharashtra, Bihar, West Bengal and Orissa accounted for 164 million poor (about 51.27 per cent of the total poor) as per the estimates for 1973-74. During 2004-05 also, these states had highest per centage of poor, i.e. 166 million (about 55 per cent of the total poor estimated at 302 million). This shows concentration of bulk of the poor in these states.

The States which had shown a substantial reduction in poverty ratio are Andhra Pradesh, Karnataka, Kerala and Tamil Nadu. These four states had 24 per cent of the country's poor during 1973-74 which reduced to 15.25 per cent in 2004-05. The economic reform process does not seem to have yielded benefits for the states like Bihar, Orissa, Madhya Pradesh and Uttar Pradesh whereas the states namely Assam, Punjab, Haryana, Kerala, Andhra Pradesh, Karnataka, Gujarat, which had high concentration of poor in the pre-reform period experienced a significant decline in the post-reform period. The decline in the poverty ratio had been the highest in the case of Gujarat, Haryana, Punjab and Rajasthan.

The Integrated Rural Development Programme and other Anti-Poverty Programmes launched by the Government have generally been conceived and formulated rightly though it is possible to point out some flaws or the other in each of them. Though the projects and programmes were rightly conceived, the shortfall occurred due to faulty implementation.[48] Irma Adelman and Sherman pointed out, "First, and perhaps surprisingly, we find that most Anti-Poverty policies eventually help the rich and middle income groups more than they help the poor. This is so even when, as in our experiments, the programmes are designed so that their initial impact is quite specific in favouring the lower income groups, and there is no diversion and favouritism in their execution. This trickle-up effect was evident in a great many different policy experiments and is difficult to avoid, second, our experience with a wide range of policies indicates that it is much easier to make income distribution worse than to improve it."[49]

C.T. Kurien has made a much more fundamental criticism of the strategy for poverty alleviation. He opined, given the structure even with the best of political will and a most committed bureaucracy, it is not possible to ensure larger benefits to the weaker sections from the Poverty Alleviation Programmes. In a country where resources are privately owned, unequally distributed and used principally to acquire control over more and more resources, the growth processes and distributive processes will be determined primarily by the given distribution of resource power in the system. The administrative interventions in this arrangement can not always be expected to be successful because they have to "negotiate through the innate economic processes of the system" and the outcome in each specific strength of the two forces viz., the intervention and the structure. In some instances the structural elements can be so pervasive that even the most carefully designed strategies may not only fail, but can turn out to be counter productive."[50]

Poverty in all complexities has been attacked in a piece meal manner through different plans and programmes, and an overall co-ordination of programmes in a multi-dimensional frame work suited to the issue of poverty is still awaited. The Poverty Alleviation Programmes have not been approximately woven with the socio-economic fabric of rural India. The demand side of one development of the rural poor which has to emerge from the clientele below the poverty line has been particularly neglected. The emphasis has been mainly on the quantitative aspects of the programmes and meeting of ambitious targets from year to year. The diluted emphasis on poverty alleviation programmes has affected the quality of assets created, the skill formation in the rural areas, the kind of employment generated and the overall impact of the programmes on the quality of life of the rural poor. India has been continuously experiencing with programmes of poverty alleviation trying to reshape and restructure the programmes on the basis of the past experience. It has been a process of learning by doing because there exists no tailor-made experience of poverty alleviation in a developing world which India can positively emulate. India's disappointments and failures in attacking poverty have made her a lot wiser and open to self-analysis and criticisms. India has improved its past strategies and approaches from one plan to the other and has shown a basic trend of shift in strategies of 'planning from above' to planning from below.[51]

The impact of various Anti-Poverty Programmes has not been satisfactory. The following are the main limitations of these programmes:

(a) There has been wrong identification of beneficiaries to the extent of 15 to 20 per cent on an all India level. This ranged from 47 per cent to 70 per cent in some states. This has been treated as one of the major shortcomings of various Poverty Alleviation Programmes;

(b) The selection of activities is wrongly done without any consideration to the ability of the beneficiaries. There are differences in infrastructural support, backward and forward linkages, etc. As a result of all these, the activities do not prove to be viable thereby affecting the impact of the programmes; and

(c) The credit delivery system is unsound, and the attitude of local level bank functionaries is far from satisfactory.

The magnitude of poverty differs widely among different States as well as among different regions and different sections of population within the State because of difference in topography, resource-endowments, and infrastructural facilities, agro-climatic and socio-economic conditions. Therefore, regional location specific studies can prove crucial in formulating the development strategy to remove the regional imbalances and socio-economic inequalities prevailing among the different sections of the population. Regional planning enables a better perception of local needs and requirements, makes better informed decision-making possible which leads to a better exploitation of local resources and potentials. The social, economic, technical, institutional and organisational problems in the overall economic growth with social justice can be better understood when viewed in the context of the specific area and segment of population. Therefore, the present study has been undertaken with a view to analyse the impact of Poverty Alleviation Programmes on the creation of productive assets, generation of gainful employment opportunities and the resultant increase in income and consumption among the weaker sections in the rural areas of Haryana.

The topography, infrastructural facilities, agro-climatic and socio-economic conditions as well as the characteristics of a particular region have a direct bearing on the levels of living of the people.

An Overview of the State Economy of Haryana

The state of Haryana came into being on 1st of November, 1966 as the 17th State of the Indian Union, as a result of the reorganization of the erstwhile Punjab State into Haryana and Punjab.[52] The Punjab-Reorganization Bill passed by the Indian Parliament on September 10, 1966, bifurcated the bilingual State of Punjab and made provision for the setting up of the new State of Haryana.[53] The State extends from 27°3′ to 31°0′ north latitude and 74°5′ to 77°6′ east longitude.[54] It is located in the Northern part of India and bounded by Uttar Pradesh and Uttrakhand in the East, Punjab in the West, Himachal Pradesh in the North and Rajasthan in the South. The State surrounds on three sides New Delhi, the Capital of the country. Most of the Haryana is in the plains with the Aravalli Mountain range starting its westward journey from here. Yamuna is the only major river that passes through this one of the greenest State of the country.[55]

At the time of formation of Haryana State on 1st November, 1966 there were seven districts viz., Ambala, Karnal, Rohtak, Gurgaon, Mahendergarh, Hisar and Jind. Thereafter new districts were notified from time to time by changing the boundaries of the districts. At present the State comprises of 20 districts viz., Ambala, Karnal, Rohtak, Gurgaon, Mahendragarh, Hisar, Jind, Bhiwani, Sonipat, Kurukshetra, Sirsa, Faridabad, Yamunanagar, Kaithal, Panipat, Rewari, Panchkula, Jhajjar, Fatehabad and Mewat.[56] Total area of the State is 44, 212 sq. km. The State is divided into 4 divisions, 47 sub-division, 67 tehsils, and 45 sub-tehsils. There are 119 Blocks in the state. Total number of villages in the State is 6955. The number of inhabited villages is 6764. Total population of the State according to Census 2001 is 211.45 lakh. The number of males is 113.64 lakh and females is 97.81 lakh, which means number of females per thousand males is 861. The rural population of the State is 150.29 lakh. This is 71.08 per cent of the total population. Urban population in the State is 61.16 lakh which is 28.92 per cent of the total population.[57]

The Decennial growth rate of urban population according to Census 2001 has been 50.82 per cent as against the overall growth rate of 28.43 per cent. The Decennial growth rate of rural population in the State is 21.12 per cent.[58] Total schedules caste population is 40.91 lakh which is 19.4 per cent of the total population. The density of population in Haryana is 478 persons per square km.[59]

The overall literacy rate of Haryana according to Census 2001 is 67.91 per cent. (78.49 per cent for males and 55.73 per cent for females) comparatively it is better than all India literacy rate which is 64.8 per cent.[60]

Out of the total population as many as 62,41,324 are main workers, 21,36,142 are marginal workers and 1,27,67,098 are non workers. The main workers constitute 29.52 per cent of the total population. The main worker is one who has worked for 183 days or more in a year in one or more than one economic activity. A person who has worked for less than 183 days in a year is considered as a marginal worker. According to Census 2001, Out of the total workers (main and marginal) 36.34 per cent are cultivators, 15.26 per cent are agricultural labourers, 2.56 per cent workers in household industry and 45.15 per cent other workers.[61]

Geo-physically Haryana falls into 2 broad natural divisions: (1) the sub-Himalayan tract, and (2) the Indo-Gangetic plain, which run in south-eastern direction, almost parallel to each other. The sub-Himalayan tract which forms a sort of grille in the north-eastern parts of Panchkula district consists of two types of hills, the higher hills and the lower hills. The former are made of two ridges, running throughout the district from the north-west to south-east, with numerous spurs branching out in all directions. These hills are known as Morni and Tipra ranges. In conformation and character, these hills belong to the outer ranges of the lower Himalayas. There are many beautiful valleys in the tract but excepting Kalka and Pinjore, none is adequately habited. The Indo Gangetic plain, the second broad natural division, is in the true sense the backbone of the State. It is a vast level plain standing nearly on the water-parting between the basins of the river Indus and the Ganga. In view of variations in deposits, the extensive plain is divided into five sub-divisions. The first sub-division, called Babbar, forms a fringe zone along the outer margin of the Shiwaliks. This has big deposits of alluvial sands brought and deposited by the rivers streams coming down the northern mountains. It is very sloppy. The second sub-division, the khaddar, occupies the levels lower to the Babbar near the river/ stream channels. Owing to its low level, it is very much prone to flooding which occurs almost every now and then. The fourth sub-division, the sandy tract, comprises the districts of Hisar, Sirsa and Mahendergarh, where wind blown sand stands piled up in the form of sand dunes at several places. The only part useful for cultivation in the sandy tracts are the ones called 'Tals,' where due to some reason or the other, sand does not collect. The fifth sub-division comprises the southern region where a number of hills stand out against the horizon and break the natural regularity of the plains. These hills are popularly called Arrawalis.[62]

Climatically, Haryana is no different from other northern states. It has three seasons in a year: The cool season, from November to February ; the hot season from March to June; and the rainy season, from late June to October. To start with the winter season, Haryana remains under the influence of cool out blowing land winds throughout the season. But the Himalayan mountain walls protect the regions as they do the rest of India from the icy-blasts from central Asia. The general anti-cyclonic conditions of winter months are sometimes interrupted by the feeble cyclones which give a little rainfall to the region. Summer months experience hot weather with desiccating hot winds (loo) and occasional dust storms. The climax of the season is reached in May and June when the region is hot like a furnace. About the middle of July the monsoon clouds begin to appear and the humidity increases rapidly till a thunderstorm announces the advent of the rains.[63] About 80% of the overall rainfall in Haryana falls between July and September. There is pronounced rainfall peak in the months of July, August and September. There is a little amount of rain during the winter season by the cyclones. It is 3 to 4 inches in the upper parts and less than an inch in the lower ones.[64]

The State has very little mineral wealth. It has no coals, gas or petroleum. Most of the minerals are found in Mahendragarh, Gurgaon, Ambala, Yamunanagar and Panchkula districts. Iron ore, limestone and slate are the only three principal minerals economically exploited at present. Other minerals are lime Kankar, China clay, dolomite, quarry and silica. Limestone and Kankar are used for feeding the cement factories in the State and also the Nangal Fertilizer Plant, Punjab. Mahendergarh district is found to be very rich in mineral resources and there is very great scope of exploitation of minerals in this area.[65]

There is a great potential of fish culture in the State. After green and white revolution, Haryana State is now on the threshold of 'Blue Revolution'. Fish culture is also being accepted by the farmers of the state as secondary occupation. Farmers have also started construction of fish tanks in their own land as measures of integration of agriculture. The Government is providing technical and financial assistance through Fish Farmers' Development Agencies to the fish farmers for fish culture. The fish production increased from 39.13 thousand tonnes in 2003-04 to 42.05 thousand tonnes in 2004-05 to 48200.00 tonnes in 2005-06. The State has net national coverage of 2260 kg per hectare of fish production.

The total area under forests in the State of Haryana is 1.56 lakh hectares which constitutes 3.5 per cent of the total geographical area. Integration of growing tree species along with agricultural crops under agro-forestry, adoption of farm forestry, massive afforestation on degraded panchayat lands and afforestation on mobile dunes with active participation of the people has resulted in increase in forest cover of the State. Thus the total forest and tree cover in the State is now 6.6 per cent as reported by Forest Survey of India in its Forest Survey Report 2003. Thus, the total forest and tree cover in the State is now 6.6 per cent as reported in Forest Survey of India Report 2003. Department envisages to increase forest and tree cover in the State from 6.6 to 10 per cent by 2010.

To meet the growing demand of timber and firewood in the State, it is necessary to rehabilitate degraded forest areas and bring new areas under forests. To achieve this objective, afforestation is being carried out under different schemes by Forest Department. Till December, 2006, 4.32 crore seedlings have been planted in the State under the state/centrally sponsored schemes. Of these 1.79 crore have been planted on forest land, common land and wasteland while the remaining 2.53 crore seedlings have been distributed free of cost by the Forest Department to various Government departments, farmers, Panchayats, Educational Institutions and public for plantation on their lands. An Externally Aided Afforestation Project of Rs. 286 crores is being implemented with the financial assistance of Japan Bank of International Cooperation. Under this project, 48800 hectares of land will be brought under afforestation and the project will last for 7 years till 2011. Although Haryana is deficient in the extent of natural forests but due to its location there is diversity of wildlife habitat found in the State. To preserve wildlife, two National Parks and ten Wildlife Sanctuaries have been constituted in the State. The State has taken lead in conservation of vultures. The only of its kind, Vulture Conservation Breeding Centre has been established at Pinjore. An Elephant Rehabilitation Centre is being established in the Shivalik area of the State.[66] Medicinal plants of different varieties have been planted under the "Vanspati Van Scheme" in the State. Government has launched a scheme for plantation of medicinal plants in the State. Ch. Devi Lal Nature Park has been developed over an area of 180 acres in village Chuharpur, district Yamunanagar with the help of Shivalik Development Agency.[67]

Energy in one form or the other is the most important input for any development and directly determines the pace of economic growth in any society. The State Government values the role of electricity in the development of State and assigns highest priority to power sector. Haryana State has limited availability of natural sources of energy. There is no hydro-generation potential in the State. Even the coal mines are far away located from the State. The total installed capacity available to the state at present is 4051.30 MW. It includes 1587.40 MW from State's own stations, 937.50 MW from jointly owned projects and the balance as share in central projects and independent private power projects. The power availability from these sources during the year 2004-05 was 21713.6 million units (MUs). During the year 2005-06 it was 26719.4 MUs and during the year 2006-07 it was 17577.42 MUs. The number of electricity consumers in the state as on March 2006 was 40 lakhs. Every year nearly 1.5 lakh new electric connections are released.[68]

Agriculture is the mainstay of Haryana's economy. About 29.6 per cent of the total income of the state comes from agriculture and allied activities. The total area under crops has increased considerably since 1970-71. The Gross Area Sown, which was 45.99 lakh hectares during 1966-67, has increased to 49.57 lakh hectares in 1971 and further increased to 64.80 lakh hectares during 2006-07. During the year 2006-07 the Gross Area Sown is likely to remain the same, i.e., 64.80 lakh hectares. A remarkable increase in food grains production is visible in Haryana since 1970-71. Production of total food grains is likely to increase from 47.71 lakh tonnes in 1970-71 to 144.43 lakh tonnes in 2006-07 showing an increase of 202.70 per cent. Haryana ranks first in the country in the export of basmati rice.

In the State there is dominance of wheat and rice crops in the gross area sown. The percentage of area under these two crops to the total gross area sown in the State has increased from 28.20 per cent during 1970-71 to 51.27 per cent during 2006-07. Wheat and rice played a major role in pushing up the agricultural production. The production of paddy which was 4.60 lakh tonnes in 1970-71 increased to 30.23 lakh tonnes in 2004-05 and 33.71 lakh tonnes in 2006-07 thereby showing the tremendous increase of 632.80 per cent. Similarly, the production of wheat which was 23.42 lakh tonnes in 1970-71 has increased to 96.97 lakh tonnes during 2006-07 reflecting an increase of 314.00 per cent. During 2005-06 the area under high yielding varieties of wheat, rice, maize and bajra was 99.7, 76.7, 44.6, and 84.2 per cent respectively.[69]

Haryana State is emerging very fast as one of the leading states in the field of horticulture. The main thrust is being given for the development of floriculture and mushroom apart from fruits and vegetables. At present the area under various horticultural crops in the state is about 4.7 per cent of the cropped area. The area and production under fruits increased considerably from 12640 hectares and 99800 tonnes respectively during 1990-91 to 27103 hectares and 236200 tonnes by 2005-06. Likewise area and production under vegetables have also increased from 55360 hectares and 802240 tonnes respectively in 1990-91 to 232660 hectares and 2984800 tonnes during 2005-06. The cultivation of flowers for commercial purpose has also been taken up at a large scale in the State. As a consequence the area under floriculture has increased from 50 hectares during 1990-91 to 5418 hectares during the year 2005-06.[70]

Haryana is the milk pail of India and is famous for its breed of "Hariana Cows" and 'Murrah Buffaloes'. The milk production in the State has increased to 54.70 lakh metric tonnes in 2006-07 as against 52.99 lakh metric tonnes in 2005-06 and is proposed to increase to 61.20 lakh metric tonnes during Eleventh Five Year Plan. The per capita availability of milk in the state has increased from 656 grams per day in 2002-03 to 660 grams per day in 2006-07 and is at the second highest position in the country against the national average of 232 grams. The State Government is laying emphasis on increasing the production capacity of the animals through genetic improvement of the animals. In order to improve the genetic stock, the special attention is being given towards preservation, multiplication and improvement of indigenous germplasm such as Murrah breed of buffaloes and Hariana and Sahiwal breeds of cows.[71]

The canal water is the main source of irrigation as well as domestic supplies to the state. The total availability of water from both the sources i.e. surface and sub-surface is much below the requirement. The availability of surface water is more or less constant with a small variation with the filling of Bhakra and Pong reservoirs and the flow in river Yamuna, whereas the availability of sub surface water is reducing due to more withdrawal than its recharging, thereby declining the ground water levels in sweet water zone. The Government has therefore been giving top priority to the works relating to the conservation and management of available water resources and the recharging of ground water schemes in the depleted zone.[72] The net irrigated area in Haryana during 2003-04 was 2969000 hectares. This constitutes 84 per cent of the net area sown. The main sources of irrigation in Haryana are Government Canals and Tube wells.[73]

Presently Haryana is one of the industrially developed states of the country and is a first choice of the domestic and foreign investors. Haryana has an edge over the other States of the country on account of the best infrastructure facilities, better law and order and cordial labour relations. At the time of formation the State had only 162 large and medium units and about 5000 small scale industries. Today, Haryana has 1290 large and medium units and about 80,000 small scale units.[74] Total number of registered working factories in 2003 in Haryana were 9047 and the estimated number of workers employed in working factories was 553000 in 2003.[75] The number of registered working factories and number of workers employed increased to 9164 and 557285, respectively in 2004. This number further increased to 9282 and 574591 in 2005.[76] Haryana is at the top of the country in the export of basmati rice. Haryana ranks third in the country in software exports in the last three years. With a view to boost exports the State Government is setting up Special Economic Zone on 3000 acres of land in Garhi Harsaru in district Gurgaon. The Special Economic Zone (SEZ) will provide all modern amenities and shall be designated duty free enclave and to be treated as foreign territory for trade and operations, duties and tariffs including custom and central excise duty.[77] So far, the State has received 72 proposals for setting up SEZs with an investment of more than Rs. 175000 crores and employment potential for more than 20 lakh persons. 49 proposals have been granted in principle/formal approval by Government of India. During the year 2006-07 (upto December 2006), 65 SEZ proposals were received with an investment of Rs. 166238 crores and employment potential for 16 lakh persons.[78]

The Cooperative Movement is the best instrument of economic and social reform. The most outstanding work of cooperative movement is reflected in the agricultural credit and agricultural marketing sectors along with the contribution made by other sectors in the upliftment of financial position of people of State. The co-operatives in the State have amply demonstrated their strength in several fields of rural economy. Presently, about 22000 cooperative societies are working in Haryana with a membership of more than 50 lakhs. The cooperative banks have disbursed loans to the tune of Rs. 4357 crores during the year 2005-06 and these banks have fixed a target of Rs. 6200 crores for the year 2006-07. The branches of cooperative banks are being increased from 358 to 560.[79]

The Haryana Khadi and Village Industries Board (HKVIB) is engaged in generating employment and now a days is engaged in implementing Khadi and Village Industry Commission's Rural Employment Generation Programme through banks with one time margin money assistance for developing viable village industry projects. The Haryana Khadi Village Industries Board has reported that Khadi and Village Industry Board of Haryana have achieved production of Rs. 6140.35 lakhs and sale of Rs. 6502.40 lakhs during the year 2006-07 giving full employment to 27677 persons and part time employment to 35349 persons.[80]

A well planned and efficient network of transport is an essential component of developing economy. Haryana Roadways has earned the reputation of being one of the best State Road Transport undertakings in the country, in the fields of operational efficiency, staff productivity, low operational cost, per effective km operated, and profit before taxes, etc. At present, the Haryana Roadways has about 3366 buses (as on 31.12.2006) being run from 20 main depots and 17 sub-depots. These services cover about 11.17 lakh kms every day and carry about 11.15 lakh passengers daily (2006-07).[81] Length of metalled road (P.W.D.) is 23013 kms and the number of villages connected with pucca roads is 6756 during 2005-06.[82]

Education is a key to development and this factor has become the most important part of every Government agenda. At present there are 5 universities and 282 colleges, 5317 High/ senior secondary schools, 2168 middle schools and 12179 primary schools.[83] A number of incentives to girls and all children belonging to weaker sections have been provided to encourage their enrolment and retention in schools. Free text books have also been provided to Scheduled Castes and Weaker section students studying in classes VI to XII in Government schools worth Rs. 165.00 lakhs annually. Total literacy campaign is being reactivated in the state. Post-Literacy Programme is being implemented in 7 districts. State Government is providing free cycles to girl students of those villages which do not have middle school.[84]

Under National Programme for Nutritional Support to primary education, centrally sponsored mid-day meal (cooked food) scheme to provide cooked food to the children for primary classes (I-V) in all Government, local bodies and government aided private schools, has been launched in the entire State from 15th August, 2004. The main objective of the scheme is to boost universalization of primary education by increasing enrolment, retention and attendance and simultaneously impacting on nutritional level of students in primary classes.

The State economy continued to record a steady growth during 2005-06. According to quick estimates, the Gross State Domestic Product (GSDP) of Haryana at constant (1999-2000) prices has been estimated at Rs. 77666.20 crores in 2005-06 as against Rs. 71879.71 crores in 2004-05 recording a growth of 8.1 per cent during 2005-06 as against 5.2 per cent during 2002-03. At current prices, the Gross State Domestic Product has been estimated at Rs. 100675.55 crore in 2005-06 as against Rs. 89431 crore in 2004-05 recording an increase of 12.6 per cent. The structural composition of the State economy has witnessed significant changes since the formation of Haryana state. Agriculture sector still continues to occupy a significant position in state economy, although the share of this sector in the Gross State Domestic Product is continuously declining. The pre dominance of agriculture sector is also responsible for instability in the growth rate of economy due to fluctuations in agricultural production. The natural calamities and fluctuations in rainfall often cause substantial loss in crop production which eventually results in fluctuations and instability in the growth rate of state economy. Moreover, rapidly increasing share of service sectors is also responsible for decline in the share of Agriculture sector. The composition of Gross State Domestic Product at constant (1999-2000) prices reveals that the share of primary sector which includes agriculture and allied sectors has declined from 31.9 per cent during 1999-2000 to 23.3 per cent during 2005-06. The share of secondary sector which also includes manufacturing sector has increased from 30.00 per cent during 1999-00 to 32.4 per cent during 2005-06. Tertiary sector which is a combination of different services like trade, transport, banking, public administration, education, health, etc. also witnessed significant increase in its share. Its share has increased from 38.1 per cent during 1999-00 to 44.3 per cent during 2005-06. The per capita net state domestic product in real terms at constant (1999-00) prices has been estimated at Rs. 29887 during 2005-06 as against Rs. 28119 during 2004-05 showing an increase of 6.3 per cent during 2005-06. At current prices, the per capita income has been estimated at Rs. 38832 during 2005-06 as against Rs. 35044 during 2004-05 showing an increase of 10.8 per cent during 2005-06.[85] As per a survey conducted by the Haryana Government in 2000, the total number of families below poverty line in the State was 826562, out of which 187785 families were in the urban areas and 638777 in rural areas.[86]

Poverty Alleviation and Welfare Schemes

The State Government has been constantly making efforts to eradicate poverty in the State by assisting people living below the poverty line through various schemes, in order to break the vicious circle of poverty. Necessary steps are being taken to identify the poorest of the poor families and distribution of pink colored ration cards under Antyodya Anna Yojana scheme of Government of India launched in Haryana during 2001-02.

Under this scheme, 35 kilograms wheat per family per month is being supplied to the Antyodya families at the rate of Rs. 2.10 per kilogram. The transportation and dealers margin is borne by the State Government. Under this scheme, the Government of India is allocating 10235 metric tonnes of wheat per month to the State of Haryana for Antyodya families. Pink ration cards have been issued to 2.89 lakh Antyodya families under this scheme in the State upto March, 2005. The State has also taken up several measures for carrying out socio-economic programmes especially for the welfare of the backward classes, handicapped persons, destitute women and weaker sections by adopting a policy of one job for one family, permits to unemployed youths for operating maxi-cabs, introduction of "Sulabh Shauchalayas", liberation of scavengers from their traditional occupation of manual removal of night-soil and universalization of education.

Among the Poverty Alleviation Programmes, Swarnjayanti Gram Swarozgar Yojana (SGSY) is a holistic Programme covering all aspects of self-employment such as organization of the poor into self-help groups, training, credit, technology, infrastructure, marketing, etc. The target group consists of families living below the poverty line. The objective of the scheme is to bring every assisted family above the poverty line. Under this scheme, total funds to the tune of Rs. 1464.09 lakhs were made available during the year 2006-07. Against the available funds, an amount of Rs. 832.10 lakhs has been utilised for assisting 5906 Swarozgaries upto the end of December, 2006.Under this scheme, an outlay of Rs. 500 lakhs has been proposed as 25 per cent State share for annual plan 2007-08.

Under Indira Awaas Yojana, 3002 houses were constructed and construction of 3242 houses was in progress at the end of December, 2006. During this period, an expenditure of Rs. 1141.13 lakhs had been incurred. Under this scheme, an outlay of Rs. 600 lakhs as 25 per cent State share has been proposed for annual plan 2007-08.

The Sampooran Grameen Rozgar Yojana (SGRY) aims to provide additional wage employment opportunities to rural poor who are in need of work. The secondary objective of the scheme is the creation of durable community, social and economic assets and infrastructural development in rural areas.

The wages to the workers are being paid in the shape of cash and kind. At present, 5 kg. of wheat at the price of Rs. 6.86 per kg. and cash wage of Rs. 62.25 per man per day are being provided to the workers engaged under SGRY. Under this scheme, total funds to the tune of Rs. 5869.19 lakhs were available upto the month of December, 2006. Against the available funds, an amount of Rs. 4157.39 lakh has been utilized for generating 34.36 lakh mandays in rural areas. The Government of India has also allocated 36818 metric tonnes food grains (wheat) to the State Government free of cost under this scheme for distribution to the workers. Against this, 22581 metric tonnes of wheat have been distributed to the workers as part of wages. Under SGRY an outlay of Rs. 2100 lakhs has been proposed as 25 per cent State share for annual plan 2007-08. More durable community assets would also be created in the villages.

The Ministry of Rural Development, Government of India had launched a scheme namely, National Food For Work Programme (NFFWP) from the year 2004-05 in Mahendergarh District. This is a 100 per cent Centrally Sponsored Scheme. Food grains are also provided by the Government of India, free of cost. The main objective of this Programme is to provide additional resources apart from the resources available under the Sampooran Grameen Rozgar Yojana (SGRY) so that generation of supplementary wage employment and providing of food-security through creation of need based economic, social and community assets in the district is further intensified. This Programme is open to all rural poor who are in need of wage employment and desire to do manual and unskilled work. Under the scheme, an assistance of about Rs. 600.00 lakh would be provided to district Mahendergarh during 2005-06 for generation of supplementary wage employment and creation of need based assets in the district. Efforts would be made to cover other poor districts of the State under the scheme.

Another new 100 per cent Centrally Assisted Scheme namely, Backward District Initiative-Rashtriya Sam Vikas Yojana (RSVY) now Backward Region Grant Fund (BRGF) has been launched from the year 2004-05 in Sirsa District. From the year 2007-08, this scheme has been extended by the Government of India to district Mahendergarh also. The main aim of this scheme is to solve the problems of poverty, low growth, poor governance in the backward district. The selection of district has been made by the Planning Commission, Government of India. The project is required to be implemented in a period of 3 years. Under this scheme, an amount of Rs. 1226.14 lakh has been spent and 656 works have been completed upto December, 2006 and 231 works are under progress.

The Swaran Jayanti Shahari Rozgar Yojana (SJSRY) provides gainful employment to the urban un-employed and under-employed poor beneficiaries through setting up of self-employment ventures providing wage employment through skill development training .The scheme is funded in the ratio of 75:25 by the Centre and the State Government. During the year 2006-07, 1737 individual beneficiaries and 58 groups relating to Development of Women and Children in Urban Areas (DWCUA) were provided loan and subsidy, 5380 persons were provided training, 59 Thrift and Credit Societies were assisted and 0.39 lakh mandays were generated upto 31.12.2006. There is a provision of Rs. 412.50 lakh in the State Budget 2007-08 for the scheme.

The scheme of Integrated Housing and Slum Development Programme (IHSDP) was introduced by the Government of India by replacing National Slum Development Programme (NSDP) and Valmiki Ambedkar Awas Yojana (VAMBAY) in December, 2005 to provide adequate and satisfactory water supply, sanitation, primary education facilities, health care, adult literacy and non-formal education facilities etc. in slum areas. This is a demand based scheme and the funds are to be provided by the Government of India and State Government in the ratio of 80:20. The contribution of the beneficiary is merely 12 per cent for general category and 10 per cent for SC category for the construction/up-gradation of dwelling units. So far, project reports for 31 towns have been submitted to the Government of India out of which 12 projects with a total financial outlay of Rs. 235.74 crores have been approved.

Old Age Allowance Scheme prevalent in the State has been based on economic criteria and the eligibility age is 60 years or more so as to give the benefit to the really poor and needy persons. Under this scheme, pension amounting to Rs. 300 per month is given to the eligible senior citizen of Haryana domicile. The norms of the existing scheme have also been relaxed to widen its scope. 1074610 eligible senior citizens have been covered under the scheme upto 31st December, 2006.

Widow Pension Scheme is also being implemented to provide security and financial assistance to widows and destitute women. Under this scheme, widows and destitute women aged 18 years and above, who have no other financial support, are provided pension of Rs. 350 per month. A total of 389481 such women had been benefited upto December, 2006. In addition, the State is running 3 women homes at Karnal, Rohtak and Faridabad for young widows and destitute women and their dependent children to rehabilitate and provide the facilities of boarding, lodging, education and vocational training in various trades.

The State has also taken a number of steps for rehabilitation of blind, deaf, handicapped and mentally retarded persons. As many as 106995 physically handicapped persons are being provided pension at the rate of Rs. 300 and Rs. 600 (Rs. 600 per month only for 100 per cent physically handicapped) per month upto December, 2006. Scholarships ranging between Rs. 100 to Rs. 750 per moth are being given to handicapped students. The un-employment allowance to the educated handicapped persons are being given between Rs. 200 to Rs. 300 per month. The rate of unemployment allowance has been enhanced in 2004 from Rs. 200 to Rs. 400 and Rs. 300 to Rs. 600 for only blind persons.

In the area of social security, a scheme known as Rajiv Gandhi Parivar Bima Yojana, launched from 1 April, 2006 to provide social security to the citizens of the State. Under this scheme, dependants of the bread earner of a family in the age group of 18-80 years except employees of Government and its Public Sector Undertakings, Cooperative Institutions, Universities and Government Aided Institutions and Income Tax Payees are provided compensation of Rs. 1.00 lakh in case of unnatural death or permanent total disability due to accidents like rail or road or air accidents, tractor or farming equipment, riot, earthquake, strike, terrorist activity, storm, cyclone, snake bite, drowning, poisoning, electrocution, falling from height, collapse of house or building, fire, explosion, murder, attack of animals, stampede and suffocation, lightening, frost bite, sun burn (loo), burn injuries, death or permanent total disability due to any other unnatural event, within 72 hours of the submission of claim form. Similarly, Rs. 25,000 to Rs. 50,000 is also given on the basis of disability per centage. 980 cases have been covered upto 31st December, 2006 under this scheme.

The Samman Pension is being paid to the freedom fighters and their widows. It has been increased from Rs. 3,500 per month including fixed medical allowance to Rs. 5,125 at the pattern of Swatantrata Sainik Samman Pension Scheme 1980. The benefits are available to dependents of martyrs of armed forces and have been extended to martyrs of paramilitary forces.

Under Indira Gandhi Priyadarshani Viwah Shagun Yojana, the Scheduled Castes persons living below the poverty line will be given Rs. 15,000 at the time of marriage of their daughter and the persons of other sections of society will be given Rs. 5,100 for this purpose. Keeping in view the miserable economic conditions of the widows, Rs. 15,000 are also given to the widows of all sections of the society living below poverty line under this scheme from August, 2006.

The Department of Women and Child development is functioning in the State for overall development and empowerment of women and children. Integrated Child Development Services (ICDS) has been expanded as a step towards universalization of ICDS, the total number of sanctioned ICDS projects in the states has risen from 116 to 128 with 16359 Anganwari Centres, including 10 urban projects. Under this scheme, services like Supplementary Nutrition, Immunization, Health Check Up, Referral Services, Non-Formal Pre-School Education and Health and Nutrition Education are being provided to children below 6 years of age, pregnant and nursing mothers and other women in the age group of 15-45 years in an integrated manner through the network of Anganwari Centres. During the year 2006-07, a sum of Rs. 4608.16 lakhs have been spent on ICDS and Rs. 4376.42 lakhs on supplementary nutrition upto December, 2006. A sum of Rs. 17199.72 lakhs has been proposed in the budget for the year 2007-08 for implementation of ICDS scheme including a sum of Rs. 8250.99 lakhs for supplementary nutrition.

In order to eradicate malnutrition among children, two new schemes namely "Improving Infant and Young Child

Feeding" and "Best Mother Awards" have been started from the year 2005-06. A sum of Rs. 19.16 lakhs was provided in the budget to cover 2346 mothers during the year 2006-07.

The Women and Child Development Department is implementing many others programmes/schemes launched by State/Central Government. Kishori Shakti Yojana is being implemented and it has become the second biggest scheme of human resources development after Integrated Child Development Services Scheme for improving the health and nutritional status of adolescent girls in the age group of 11-18 years and to train and equip them to improve home-based and vocational skills and to promote awareness of health, hygiene, nutrition, home management, child care, etc. Under this scheme, services are provided through formation of Balika Mandals for 6 months in 10 per cent of Anganwari Centres. At present 1622 Balika Mandals have been formed. The girls are also provided supplementary nutrition at the rate of Rs. 5 per girl per day. 60291 girls have been provided supplementary nutrition and training. A sum of Rs. 320 lakhs has been proposed in the budget for the year 2007-08 out of which Rs. 250 lakhs are under supplementary nutrition.

To remove the sense of economic insecurity in the minds of parents who have only daughters, Ladli Social Security Pension Scheme is being implemented from November, 2006 under which pension at the rate of Rs. 300 per month will be paid to the families from the 55th birthday of the father or mother till their 60th birthday, i.e. for five years. Thereafter, they will be eligible for old age allowance.

The Haryana Scheduled Castes Finance and Development Corporation provides loan/benefit to only those identified Scheduled Caste families whose annual family income does not exceed Rs. 20,000 in rural areas and Rs. 27,500 in urban areas for various bank assisted income generating schemes such as dairy farming, sheep rearing, piggery, kiryana shop, animal driven carts, leather and leather goods making, tea shop and bangles shop, etc. In case of National Scheduled Caste Finance and Development Corporation (NSFDC) assisted schemes such as purchase of Light Commercial Vehicles, Auto-Rickshaw (Diesel), Car Taxi (Diesel-5 Seater) and Jeep (Diesel-10 Seater), etc., the income ceiling is Rs. 40,000 per annum in rural areas and Rs. 55,000 per annum in urban areas. There is no income limit under National Safai Karamcharies Finance and Development Corporation (NSKFDC) Schemes, only occupation is the criteria for eligibility.

Haryana Backward Classes and Economically Weaker Section Kalyan Nigam is working for the economic upliftment of backward classes, minority communities and handicapped persons. Against a target of Rs. 3.4 crores for providing financial assistance to 1180 persons of backward classes during 2006-07, loan of Rs. 342.05 lakhs to 1279 persons of backward classes has been given upto 31.12.2006. A target of Rs. 4.88 crore is fixed for providing financial assistance to 940 persons of Minority Communities during the year 2006-07 and the Nigam has managed to disburse loan worth Rs. 563.35 lakh to 1063 persons of Minority Communities upto 31.12.2006. Against the target of providing financial assistance of Rs. 5 crores to 800 handicapped persons during 2006-07, Rs. 158.02 lakhs have been given to 316 handicapped persons upto 31st December, 2006.[87]

An Overview of the District Economy of Yamunanagar

The Yamunanagar district, named after its head quarter town came into being on 1st November, 1989 exactly 23 years after the State came into existence. The Yamunanagar town which is located on the banks of Yamuna River was known as Abdulapur before partition. Yamunanagar district has been carved out of old Ambala district. The district has border with Himachal Pradesh and Uttar Pradesh.[88] The district enjoys the unique privilege of serving as gateway to the state of UP. The district is bounded by Saharanpur district of UP in the East, Ambala district in the West, Sirmour district of HP in North and Karnal and Kurukshetra district in the South. A major part of the district is plain except northern part which is covered by Shivalik hills.

The agricultural land in the district is quite fertile and major crops of the district are sugarcane, wheat and rice. The district is said to be sugar bowl of Haryana as one of the biggest Sugar mill of Asia is located in the city. The other major industries in the city are that of Engineering goods, Paper, Automobile, Steel-Rolling, Agricultural implements and Leather goods, etc. The Jagadhri town which is just adjacent to the head quarters is famous for its brass utensils all over India. The small scale industries of steel and aluminum are also developing in the town and state government has also approved a plan to establish thermal plant in Yamunanagar.[89]

The district has an area of 1768 square Kms according to Census 2001.[90] The district comprises two tehsils viz., Jagadhri, Chhachharauli and four sub-tehsils viz., Bilaspur, Radaur, Sadhaura and Mustafabad. Administratively the district has one sub-division, i.e. Jagadhri. From the development point of view, the district is divided into six blocks viz., Bilaspur, Chhachharauli, Jagadhri, Radaur, Sadhaura and Mustafabad.[91] The district has 639 villages out of which 613 are inhabited and 26 uninhabited villages. Number of towns in the district is 11 according to Census 2001.[92]

Total population of Yamunanagar district increased from 806279 in 1991 to 10,41,630 in 2001. Out of total population 559444 are males and 482186 are females. The rural population according to the Census 2001 constituted 648608 (62.27%) out of which 347540 are males and 301068 are females. The urban population is 393022 (37.73%) out of which 211904 are males and 181118 are females.[93] Scheduled caste population of the district which was 205155 during 1991 (24.96%)[94] increased to 255550 during 2001 which is 24.50 per cent of the total population.[95]

According to the Census 2001 there are 280728 main workers, 55805 are marginal workers and 705097 are the non workers. Main workers are 26.95 per cent of the total population. Out of the total working population (Main + Marginal Workers) 58,701 are cultivators, 54,470 are agricultural labourers, 10831 are in the household industries and 212531 are the other workers.[96]

The density of population of the district which was 456 persons per square kms. in 1991 increased to 589 persons per square kilometers in 2001.[97]

The literacy per centage in the district is 71.63 per cent (78.82% for males and 63.39 for females) which was 60.53 per cent (69.76 for males and 50.07 for females) during 1991. The literacy rate in Yamunanagar is above the State average of 67.91 per cent.[98]

The Yamunanagar district which ranks tenth in the State accounts for 4.66 per cent of the total population of the State as per 2001 Census. In terms of its ranking in population size in India its rank falls at 414th place out of 593 districts in India. The growth rate of population in district was 40.82 per cent during 1951-61 as against 33.79 per cent for the state as a whole. In the succeeding decades, it was 29.24 per cent during 1961-71, 32.26 per cent in 1971-81, 27.41 per cent during 1981-91 and 21.84 per cent during 1991-2001 in comparison to growth rate of population for the state as a whole which is 28.06 per cent. The relative lower growth rate of population may be attributed to success of family welfare programmes, out migration and sluggish growth of industries which discouraged immigration.

Yamunanagar district has recorded a considerable decrease in sex ratio from 883 in 1991 to 863 in 2001 a decline of 20 points. The decline is relatively more in the child sex ratio (0-6 age group) from 888 in 1991 to 807 in 2001. In the rural areas of district the sex ratio has declined to 869 in 2001 from what it was in 1991 (884). The main reason for low sex ratio may be due to out migration and medical facilities available in town of Jagadhri and Yamunanagar.[99]

The climate of the district is different during the year with the seasons of winter, summer and monsoon. Normally the months of November to February are cold, whereas the hot weather is pronounced from March to the advent of the monsoon. The monsoon mostly breaks in the last weak of June or first week of July. Hills of Shivalik in the north also influence the local weather.

The annual rainfall varies from year to year. The months of July and August are the wettest. The rainy season in the district generally begins in the later half of June and till end of September. Occasionally showers are continual in October and November after which there is usually little rain until the winter showers caused by western winds. Annual rainfall was 1110 mm during 2004-05.[100]

The main river of the district is Yamuna by which the name of district came to existence. The other main rivers of the district are Chitang, Pathrola, Som, Markanda, Sarswati, Makti and Rakshi. All these rivers came from different areas of

Yamunanagar. Almost all the rivers in the district are seasonal and tributaries to the main rivers.

The main forest product in the district is Safeda, Shisham, Kikar, Neem, Khair, Sagwan, Sain, Sal, Sandan, Bahera, Teak, Bamboo, Pulp and Bhabhar. The important market in the district where the major portion of the forest product is consumed is Yamunanagar. The forest-based industries at Yamunanagar are paper mill, saw mill, hard board, straw board & plyboard factories, sugar mill, packing case industry and furniture market. Jagadhri, the sister town of Yamunanagar, is one of the main fuel wood consuming centres. The fuel wood is mainly used in metal industry and brick making. Chhachharauli has a local market for Bhabbar and Ban all made from it. The main marketable forest produce and the tract are Kalesar, Kalanaur and Kotkalsia. Total forest area in the district is 218 sq. kms. This is 12.33 per cent of the total geographical area.[101]

The situation is satisfactory regarding the transportation, communication, housing, defence, power, medical and public health, education, ware housing, marketing and banking, etc.

There are 923 primary schools, 65 middle schools, 92 high/ senior secondary schools in the district.

Among the medical and health facilities there are 6 hospitals, 17 dispensaries, 19 primary health centres and 112 sub-centres. The metallic road length of the district is 941 km, surfaced road 937 km and unsurfaced road 4 kms. The total length of railway tracks in the district is 34 km. [102]

Yamunanagar district has a network of 119 bank branches. Punjab National Bank is the lead bank in the district. There are 90 branches of Commercial Banks, 4 Primary Co-operative Agriculture and Rural Development Banks, 17 branches of Yamunanagar District Central Co-operative Bank and 8 branches of Regional Rural Banks. Out of 119 bank branches in the district 11 branches are in Bilaspur block, 71 in Jagadhri, 5 in Sadhaura, 16 in Chhachharauli, 11 in Radaur and 5 branches are in Mustafabad block.[103]

Electricity supply is available in all the urban, semi-urban and all villages of the district. Water supply is also available in all urban and semi-urban areas and in some villages of the district, but in many villages the water supply through taps is not available. The villages get water from wells, rivers, and hand pumps for their daily needs.

Economy of the district which was mainly agrarian in the past, is transforming but very slowly. Big industries relating to brassware, sugar, paper and allied activities were well established here since ages but have not grown. With working population 32.29 per cent in 2001 which was 27.88 per cent in 1991, the district ranks 18th among 20 districts of Haryana. Due to special emphasis given on to net the work of females, work participation rate has increased from 2.75 per cent to 11.38 per cent in the district over the decades. Similar emphasis was also laid on to net the marginal workers resulting in major change.

There were only 0.30 per cent marginal workers in 1991 whereas 5.23 per cent marginal workers were reported during 2001. Yamunanagar district has a very big army of non-workers (67.71%) and is second to Ambala district in this regard. Women work participation is also the lowest in these two districts. The main reason for low reporting of women workers can be attributed to the concentration of Punjabi population which shifted here after partition. Only 33.03 per cent workers were engaged in agricultural pursuits and 3.07 per cent were engaged in household industries whereas a major part (63.90 per cent) of workers were pursuing other occupations. Of the total female workers 76.96 per cent were reported in other work category. In rural areas 49.87 per cent of the total workers are engaged in agricultural activities and only 2.79 per cent are in household industry. Whereas in urban areas 92.57 per cent of total workers are engaged in other workers' category.

In the Yamunanagar district, out of total persons, 27.06 per cent are main workers and 5.23 per cent marginal workers. Work participation rates for the district was the lowest among the districts of State in 1991 census which unfortunately still continues during 2001 Census also, though the work participation rate has gone up from 2.21% in 1991 to 6.89% in 2001 for female main workers. Similarly, work participation of female marginal workers has also increased from 0.54 per cent to 4.49 per cent. When we compare rural and urban statistics of 2001 we find work participation rates for both males and females among marginal workers are quite high. The female work participation rate among main workers is also higher in the rural areas.

Yamunanagar district ranks 18th among the twenty districts so far as work participation rate is concerned and also ranks 18th for female work participation rate in 2001 Census. It shows relative stagnation in spite of high fertility of land, industrially developed area with sufficient rainfall coupled with underground sweet water. Relatively low per centage of workers also conveys the growing magnitude of unemployment.[104]

Industry sector is one of the important sectors of the economy. Government has laid special emphasis on development of this sector due to its valuable contribution to the economic development of the country viz. national income, greater employment opportunities, potential for export and equal distribution of resources, etc. In the liberalised industrial policy, the Government has announced a number of measures to boost industrial growth, viz. delicencing, liberal imports, speed flow of credit to the industry and incentives for capital investment.

Small Scale Industry (SSI) as an important segment of priority sector lending is getting lot of attention by the central and state governments for its sustained growth. Small scale industry plays a very important role in providing better opportunities for the unemployed, decentralisation of economy, increased share of export, increasing productivity, better utilisation of natural and local resources and also helpful to decrease the per centage of poverty. The small scale sector comprises of: tiny units comprising of villages and cottage industries, artisan-based units and other small scale industries.

The Yamunanagar district is well placed for development and growth of industry. The infrastructural facilities available in the district are: Industrial Estate Developed by the Haryana State Industries Development Corporation is existing at Yamunanagar itself and now Haryana State Industries Development Corporation is carving out industrial area at Manakpur. Moreover, suitable land is easily available throughout the district at reasonable rates for setting up new industrial units; quality marketing centre with common facility workshop is existing at Jagadhri. The centre provides facilities like anodising, heat treatment and mechanical testing of metal; District Industries Centre, Yamunanagar is headed by the General Manager and plays pivotal role in development of Small Scale Industries, tiny and village industries. The District Industries Centre provides following facilities to the entrepreneurs : Registration of small industries on provisional and permanent basis, entrepreneurial guidance with regards to selection of project and getting back credit, provision of financial incentives as announced by State government from time to time, supply of project report, implementation and monitoring of Rural Industries scheme of the State government. Under single windows service concept, the District Industries Centre tries to sort out all types of problems being faced by the entrepreneurs in successful implementation of their projects, etc. There is one polytechnic at Damla and two ITIs (one at Chhachharauli and one at Yamunanagar) in the district. Yamunanagar and Jagadhri are connected with the railway network and good transport facilities are available in the district. Power and labour are available in the district and people of the district possess entrepreneurial qualities.

About 8376 small scale Industries units are registered with District Industries Centre, Yamunanagar. Out of the total number of Small Scale Units registered, 2502 units have been set-up under Rural Industries Scheme of the State government. These units provide employment to 36900 persons. Most of the units at Jagadhri are engaged in metal forming activity whereas at Yamunanagar agro and forest-based units dominate the scene. Quite a good number of units are engaged in fabrication of sugar, chemical and paper machinery.[105]

Out of the total area 12500 hectares is net sown area.[106] Per centage of net irrigated area to net area sown is 90.4 per cent in 2004-05 which was 90.4 per cent in 2003-04, 87.2 per cent in 2000-01 and 79.8 per cent in 1995-96.[107] Whereas, the per centage of Gross area irrigated to Gross area sown is 91.6 per cent.[108] Rice is grown in 58700 hectares, maize in 1900 hectares, wheat in 72300 hectares, oil seeds in 3300 hectares, sugarcane in 38400 hectares, pulses (rabi and kharif) in 2900 hectares and potato in 1300 hectares.[109]

On a comparative basis there is a lesser quantity of cultivable land in Chhachharauli, Bilaspur and Sadhaura blocks. In Chhachharauli block most of the land is stony and there is absence of irrigation facilities. Larger area is covered by forests. Some land of Sadhaura block is also stony and there is lack of irrigation facilities.

The cultivators have mostly started using improved quality seeds, fertilizers, insecticides, pesticides, etc. and due to interest in revitalisation of farming there is a regular increase in the number of pump sets, electric tube wells, tractors, implements, etc. But as the size of land holding is small agricultural machines like harvesters, combine etc. could not become popular. There has been a steady rise in the yield of crops per hectare during the period 1999-02 to 2003-04.

The horticulture has remained neglected sector in entire district. Lack of co-ordination between commercial banks and State level agencies has been identified as one of the constraint factor. But with the creation of separate directorate, it is hoped that the average area under horticultural crops will increase manifold. Due to comparable better returns, farmers are shifting to more paying horticultural crops which are capable of providing greater employment opportunities and produce value addition.[110]

The canal irrigation facility is only available in some parts of the Chhachharauli block. Rest of the blocks are completely dependent on the underground water for meeting irrigation water requirement. Gradually the farmers are shifting to deep tube well, as the ground water level in many parts has fallen considerably. But the unscientific and excessive exploitation of ground water have rendered most parts of the district among dark/grey areas. In the watershed management, an integrated approach is taken up for development of resources. In term of resources development it starts with water, then extends to the resources of fuel, fodder, horticulture, livestock and all associated components. Major parts of the district particularly Sadhaura and Bilaspur blocks are affected by deep soil erosion, resulting in vast stretch of degraded lands unfit for producing agricultural products. The area is quite rugged and needs special technology for reclamation. To check further degradation of land and to reclaim already degraded land, a World Bank-aided project is running in the district.[111]

Animal husbandry activities like dairy, poultry, goat rearing and sheep rearing are playing important role in socio-economic development of the rural areas. As per the Livestock Census 1992 the livestock population was 392972 and that of puppetry birds was 729116 in the district. In order to increase milk, egg and meat production in the district the department is undertaking a number of developmental programmes. Special dairy development programme is undertaken under the auspices of milk commissioner (Mini Dairy) with the following objectives, (i) to provide self-employment to educated unemployed youth and ex-servicemen, (ii) to raise socio-economic standard of weaker sections of society, and (iii) to meet the requirement of quality, dairy products and balance diet to all sections of the society through modern and scientific methods of dairy farming.[112]

During 2001, 31320 families (i.e. 32.34 per cent) in the rural areas of the district were below poverty line[113] against the state average of 30.34 per cent. At present various anti-poverty and development programmes are in progress in the district. The development programmes implemented in the district can be classified into two groups viz. *(a) Bankable Schemes* implemented by different district development agencies. These schemes mainly fall under the Central Government and State Government sponsored programmes. Most of them deal with the overall socio-economic development of rural areas and the deprived sections of the society. The different development programmes/schemes under it are Rural Industrial Scheme, Prime Minister Rojgar Yojana, Bio-gas, Intensive Cattle Development Programme, Mini Dairy, Fish Farming, Development Programmes for Scheduled Castes, Development Programme for Women. Different ongoing schemes for Ex-servicemen, Schemes for development of Khadi and Village Industries, Special Food Grain Production Programme, Oil-seeds Production Programme and Investment Credit to Small Scale Industries, *(b) NABARD approved schemes.* These schemes are formulated on compact area basis by the concerned banks and thereafter got approved from National Bank for Agriculture and Rural Development (NABARD). It is implemented over a period of 5-6 years. All these schemes fall under the non-automatic refinance schemes of NABARD.[114]

Out of 65367 land holdings in the district 31583 are less than one hectare which is 48.3 per cent, 13143 are between 1 to

2 hectares which is 20.1 per cent and 20641 are above 2 hectares which is 31.6 per cent.[115]

As the per centage of small and uneconomic holdings, i.e. land holdings upto 1 hectare is high as compared to large sized holdings, therefore, it is suggested to encourage agricultural-based industries so as to provide additional sources of income and employment to small, marginal farmers and landless agricultural labourers of the district.

Notes and References

1. Gopal Kadekod, and Mary Gregory, Income Distribution, Growth and Basic Needs in India, Vikas Publishing House, New Delhi, 1979, pp. 3-4.
2. S.K. Rao, A Note on Measuring Economic Distances Between Regions in India, *Economic and Political Weekly,* Vol. 8, No. 17, Bombay, (April 28, 1983), p. 793.
3. P.S. Mundinanani, Regional Disparities in India, *Yojana,* Vol. 27, No. 19, New Delhi, October 16-31, 1983, pp. 3-4.
4. M.L. Patel, Dilemma of Balanced Regional Development, Progress Publishers, Bhopal, 1975, p. 18.
5. B.S. Minhas, Planning and Poor, S. Chand and Company, New Delhi, 1974, p. 7.
6. Claus, H.R.H. Prince, One World and Many, *Development Journal of the Society for International Development,* No. 2, Rome, 1991.
7. K.A. Jalihal and M. Shivanthi, Pragmatic Rural Development for Poverty Alleviation, A Pioneering Paradigm Concept Publishing Company, New Delhi, p. 37.
8. Food and Agricultural Organization (FAO), Population and Agricultural Development, Rome, 1977.
9. Raghbendra Jha, Growth Inequality and Poverty in India : Spatial and Temporal Characteristics, *Economic and Political Weekly,* Vol. XXXV, No. 11, Bombay, March 11, 2000, pp. 921-28.
10. V.M. Dandekar and Nilakantha Rath, Poverty in India, Indian School of Political Economy, Bombay, 1971, p. 1.
11. Mansoor, Ali, Missing Links in Indian Planning, Light and Life Publishers, New Delhi, 1979.
12. C.T. Kurien, Poverty, Planning and Social Transformation, Allied Publishers, New Delhi, 1978, pp. 1-2.
13. United Nations, Economic and Social Commission for Asia and Pacific (ESCAP), The Rural Poor, Bangkok, 1985. pp. 2-3.
14. Neela Mukherjee, Lessons of Poverty Alleviation Programmes, *Yojana,* Vol. 34, Nos. 14 and 15, New Delhi, 1990, p. 37. Also see Vivek Ranjan Bhattacharya. *New Face of Rural India—March of New Twenty Point Programme,* Metropolitan Book Co. Pvt. Ltd., Delhi, 1982, p. 443.
15. P.D. Ojha, A Configuration of Indian Poverty: Inequality and Levels of Living, *Reserve Bank of Indian Bulletin,* Vol. 24, Bombay, 1970, pp. 16-27.

16. Department of Economic and Social Affairs, Poverty Unemployment and Development Policy : A Case Study of Selected Issues with Reference to Kerala, United Nations, New York, 1975, p. 7.
17. A.K. Sen, Poverty, Inequality and Unemployment: Some Conceptual Issues in Measurement, in Poverty and Income Distribution in India (ed.). T.N. Srinivasan and P.K. Bardhan, Statistical Publishing Society, Calcutta, 1974, pp. 67-68
18. V.M. Dandekar and Nilakantha Rath, Poverty in India, Indian School of Political Economy, Bombay, 1971.
19. Raj Krishna, Unemployment in India, *Indian Journal of Agricultural Economics*, Vol. 28, No. 1, Bombay, January-March, 1973.
20. Mahendra, P. Desai, Problems of low-Income Sections in Rural Areas, In *Rural Development for Weaker-Sections*, Seminar Series—XII, Indian Society of Agricultural Economics, Bombay, 1974, pp. 58-59.
21. I.Z., Bhatty, Inequality and Poverty in Rural India, in T.N. Srinivasan and P.K. Bardhan (ed.) *Poverty and Income Distribution in India*, Statistical Publishing Society, Calcutta, 1974, p. 292.
22. Amartya Sen, On Economic Inequality, Oxford University Press, London, 1973, pp. 37-38.
23. C.T. Kurien, Poverty Planning and Social Transportation, Allied Publishers Pvt. Ltd., New Delhi, 1978, p. 122.
24. Government of India, First Five Year Plan (People's Edition), 1953, p. 1.
25. Government of India, Planning Commission, *Review of the First Five Year Plan* (1951-56), New Delhi, 1957, pp. 1-8.
26. Government of India, Planning Commission; *Second Five Year Plan* (1956-61), New Delhi, 1956, pp. 22 and 26.
27. Government of India : Planning Commission; *Third Five Year Plan* (1961-66), New Delhi, 1961, pp. 1 & 2, 10.
28. Government of India: Planning Commission, *Fourth Five Year Plan* (1969-74), New Delhi, 1969, pp 15-17.
29. Government of India: Planning Commission, Towards An Approach to the *Fifth Plan*, New Delhi, 1972, p. 7.
30. Government of India : Planning Commission, *Sixth Five Year Plan*, New Delhi, August, 1980, p. 51.
31. *Ibid.*, p. 34
32. Government of India: Planning Commission, *Sixth Five Year Plan*, (1980-85), New Delhi, 1980, p. 34.
33. M.L. Sharma, T. M. Dak and O.P. Verma, IRDP Retrospect and Prospect, *Kurukshetra*, Vol. XXXVIII, No. 2, New Delhi, 1989, pp. 18-19.
34. Government of India, Planning Commission, *Seventh Five Year Plan*, (1985-90) New Delhi, 1985, p. 4.
35. Government of India, Planning Commission, *Eighth Five Year Plan*, Volume II, Delhi, 1992 p. 36.
36. Government of India, Planning Commission, *Ninth Five Year Plan*, (1997-02), New Delhi, Volume II, p. 10.
37. Government of India, Planning Commission, *Tenth Five Year Plan*, (2002-07), Vol. II, Delhi, 2003, p. 294.
38. Government of India, Planning Commission, *Tenth Five Year Plan* (2002-07), Volume II, Delhi, 2003, p. 298.

39. *Ibid.*, p. 299.
40. Government of India, Planning Commission, *Tenth Five Year Plan* (2002-07), Vol. II, Delhi, 2003, pp. 294-95.
41. Rural Development in Haryana, *Udyog Yug*, Vol. 24, No. 4, April 2002, Chandigarh, p. 21.
42. Government of India, Planning Commission, *Tenth Five Year Plan* (2002-07), Vol. II, Delhi, 2003, p. 302.
43. Government of India, Planning Commission, *Report To The People*, 2004-07, New Delhi, 2007, pp. 10-32.
44. Government of India, Planning Commission, *Ninth Five Year Plan*, (1997-2000), Vol. I, New Delhi, 1997, p. 29.
45. Government of India, Planning Commission, *Seventh Five Year Plan* (1985-90), New Delhi, 1985.
46. Government of India, Planning Commission, *Himachal Pradesh Development Report*, New Delhi, 2005, p. 390.
47. Government of India, Planning Commission, Towards Faster and More Inclusive Growth, An Approach to the Eleventh Five Year Plan (December 2006), New Delhi, p. 71.
48. M.V. Rajshekharan, Does IRDP Need Revamping? *Kurukshetra*, Vol. XXXVIII, No. 2, November 1989. New Delhi, pp. 13-16.
49. Irma Adelman and Sherman Robinson, Income Distribution Policies in Developing Countries—A Case Study of Korea, Oxford, 1978, p. 191.
50. C.T. Kurien, Reconciling Growth and Social Justice : Strategies Versus Structure, in M.L. Dantwala, Ranjit Gupta and Keith C.D. Souza (eds.), *Asian Seminar on Rural Development—The Indian Experience*, New Delhi, 1986, p. 382.
51. Neela Mukherjee, Lessons of Poverty Alleviation Programmes, *Yojana*, Vol. 34, Nos. 14 and 15, New Delhi, August 15, 1990, p. 40.
52. S.P. Gupta, Three Decades of Haryana—A Descriptive Study, Esspee Publications, Chandigarh, 1999, p. 3.
53. Panjab Boundary Commission Report, Para 136, Point 3, May 31, 1966, p. 49.
54. National Council of Applied Economic Research, 1970, p. 1.
55. Government of India, Ministry of Textiles and the Craft Council Haryana—Faridabad, Crafts of Haryana, New Delhi, 2002-03, p. 1.
56. Government of Haryana, (Economic and Statistical Organization),Statistical Abstract of Haryana, Chandigarh, 2005, p. 31.
57. Government of Haryana, (Economic and Statistical Organization), Statistical Abstract of Haryana, Chandigarh, 2005, p. 23.
58. *Ibid.*, p. 745.
59. *Ibid.*, p. 23.
60. Government of Haryana, (Economic and Statistical Organization), Statistical Abstract of Haryana, Chandigarh, 2005, p. 96.
61. Government of Haryana, (Economic and Statistics Organization), Statistical Abstract of Haryana, Chandigarh, 2005, pp. 54-55.
62. K.C. Yadav, Modern Haryana—History and Culture, 1803-1966, Manohar Publishers, Delhi 2002, pp. 15-16.
63. Hisar District Gazetteer, Revenue Department, Haryana, Chandigarh, pp. 16-17.

64. Report of Haryana Development Committee 1966, p. 46.
65. S.P. Gupta, "Three Decades of Haryana—A Descriptive Study, Esspee Publications, Chandigarh, 1999, p. 13.
66. Government of Haryana, (Economic and Statistical Organisation), Economic Survey of Haryana (2006-07), Chandigarh, 2007, pp. 38-40
67. Government of Haryana, (Economic and Statistical Organisation), Economic Survey of Haryana (2004-05), Chandigarh, 2005, p. 24
68. Government of Haryana, (Economic and Statistical Organisation), Economic Survey of Haryana (2006-07), Chandigarh, 2007, pp. 46-47.
69. Government of Haryana, (Economic and Statistical Organisation), Economic Survey of Haryana, (2006-07), Chandigarh, 2007, pp. 27-31.
70. Government of Haryana, (Economic and Statistical Organisation), Economic Survey of Haryana, (2006-07), Chandigarh, 2007, pp. 34-35.
71. *Ibid.*, pp. 36-37.
72. Government of Haryana, (Economic and Statistical Organisation), Economic Survey of Haryana (2004-05), Chandigarh, 2005, p. 27.
73. Government of Haryana, (Economic and Statistical Organisation), Statistical Abstract of Haryana, Chandigarh, 2007, p. 266.
74. Government of Haryana, (Economic and Statistical Organisation), Economic Survey of Haryana (2006-07), Chandigarh, 2007, p. 51.
75. Government of Haryana, (Economic and Statistical Organisation), Statistical Abstract of Haryana, Chandigarh, 2005, p. 26.
76. Government of Haryana, (Economic and Statistical Organisation), Statistical Abstract of Haryana, Chandigarh, 2007, p. 371.
77. Government of Haryana, (Economic and Statistical Organisation), Economic Survey of Haryana (2004-05), Chandigarh, 2005, p. 36.
78. Government of Haryana, (Economic and Statistical Organisation), Economic Survey of Haryana (2006-07), Chandigarh, 2007, p. 52.
79. Government of Haryana, (Economic and Statistical Organisation), Economic Survey of Haryana (2006-07), Chandigarh, 2007, p. 40.
80. *Ibid.*, p. 55.
81. *Ibid.*, p. 63.
82. Government of Haryana, (Economic and Statistical Organisation), Statistical Abstract of Haryana, Chandigarh, 2007, p. 27.
83. Government of Haryana, (Economic and Statistical Organisation), Statistical Abstract of Haryana, Chandigarh, 2007, p. 26.
84. Government of Haryana, (Economic and Statistical Organisation), Economic Survey of Haryana, 2004-05, Chandigarh, 2005, p. 63
85. Government of Haryana, (Economic and Statistical Organisation), Economic Survey of Haryana, 2006-07, Chandigarh, 2007, pp. 1-3.
86. Government of Haryana (Directorate of Census Operations), Census of India 2001, Series-7, Paper-3, Provisional Population Totals, Chandigarh, 2001, p. 128.
87. Government of Haryana, (Economic and Statistical Organisation), Economic Survey of Haryana, Chandigarh, 2005, pp. 5-12.
88. Census of India, 2001, Series 7, Paper-2, (Government of Haryana), Provisional Population Totals, Chandigarh, p. 91.
89. District Credit Plan, Yamunanagar, (2004-05), Punjab National Bank, Chandigarh, April 2004, p. 5.

90. Government of Haryana, (Economic and Statistical Organization), Statistical Abstract of Haryana, Chandigarh, 2005, p. 39.
91. Government of Haryana, (Economic and Statistical Organisation), Statistical Abstract of Haryana, Chandigarh, 2005, p. 14.
92. *Ibid*. p. 38.
93. *Ibid*., pp. 37-40.
94. Government of Haryana, (Economic and Statistical Organisation), Statistical Abstract of Haryana, Chandigarh, 2003, p. 63.
95. Government of Haryana, (Economic and Statistical Organisation), Statistical Abstract of Haryana, Chandigarh, 2005, p. 61.
96. *Ibid*., p. 54-57.
97. Government of Haryana (Economic and Statistical Organisation), Statistical Abstract of Haryana, Chandigarh, 2005, p. 746.
98. *Ibid*., p. 772.
99. Government of Haryana, (Directorate of Census Operations), Census of India, 2001, Series 7, Paper-2, Provisional Population Totals, Chandigarh, 2001, p. 91.
100. District Credit Plan, Yamunanagar (2004-05), Punjab National Bank, Chandigarh, April 2004, p. 7.
101. Government of Haryana, (Economic and Statistical Organisation), Statistical Abstract of Haryana, Chandigarh, 2005, p. 318.
102. District Credit Plan, Yamunanagar, (2006-07), Punjab National Bank, Chandigarh, April 2006, p. 8.
103. District Credit Plan, Yamunanagar (2006-07), Punjab National Bank, Chandigarh, April 2006, p. 11.
104. Government of Haryana, (Directorate of Census Operations), Census of India, 2001, Series 7, Paper-2, Provisional Population Totals, Chandigarh, 2001, p. 164.
105. District Credit Plan, Yamunanagar, 2004-05, Punjab National Bank, Chandigarh, April 2004, pp. 95-97.
106. Government of Haryana, (Economic and Statistical Organisation), Statistical Abstract of Haryana, Chandigarh, 2004, pp. 212-13.
107. Government of Haryana, (Economic and Statistical Organisation), Statistical Abstract of Haryana, Chandigarh, 2006, p. 760.
108. *Ibid*., p. 758.
109. *Ibid*., pp. 228-36.
110. District Credit Plan, Yamunanagar, (2006-07), Punjab National Bank, Chandigarh, April 2006, p. 80.
111. District Credit Plan, Yamunanagar, (2006-07), Punjab National Bank, Chandigarh, April 2006, p. 82.
112. District Credit Plan, Yamunanagar (2004-05), Punjab National Bank, Chandigarh, pp. 91-93.
113. Government of Haryana, (Directorate of Census Operations), Census of India, 2001, Series 7, Paper-2, Provisional Population Totals, Chandigarh, 2001, p. 128.
114. District Credit Plan, Yamunanagar, (2004-05), Punjab National Bank, Chandigarh, April, 2004, pp. 75-76.
115. Government of Haryana, (Economic and Statistical Organizations), Statistical Abstract of Haryana, Chandigarh, 2004, p. 218.

2

Review of Literature

This chapter deals with the review of studies conducted by the Government agencies as well as individual scholars for the evaluation of various Poverty Alleviation Programmes with a view to achieve a deep insight into the implementation of these programmes and their resultant overall performance, the causes of their success and/or failure with respect to the selection of beneficiaries as well as the distributional aspect.

This chapter has been divided into two sections. Section I deals with the review of macro-level studies conducted on poverty and poverty alleviation programmes by the Government agencies and the micro level individual studies have been reviewed in Section II.

SECTION I

2.1 REVIEW OF MACRO LEVEL STUDIES CONDUCTED BY THE GOVERNMENT AGENCIES

This section deals with the review of empirical studies conducted by government agencies related to the impact of Poverty Alleviation Programmes on different aspects of levels of living viz. distribution of assets, income, pattern of consumption, magnitude of unemployment etc. as well as general level of living of weaker sections in rural areas of Haryana.

The National productivity Council, (1984)[1] by conducting a concurrent evaluation study on Integrated Rural Development Programme in Bhiwani District of Haryana pointed out certain anomalies in providing assistance on the basis of criteria 'poorest among the poor' first. The scheduled castes and scheduled tribes families were given priority in giving benefits of the programme. The assistance provided to scheduled castes and scheduled tribe families was only marginally more than the assistance provided to other general caste beneficiaries. There was lack of co-ordination among various agencies and departments implementing Integrated Rural Development Programmes, providing minimum needs and infrastructure. The study concluded that 80.89 per cent beneficiaries belonged to the land based activities i.e. agriculture and animal husbandry. The percentage of irregularity in loan repayments among beneficiaries from different sectors have been worked out 65.00, 75.92, 71.43 and 75.0 per cent in agriculture, animal husbandry, industry/business and tertiary sectors respectively. About 58.71 per cent families had crossed the poverty line. About 28.86 per cent of these families had derived more than 50 per cent of their net annual income from the assistance provided to them under Integrated Rural Development Programmes. About 80.25 per cent of families received less than Rs. 1400 as subsidy.

Agricultural Finance Corporation Limited, Bombay (1984)[2] conducted a concurrent evaluation and impact study of IRDP in Rohtak district of Haryana. The study was sponsored by Development and Panchayat Department, Government of Haryana. The study pointed out that about 26.2 per cent of beneficiaries assisted in the sample blocks were ineligible for getting assistance under Integrated Rural Development Programme. About 35 per cent of beneficiaries assisted under the programme were not from the list of selected beneficiaries and were included on *adhoc* basis. Gram Sabha and officials of financial institutions were not involved in the selection of beneficiaries. However adequate coverage had been given to scheduled caste families. Beneficiaries were fully involved in the selection of the scheme for providing assistance under

Integrated Rural Development Programme. There was a lack of co-ordination among the various agencies at the focal point level in the implementation of Integrated Rural Development Programme. Nearly 70 per cent of loan applications were not disposed off within the time limit prescribed by the Reserve Bank of India. Further 62.5 per cent beneficiaries were regularly making payments of their dues. There was an increase in the income of the majority of the sample beneficiaries after assistance was provided to them under Integrated Rural Development Programme and about 55 per cent families have crossed the poverty line.

Programme Evaluation Organisation of the Planning Commission 1985 (PEO Study)[3] stated that 26 per cent of the selected beneficiaries were already above the poverty line in terms of the norms of annual income of Rs. 3500 of a family of five persons and did not qualify for provision of benefit under the programme. About 88 per cent of selected households increased their income by 10.6 per cent. 77 per cent reported an increase in their consumption level and 23 per cent reported an increase in the family assets and 64 per cent felt their over all status in the village society has been elevated.

The Economic and Statistical Organization, Haryana (1987),[4] conducted an evaluation study on Integrated Rural Development Programme in four districts of Haryana i.e. Kurukshetra, Faridabad, Hisar and Mahendergarh during 1981-82 to 83-84. This study revealed that 61 per cent beneficiaries belonged to scheduled caste/scheduled tribe families. About 41.65 per cent of the beneficiaries were already having income more than the ceiling limit of Rs. 3500 per annum so they were not eligible for benefits under the programme. About 29 per cent beneficiaries had to spend excess amount on raising the assets and 71 per cent beneficiaries had to spend money to bribe the officials for expediting the payment of loans/subsidies and for obtaining the assets under Integrated Rural Development Programme. About 40.5 per cent beneficiaries were found to be defaulters in the payment of loan instalments. About 55.1 per cent crossed the poverty line and 44.9 per cent remained below the poverty line. The percentage of scheduled caste/scheduled tribes crossing the poverty line was higher than non scheduled caste/scheduled tribe families. The average annual income of majority of beneficiaries increased and incremental income per household varied from Rs. 969 to Rs. 3673 under different schemes. According to this study small scale industries and trade schemes proved to be highly remunerative and the total number of mandays employed increased between 11 to 13 per cent of all the schemes.

The Programme Evaluation Organisation (1987)[5] conducted an evaluation study of the scheme for provision of house-sites-cum construction assistance to the rural landless labourers. It has been pointed out that about 48 per cent beneficiaries were allotted house-sites/houses within three months from the date of identification. Out of remaining 52 per cent, 15 per cent received allotment within six months and about 20 per cent within 2 years and the remaining 17 per cent got after 2 years. The study revealed that majority of the beneficiaries, 9 out of every 10 were satisfied with the method of identification. In non progressive States this percentage of satisfaction was lower (80.0%). The main reason for dissatisfaction reported by the beneficiaries in both progressive and non progressive States were that: (i) they were not consulted at the time of identification (54.2%), (ii) local bodies like Panchayats/Gaon Sabha were not consulted for identifying the beneficiaries (36.1%), (iii) Adhoc nature of identification was done by the concerned officials (40.2%), (iv) no systematic procedure was followed in the matter of identification (36.1%), (v) decision influenced by vested interests (34.7%). One of the main objectives of the study was to assess social impact on the target group beneficiaries. More than 62 per cent of the beneficiaries reported improvement in health, living conditions and social status. The main reasons reported by them were: (a) availability of open space and area, (b) better environment, clean surroundings, (c) better accommodation to have rest at home, (d) availability of safe drinking water, (e) ownership of the house giving better social atmosphere etc. It was reported by one third of the beneficiaries that the scheme had improved their work efficiency and income.

State Bank of Patiala (1987)[6] by conducting an evaluation study on Finance Under Rural Development programmes, concluded that 42 among 100 person seem to have crossed the poverty line but according to these beneficiaries, the additional income so generated has not improved their living conditions to the desired extent since the market price of essential consumer goods has increased so much that the additional income generated has been nullified. However, almost all the beneficiaries under the scheme admitted that they increased their annual income and now they were living in somewhat better conditions than those before obtaining of loans under the Integrated Rural Development Programme. Regarding the utilization of the loans the report concluded that in 98 cases the funds at the initial stage were utilized properly, while in two cases animals were reportedly disposed off immediately after purchase within the same cattle fair. About 19 borrowers later on disposed off their assets and utilized the sale proceeds for some other purposes. Thus these 19 borrowers actually misutilzed the funds.

According to concurrent evaluation of Integrated Rural Development Programmes conducted by the Department of Rural Development (1990)[7] stated that about 29 per cent of the sample beneficiaries belonged to scheduled caste, 16 per cent to scheduled tribe and 20 per cent were women. The coverage of Scheduled Caste/Scheduled Tribes was significantly higher than the stipulated target of 30 per cent at the national level. The beneficiaries also included 5 per cent families of ex-bonded labourers, 0.4 per cent of handicapped and 1 per cent of the assignees of surplus land. Nearly 87 per cent of the families belonged to the destitute and very-very poor group. About 9 per cent families belonged to the destitute group. About 67 per cent beneficiaries were selected in the meetings of Gram Sabhas. In the opinion of the beneficiaries, the assets provided to them were of good quality in 80 per cent cases. About 81 per cent beneficiaries had found the assistance (subsidy + credit) sufficient for acquiring the assets. About 37 per cent beneficiaries had no overdues and 30 per cent beneficiaries had overdues less than Rs. 1000. About 67 per cent beneficiaries had overdues upto Rs. 1000. This compares well with the findings of National Bank for Agricultural and Rural Development (1985) according to which recovery is estimated at 69 per cent. The assets had generated additional income of more than Rs. 2000 in 43 per cent cases, between Rs. 1001 and Rs. 2000 in 18 per cent cases and between Rs. 501 and Rs. 1000 in 9 per cent cases. The total annual family income of the beneficiaries (from the asset and other sources) had increased by more than 50 per cent of their initial annual income in 71 per cent cases. Such increase in annual income was even more than 100 per cent of their initial income in 47 per cent cases. However, the increase in the total annual income of the beneficiaries was more than 50 per cent of their initial annual income, in 42 per cent cases such increase was even more than 100 per cent of the initial assessed annual income in 19 per cent cases. The old beneficiaries had crossed the poverty line of Rs. 3500 in 80 per cent cases and revised poverty line of Rs. 6400 in 28 percent cases at the national level. The families belonging to the destitute and very poor groups had crossed the poverty line of Rs. 3500 in 64 per cent cases and the revised poverty line of Rs. 6400 in 16 per cent cases at the national level.

The Programme Evaluation Organisation (PEO) 1992[8] undertook a quick study of Jawahar Rojgar Yojana with a view to assess the extent to which the Yojana helped in providing gainful employment to the target group; to analyse the type of assets created under the Yojana including their quality and usefulness; comprehend the arrangement for the problems encountered in the implementation of the Yojana. The study was taken up in ten states which had a little over 90 per cent of the rural poor. From each of 10 States, 20 Districts, 40 Gram Panchayats and 600 beneficiaries, who worked under Jawahar Rojgar Yojana and received wages were selected but 2 could not be convassed due to non availability; 42 per cent were scheduled caste, 21 per cent scheduled tribe, 37 per cent other. Women beneficiaries were 23 per cent. This study was conducted from last week of November, 1991 to the first week of January, 1992. It was observed that the percentage achievement in terms of mandays of employment generated was more than the percentage utilisation of total funds available during the years 1989-90 and 1990-91 at all levels. It was also observed that proportion of mandays of employment of scheduled caste and scheduled tribes to total mandays of employment generated was more than 50 per cent. But the women's share remained 22 to 25 per cent upto the district level. However at the selected Gram Panchayat level it was 15 to18 per cent only. About 35.9 per cent of the total population in all the selected Gram Panchayat was available for employment. Of these 14.8 per cent and 14.3 per cent were actually employed during 1989-90 and 1990-91 respectively. However, in the first half of 1991-92 only 3 per cent of those available for employment were employed. This shows that Yojana had provided negligible employment during the first half of the year and major work was left to be done during the second half. Nearly 89 per cent of the selected beneficiaries had expressed that assets created were useful. About 30 per cent each of selected States reported that the prescribed wage; material ratio in respect of pucca work was not workable and that the supervision and monitoring were inadequate. It was found that number of persons available for employment and who actually got employed under Jawahar Rojgar Yojana was not maintained at any level. It was suggested that such information may be maintained in the interest of proper planning and execution of Yojana. It was further suggested that assets as per the felt need of the area may be taken up and illustrative list should serve only as a guideline. However in construction of assets like veterinary hospital, bus shelter, social forestry, anganwadis, etc., the sectoral departments may take the responsibility and Jawahar Rojgar Yojana funds should serve as an additionality. It was suggested that the Yojana be implemented on selectivity basis-in the areas of concentration of the poor. This is important particularly at the Gram Panchayat level.

Programme Evaluation Organization (2000)[7] undertook the evaluation study of Employment Assurance Scheme to assess the performance, appropriateness of implementation methods adopted by the States, the extent of coverage of target group and the impact of Employment Assurance Scheme on the beneficiaries. A multi-stage sample design was adopted for the study. About 1120 beneficiary households, 112 villages, 56 blocks spread over 28 districts of 14 States were selected. It was found that the utilization of Employment Assurance Scheme funds was extremely low. Lack of planning, untimely release of funds, both from the Centre to District Rural Development Agency and from District Rural Development Agency to blocks, and other factors such as inability of the States to generate matching resources were the important factors responsible for low utilization of Employment Assurance Scheme funds. The study revealed that about 69 per cent of the beneficiaries got less than 30 days of employment in a year and another 17 per cent got employment between 30 and 50 days. The overall average for the 14 states worked out to 31 days/year. Thus the high rates of employment generation as reported in official statistics, was not supported by the information obtained from the beneficiaries. At the All India level, more than three fourths (78.48%) of the sample Employment Assurance Scheme beneficiaries belonged to the daily wage earning class, with agricultural wage earners constituting more than 55 per cent of Employment Assurance Scheme beneficiaries. It was further found that non poor were also receiving benefits of Employment Assurance Scheme. This observation was supported by the fact that a large proportion of Employment Assurance Scheme beneficiaries in some States were non-poor cultivators, non-agricultural labourers and self-employed. This is violation of Employment Assurance Scheme guidelines. It was noticed that 87.5 per cent of the beneficiaries got employment for 2 years. Majority of Employment Assurance Scheme beneficiaries earned less than Rs. 1000 and got less than 30 days of employment, but even this meagre benefit did not accrue to them each year. The study suggested that the objectives of generation of sustained and gainful employment, supplementing the income of the rural wage-earning class in agricultural lean Employment Assurance Scheme and improving the well being of the rural poor through Indira Awas Yojana have not been realized. The Indira Awas Yojana is a demand driven scheme, but the method of planning and implementation adopted is "top-down" instead of "bottom-up". The implementation method adopted is not consistent with the objectives of the scheme. It is suggested that both the wage employment seekers and the users of assets need to be involved in the identification of schemes/projects that are useful and productive for the community, and would have the potential of generating sustainable and gainful employment. This is possible only if the Gram Sabha is vested with the responsibility of preparing the list of the wage employment seekers and in the identification of projects useful to the community.

Concurrent evaluation of Indira Awas Yojana (2001)[10] was undertaken by the Ministry of Rural Development. It covered

53,153 Indira Awas Yojana beneficiaries in the States and 590 in the Union Territories. The main objectives of the study were: (a) assessing the implementation and policy environment of the programme, (b) understanding the socio-economic conditions of the beneficiaries and ascertain the procedure of their selection for assistance under the scheme, and (c) evaluating the impact of the programme on the beneficiaries. The evaluation was carried out in 25 states and 5 union territories. About 57 per cent of the beneficiaries belonged to scheduled caste. The share of scheduled tribe beneficiaries was 22 per cent. Nearly 70 per cent of the primary beneficiaries of the Yojana were found to be illiterates. For every 1000 males there were about 553 female beneficiaries, 28 per cent of the scheduled caste/scheduled tribes women covered in the survey were found to be household heads. The average annual income of beneficiaries for the entire sample worked out to be Rs. 11062, which was quite close to the poverty line income level of Rs. 11000 per annum. While 63 per cent of the beneficiaries across the States reported their annual income as less than Rs. 11,000. About 64 per cent in Union Territories reported it as above Rs. 11,000. In more than three quarters of the cases, selection of beneficiaries had been made by Gram Sabhas. The role envisioned for people's assemblies at the village level in selecting the eligible beneficiaries had been performed by political parties and government functionaries in about 18 per cent of the cases overall and more markedly in States like Bihar and Andhra Pradesh and Union Territories of Pondicherry. About 70 per cent of the houses across States and Union Territories had been constructed anew, and nearly 28 per cent after dismantling the old structures. About one per cent of cases were also reported where beneficiaries had used Indira Awas Yojana assistance for house renovation, though it is not eligible for assistance under the scheme. At all India level, 47 per cent of the Indira Awas Yojana houses were reportedly constructed by the beneficiaries themselves and the rest 53 per cent by external agencies like contractors, village panchayats, voluntary agencies and government departments. Under the employment content of housing programmes that depend on intensive use of labour was quantified in two ways: (1) as physical units like mandays or man-years, and (2) as a ratio of wages to total housing cost (net of land value). As for the former measure, on an average 53 mandays of family labour and 57 mandays of hired labour had been put in to construct an Indira Awas Yojana house. The corresponding figure for Union Territories were 82 and 44 respectively. When applied second method it was found that (1) in majority of States cost ratio of labour and material was favorable to the latter, and (2) the share of cost of family labour was invariably low in all the States. In only 3 out of 14 States, the family labour constituted more than 10 per cent of the total building cost. Despite the inadequacies in implementation, 86 per cent of the beneficiaries had expressed their satisfaction with the constructed houses. The satisfaction level was high in states like Tripura, Andhra Pradesh, Sikkim, Nagaland, Goa, Haryana, Himachal Pradesh and the Union Territories of Dadra and Nagar-Haveli and Daman and Diu. In Kerala, Arunachal Pradesh, Tamil Nadu and Union Territories of Pondicherry nearly a third of the beneficiaries were not happy with the houses. It was suggested that Panchayats should play a more constructive role in the schemes like Indira Awas Yojana, the primary intention of which is to help the poor and the vulnerable, both by giving them decent shelters and by generating some employment. They are to be more actively involved in information dissemination, pre-construction inspection/verification of house sites, as also monitoring of implementation of schemes. Panchayats can also take responsibility of supplying skilled manpower and low cost technology.

Himachal Pradesh Planning Department (2002)[11] conducted an evaluation study on Integrated Rural Development Programme to make an impact assessment of the programme, mainly to observe perceptible changes in the target groups particularly benefited families in terms of their annual income, upliftment of socio-economic status and efficacy of the programme in bringing down the incidence of poverty among the identified poor families. Out of 72 blocks in the State, 24 blocks were chosen on systematic random sampling basis. A total of 556 beneficiaries were selected. Out of the total beneficiaries 69.51 per cent were males and 30.49 per cent were females; 35.15 per cent belonged to scheduled castes and 13.20 per cent to scheduled tribes and remaining 51.65 per cent were from other categories, 83.50 per cent of the Integrated Rural

Development Programme beneficiaries were marginal farmers, 4.27 per cent small farmers and 12.23 per cent were landless. Out of 515 sample beneficiaries, 6.41 per cent were having annual income upto Rs. 1000; 34.95 per cent were in the annual income range between Rs. 1001 to Rs. 3500; 24.47 per cent were in the income group of Rs. 3501-4800 whereas 34.17 per cent beneficiaries were having annual income above Rs. 4801. Out of the total sample beneficiaries, 89.13 per cent reported that a household survey was conducted prior to their selection to the Integrated Rural Development Programme whereas 10.87 per cent replied in negative. It was found that of the total beneficiaries 51.66 per cent were assisted under primary activities; 7.44 per cent under secondary sector activities and remaining 40.90 per cent under tertiary sector activities. About 98.43 per cent faced no difficulties in obtaining loan/subsidy. It was found that 42 family members of the beneficiaries were assisted under other programmes like Indira Awas Yojana, Gandhi Kutir Yojana, Training of Rural Youth for Self-Employment, Prime Minister Rojgar Yojana, etc. in six districts. About 73.19 per cent beneficiaries were not able to derive annual income of Rs. 11,000 from the assets given to them whereas 26.81 per cent succeeded in generating annual income more than Rs. 11,000 from the assets given to them. It was found that out of 181 beneficiaries who preferred wage employment, maximum 130 (i.e. 71.82 per cent) desired wage employment for more than 9 months in a year.

SECTION II

2.2 REVIEW OF MICRO LEVEL STUDIES CONDUCTED BY INDIVIDUAL RESEARCHERS

In this section the micro level empirical studies conducted by individual researchers on the different aspects of the poverty alleviation programmes have been reviewed.

Apte (1976)[12] conducted an empirical investigation in 15 Kolaba villages in Kolaba district of Maharashtra; in order to study the natural and other resources, the existing pattern of employment and earnings, institution of the villages and various economic activities in the region. He stated that though the Government had implemented several schemes for the upliftment of the scheduled tribes yet these people had not been benefited from these programmes either because they were not aware of these programmes or were unable to complete the required formalities for getting credit as well as other facilities. They need guidance from voluntary workers; and even by paid workers, if necessary. Therefore, detailed economic investigations are necessary to identify suitable persons to take up the challenge either as volunteers or paid workers to implement schemes for tribal development.

Sharma (1978)[13] conducted an empirical investigation for five blocks in Tehri Garwal district of Uttar Pradesh to study the effects of planning on the tribal poor. He stated that the difficult and rugged nature of terrain precluded easy accessibility and isolated the tribals from rest of the world. Agricultural production was low due to the unfavourable climatic conditions, lack of irrigation facilities, continuous use of primitive methods of cultivation and less area for cultivation in the isolated small holdings. The hill areas and tribal areas constituted special problem areas as they were backward and inaccessible and also neglected and exploited for centuries.

Gupta and Aggarwal (1980)[14] concluded that the assistance provided by Marginal Farmers and Agricultural Labourers Agencies for various types of enterprises had contributed to an overall increase in the income of the marginal farmers and agricultural labourers. The average family income of beneficiaries increased by 73.56 per cent within 4 years of their participation in the programme. Dairy was found to be more profitable than other types of assistance. In 1971-72, before availing themselves of the assistance, most of the beneficiaries were below the poverty-line, i.e., their annual per capital income was below Rs. 3500, but in 1975-76 after they had utilised the assistance, their income rose quite significantly and not remained under the poverty-line. Participation in the programme had not only led to new employment opportunities for the family members who were otherwise unemployed but also with the improvement in economic status the education level of family members rose. Beside the living standard of all categories of beneficiaries had improved. The researchers further suggested that to make better and optimum use of assistance taken by the participants, it is necessary to solve their problems relating to: (1) costly raw material, (2) lack of transportation facilities, (3) harassment and high taxes charged by the officers at state barriers, (4) lack of regular market and less remunerative prices of various enterprise products, and (5) dearth of storage facilities with the respondents.

Yadav and Mishra (1980)[15] examined the impact of the Tribal Development Programmes on employment, income and asset formation in Bastar district of Madhya Pradesh. They collected primary data from 50 families (25 beneficiaries and 25 non-beneficiaries) for the period 1974-75 to 1978-79. The employment opportunities of beneficiary and non-beneficiary families had increased during the period of study. The employment of the beneficiaries had increased by 26.17 per cent against 13.40 per cent for the non-beneficiaries during the period 1974-75 to 1978-79. During the same period more employment opportunities had been generated in almost all occupations. The increase in employment opportunities in crop production accounted for 20.57 per cent in case of beneficiaries against an increase of 5.05 per cent for the non-beneficiaries. The increase in non-farm employment was 33 days (i.e. 25%) for the beneficiary families against 15 days (i.e. 9.79%) for the non-beneficiary families. The total income of an average beneficiary increased by 36.87 per cent while that of non-beneficiaries rose by 20.09 per cent. The farm income of the beneficiaries increased by 31.45 per cent against an increase of 10.53 per cent in the case of non-beneficiaries. The non-farm income of the beneficiaries and non-beneficiaries rose by 49.66 and 47.99 per cent respectively. The total value of assets of an average beneficiary family was Rs. 8,782 in 1974-75 and it increased to Rs. 9,554 in the year 1978-79 showing an increase of 8.79 per cent during study period. However, still there exists a lot of scope to widen employment and income opportunities to the tribal families by altering certain programmes.

They also stated that the value of inputs given in grants and subsidies to the beneficiaries come out Rs. 48,464, i.e., nearly 43 per cent of the total value which mainly comprised the value to diesel pumps given on the basis of 75 per cent subsidy and the benefits accrued to only 5 families, grants for poultry units ranked second and accounted for nearly 27 per cent of the tribal value of subsidies and grants, benefiting only 4 of the sample households. However, paddy seeds and chemical fertilizers were availed by all the beneficiaries and their total value represented 13 per cent of the total value of grants and subsidies. The sample beneficiaries were distributed fruit plants worth Rs. 2500 but hardly 20 of them survived. Secondly, though the agency spent Rs. 13,142 for the establishment of poultry units, not a single unit was found in operation at the time of survey.

Shina and Singh (1981)[16] examined the impact of Small Farmers Development Agency on the small and marginal farmers in Champaran district of Bihar. They have analysed the phenomenon of poverty and suggested extension of new programmes like Small Farmers Development Agency. Regarding the performance of Small Farmers Development Agency they stated that it is evident that the Small Farmers Development Agency has brought about a positive impact on the economy of small and marginal farmers. If all the small and marginal farmers participate in the Agency's development programmes, they can definitely increase their income level at par with that existing between these groups.

Sundram (1981)[17] conducted two empirical investigations regarding identification of beneficiaries. In case of the Kazhakoottam Block in Trivandrum district of Kerala State, he found that the identification of the eligible beneficiary households was not systematic and exhaustive. There was also no public participation in the selection of beneficiaries. In case of Utnigramerur block in Chingleput District of Tamil Nadu the study revealed that the initial identification of the eligible families had not been done systematically, that control and monitoring functioning at the field level required great improvement, and that follow-up contacts with the beneficiaries had been neglected. The study traces these inadequacies to ill-equipped departmental machinery and underlines the need for organizational and administrative changes in this context. This study has also drawn attention to the lack of area specifications in the schemes adopted, the failure to use resource inventory information for scheme formulation and lack of efficiency in extension services. Further the local level planning on a systematic basis has not yet taken off, though considerable experience has been acquired in implementing beneficiary-oriented programmes.

Deshpande (1982)[18] conducted an empirical investigation of 153 tribal workers working on the Development Projects, to study the impact of Employment Guarantee Scheme on poverty and bondage among the tribals of Thane district in Maharashtra. The 90 per cent of the workers belonged to three adivasi groups and more than 72 per cent of the workers were illiterate. Those who sought wage-employment under the Employment Guarantee Scheme were not necessarily the landless workers. They sought wage-employment as they were unable to harvest second crop on their lands and grain-stock built up on the basis of Kharif season alone was too inadequate to meet out their domestic needs. Consequently, even farmers with relatively larger holdings were found seeking employment whenever possible. He stated that though Employment Awareness Scheme was the main source of employment, yet not many benefited from this programme. For half of the workers, work was available for less than 50 days during the year, for another third, it was available for 100 days at the most. With all the sources of getting wage work, the problem of unemployment was not solved. The period of unemployment varied from one month to about three months in a year. On an average the period of employment offered under the Employment Guarantee Scheme was quite small and could not help to eliminate unemployment completely. Nor could it help adivasi to reduce their dependence on farm-employers who offered employment but exploited the adivasi considerably.

Noorbasha *et. al.* (1983)[19] in their study concluded that identification of the beneficiaries by District Rural Development Agency is not a novel concept in the field of rural subsidy programmes. It is only a new bottle filed with old wine of Small Farmer Development Agency and hence has all the inherent loopholes. Therefore, the identification programme is found false and lengthy in numerous cases and, ultimately, it is the Regional Rural Bank which has to battle with multitudes of defaulters. Moreover, for the reason that the District Rural Development Agency is also blessed with some political colouring with the involvement of the Village Block Development Officers the fruit of the District Rural

Development Agency and Regional Rural Bank have not percolated down to the deserving sections. They suggested that District Rural Development Agency must act only as the subsidising agent and not as an identifier, for the simple reason that it is only the lending banker who assumes the risk of supervision and recovery from his customer. This will save District Rural Development Agency from a time and money consuming process.

Nayak and Prasad (1984)[20] have found that the scheduled castes and scheduled tribes have a lower standard of living than the non scheduled caste/scheduled tribes in Karnataka. The increase in the inequality for scheduled caste/scheduled tribes is higher than the non scheduled caste/scheduled tribes due to differential utilization of Government benefits. A small percentage of scheduled caste/scheduled tribes in the urban sector have better living condition than the non-scheduled caste/scheduled tribes while majority of them suffer relatively more. The mobile persons among them segregate themselves from their fellowmen.

Pathy (1984)[21] after analyzing the impact of development on tribal welfare in Gujarat stated that barely 10 per cent of the tribals had benefited from development programme. Further, within this group it was only the landlords and rich peasants who had profited more than truly needed for whom the programmes were meant.

Parvathamma (1984)[22] has conducted a socio-economic survey of scheduled caste and tribes in Karnataka and found that they are living in rural areas, segregated from higher caste society in separate colonies. The majority of them have their own mud houses or slightly better constructed houses. Most of them are living in abject poverty and work as landless agricultural labourers. Some others are engaged in unclean jobs. Most of the households have two to four working members. But in terms of their monthly contribution to the family income, it is very low. As many as 77 per cent households are said to have Rs. 200 or less per month income, among them, 14 per cent have only Rs. 50 or less monthly income. The level of education and politicization of scheduled caste/scheduled tribes in Karnataka is very low. They think that large economic concessions like land, education and employment may help them to improve their present conditions.

Subbarao (1985)[23] examined critically the impact of Integrated Rural Development Programme on the basis of field work done by various agencies like National Bank for Agriculture and Rural Development. He found that wrong identification of beneficiaries is one of the major causes of the failure of the programme. The wrong identification is related not so much to the efficiency of administrative infrastructure as the method adopted in identification of the poor. The difficulty also arose because of the absence of any preparatory work and the anxiety for target fulfilling.

Satyanarayan and Peter (1985)[24] in their study concluded that among various apparent constraints, uneven, untimely and inadequate financial and supervising support for the Integrated Rural Development Programme schemes, the traditional dominance of the rich and powerful political personal links in the rural area, expanding population, illiteracy and unemployment, inherent inferiority complex and lack of enthusiasm and confidence among the rural poor are the significant factors mainly responsible for the overall hindrance in the process of poverty alleviation. In the presence of such chronic rural problems, the responsible job of managing the Integrated Rural Development Programme schemes has rendered helpless the socially weaker group of village level workers. As a result, the alignment in the planning and implementation of the Integrated Rural Development Programme schemes could not be properly organized. Identification of the beneficiaries has been made the responsibility of ill-paid village level workers or primary school teachers. As a result, all who dominate them could be enrolled as beneficiaries. On the other hand the procedures laid down for obtaining the bank assistance are cumbersome and can be managed by affluent class. Thus, the deserving poor always get eliminated from the scene.

Chandakavate (1985)[25] conducted a study in Singdi taluka of Bijapur district in Karnataka to make an evaluation of Integrated Rural Development Programme. He observed that identification of suitable beneficiaries for assistance and their categorization is found defective. A formal discussion with the beneficiaries revealed that about 7 per cent of the families surveyed were ineligible as they were above the poverty line. These families have either government/private job holders as members or have big landholdings. Some small and marginal farmers have been assisted under the same programme treating them as separate families. Bankers were not a party in the identification of the beneficiaries. An unpleasant aspect of the programme was the poor recovery performance. It was revealed that 6 per cent of the beneficiaries fully repaid their loan. About 36 per cent of them had not repaid at all and the remaining beneficiaries had partly paid the loans.

Tewari (1985)[26] made an attempt to study the shortcomings of the Integrated Rural Development Programme by using the secondary data. Due to the storage of staff, the functionaries concentrated on such assistance which would render quick and conspicuous results, and they had no time to ascertain beneficiaries' genuine interest or for innovating activity. Normally, the time taken in getting the loan ranged from 3 to 6 months. In some cases, it was reported to be even more than 6 months. This problem of delay in sanction of loan can be overcome to a great extent by simplifying the procedure of loan advancement. To implement the schemes the banker takes lot of time for screening, sanction of letter, guarantee, subsidy, margin-money and fulfilling other formalities, etc.

Zaidi (1985)[27] evaluated the implementation and performance of Rural Development Programme. Regarding identification of beneficiaries he pointed out that a base-line survey of rural households and thereafter credit camps for identification of beneficiaries are the pre-requisites of Integrated Rural Development Programme, but at several places like Aligarh District (U.P), the programme was started as early as 1977-78, but both the pre-requisites were not fulfilled. The problem resulted in 'wrong identification of beneficiaries which accounted even to as high as 50 per cent.

Jain *et. al.* (1985)[28] analysed the performance of different development programmes in different districts of the country. Regarding Isagarh block of Guna district of Madhya Pradesh, they stated that persons were trained from Training of Rural Youth for Self-Employment programmes in the block. There is only one training centre which is situated in Isagarh and women are trained in stitching and tailoring. There is no arrangement for marketing the crafts that they produce. Henee, they are encouraged to stitch miniature garment sample and baby clothes which are then stuck in an album which they have to maintain. The sewing machines that are bought with the loans sanctioned at the end of the tailoring are soon sold at a premium in the market. Even if an enterprising trainee wishes to start a tailoring shop in Isagarh, she would be put out of business by the heavy competition offered by the already saturated market. This clearly shows the poor understanding of the programme by the organizers. The wrong selection of trade is the shortcoming of this programme.

Reddy *et. al.* (1985)[29] in their study of Andhra Pradesh concluded that the policy for small farmers' development could not create a significant impact on the target groups. The schemes proved to be too ill-organised to be viable. Infact, some of the schemes proved to be counter-productive. The agricultural labourers are not only bypassed but are put to great misery. The administrative machinery is not properly oriented, nor is it vigorous to help the poor. The middlemen, as a result, have been appropriating the benefits. The poor as a class are yet to develop participative culture to overcome the serious limitations of a public policy and an in-egalitarian socio-economic system. Thus, the small Farmers' Development Agency is another important public institution which failed like Green Revolution to make a positive impact on the rural poor.

Dogra (1986)[30] observed many malpractices prevailing in Integrated Rural Development Programme and District Rural Development Agency in his study of Manika block in Palamman district. He stated that assets are taken mainly from established contractors. He further concluded that the various assets to be distributed, such as goats, cows, bullocks, pumping sets, etc., are decided upon and contracts established with the various contractors and middlemen who specialise in supplying one or more such assets for Integrated Rural Development Programme.

Khatkar (1986)[31] conducted a study in Rewari block of Mahendragarh district of Haryana. The main objective of the study was to examine the identification of beneficiaries and impact of Integrated Rural Development Programme. Taking 70 beneficiaries of Integrated Rural Development Programme this study pointed out that only 37.1 per cent of the beneficiaries are properly identified while 48.6 per cent of them are misidentified. Over 14 per cent of the beneficiaries misutilzed all Integrated Rural Development Programme assistance resulting in outright leakages.

Thippaih *et. al.* (1986)[32] ventured a study in two block of Dharwad district of Karnataka State to evaluate Integrated Rural Development Programme. They pointed out that teachers and village level workers are assigned preliminary household survey of eligible borrowers. Since they have not been trained properly to calculate the income of the households, they often mis-identify the beneficiaries. In addition to this, there has been no scrutiny of income estimates by Block and District level authorities. There were instances, where non-eligible beneficiaries were selected in Gramsabha meetings on the basis of political pressure. The researchers suggested that the persons who are in charge of identifying the beneficiaries should be properly trained in income estimation of the households. Even it could be better if they entrust this task to an expert body or a Research institute and the estimate should be properly scrutinised by District Rural Development Agencies and Block Development Offices. If banks are also associated with this work, there will be very little scope for wrong identification.

Malyadri, (1986)[33] organised a study in Rajapalem village of Kavour Taluka in Nellore district of Andhra Pradesh. Regarding bribe he comments that the beneficiaries are made to spend quite some money in this connection either to meet Village Development or Block Development Officer or Bank or District Rural Development Agency officials several times for sanctioning the loan amount. Even in the selection of beneficiaries, some bribes are known to have been taken by the officials. About 60 per cent of the beneficiaries are reported to have spent amounts between Rs. 400 and Rs. 600 in this regard, and remaining 40 per cent below Rs. 200 each. He reported that for recovery of the loan amount also there are problems. The sponsoring agencies identify the beneficiaries and ask the commercial banks to extend credit for the suggested productive activity but when the question of recovery comes, these agencies do not extend any assistance.

Singh and Deb (1986)[34] conducted an empirical investigation in order to find out the nature of people's participation in Integrated Rural Development Programme in Ludhiana and Bhatinda districts of Panjab. Their study revealed that more people from amongst the big farmers participated in larger numbers in Integrated Rural Development Programme than others. The participation of the functionaries and agricultural labourers is minimum in both the areas. They emphasized that it is imperative that efforts have to be made to create better employment opportunities for landless and small farmers under Integrated Rural Development Programme to seek more participation from rural people. If proper consideration is given to the functioning of Integrated Rural Development Programme and in formulating various facets of the scheme, it may show better participation than at present. Further, planning of Integrated Rural Development Programme may take these points into consideration.

Kaur *et. al.* (1986)[35] tried to find out the factors hindering the achievement of the objectives, envisaged in the Integrated Rural Development Programme in Haryana. Regarding selection of beneficiaries they underline that the major obstacles found in the effective implementation of the programme were: the irrational criterion adopted for the selection of the beneficiaries, which left out a large number of families living below poverty-line; wrong identification of beneficiaries which resulted in the failure of the programme in achieving its objectives.

Mishra (1986)[36] examined the question of failure of Integrated Rural Development Programme and noted that the Integrated Rural Development Programme has failed to lift the majority of the target group above the poverty line on a permanent basis. Among the problems faced by the Integrated Rural Development Programme are the problems of identification of beneficiaries, remote control owing to centralized planning and implementation, administrative problem on account of linking of subsidies with loans, target oriented approach, lack of co-ordination between Integrated Rural Development Programme agencies and other institutions, cumbersome loaning procedure, and inadequate supervision mechanism. He suggested that certain changes are essential in order to achieve the objectives with regard to Integrated Rural Development Programme. In view of the insufficient command over goods and inadequate entitlements legitimatized by the legal and institutional systems of the poor, the Integrated Rural Development Programme should be an integral part of land reform programme that tries to redistribute land to the landless or ownership rights at least to the poor tenants.

Sharma (1986)[37] made a study of scheduled castes artisans of Ambala City in Haryana. It indicates a definite change in educational, social and economic conditions of the scheduled castes artisans. The high wages of a leather worker in modern, urban industries push them into their hereditary occupations. But with industrial development the economic mobility is clear in terms of regular employment and source of income as well as their relative economic autonomy in comparison to their elder generation or their counterparts living in rural areas who still depend on land for their survival. Those with better income and living conditions can now strive for a dignified and better life.

Prasad (1986)[38] reviewed the studies conducted on the planning for the removal of poverty in India. He criticised the various policies adopted for this purpose like the trickle-down strategy, land redistribution, beneficiary-oriented programmes for the poor such as Integrated Rural Development Programme, National Rural Employment Programme and so on. The study is against the continuance of the uniform approach in different parts of the country because of wide variations in techno-economic and socio-economic conditions and makes a case for more flexible approach. He opined that poverty alleviation is possible in the next ten years or so if concerted efforts are made in terms of change in the objectives and strategy of planning and adoption of a set of interrelated policy measures. He suggested that preference should be given to more poor among the poor and proper implementation of these programmes should be emphasized so that the benefits would go to the eligible families only.

Devi (1986)[39] made an assessment of Integrated Rural Development Programme based on the information of District Rural Development Agency, Gurgaon. This study revealed that the Integrated Rural Development Programme as an anti-poverty programme is good in intention but intention alone is not enough to cater to the needs adequately. Measurement of poverty in absolute terms, i.e. in terms of per capita income required to meet subsistence needs of the family is essential but it has limited utility. There is a need to look into the various disadvantaged areas in terms of land, irrigation, possession of dry and milch animals and employment, various areas of deprivation in terms of house material possessions and essential amenities such as drinking water and electricity, as well as dependence on upper castes, local leaders and institution, officials and middlemen and various kinds of other difficulties which the poor face in obtaining the necessary inputs and services. Having defined and measured poverty purely in economic terms, there is no need to have social categories within the poor such as scheduled castes, backward classes and others. The only relevant and meaningful categories for the purpose of providing appropriate capital assistance under Integrated Rural Development Programme are landless agriculture labourers, artisans and small farmers. In fact, there is every reason to exclude small farmers with more than one hectare of land from the category of poor as they have less coercion, different priorities and more potential to develop independently without any external assistance. The more homogeneous are the poor in their needs and priorities, the more efficient will be the transfer of Integrated Rural Development Programme inputs to them and the more effective will be the programme.

Gupta (1986)[40] conducted a study on the functioning of the Integrated Tribal Development Project in Birbhum district of West Bengal. He concluded that irrigation facilities provided under Integrated Tribal Development Project were for the benefits of non-tribals, than the tribals. Tribals were less beneficiaries. The Large size multi-purpose societies had been set up under Integrated Tribal Development Project in the district, but only 20 per cent workers in the various multi-purpose societies were tribals. He stated that some of the tribals received goats, pigs or cows under the Integrated Tribal Development Project. A large amount had been spent on forestry under Integrated Tribal Development Project. Waste land had been distributed to farmers in every village. He remarked that the administrative structure on Integrated Tribal Development Project suffered from a number of limitations viz. the lack of control over resources, the complete absence of proper initiative and the complete failure of its monitoring system. He remarked that the development programmes which started around political issues had limited potentialities.

Bose (1986)[41] studied the tribal development of Kerala and observed that in spite of the preference given and schemes undertaken for the welfare of the tribals, the condition of the tribal people still remained the same. He found that there was a great disparity in the economic, social and educational development among these communities. The most deserving poor sections and backward areas had suffered due to utter neglect by the Government officials engaged in the implementation of poverty alleviation programmes in the tribal areas.

Tulsyan (1987)[42] conducted a study on the implementation of Integrated Rural Development Programme in Alauli block of Khagaria district in Bihar. He states that the District Rural Development Agency is not working efficiently in making Annual Action Plan (AAP) especially with regard to the agriculture sector. There is no doubt that the achievements are being sent to the Government from time to time, but that are not based on real facts but on common sense estimation. It is the subsidy element in the Integrated Rural Development Programme loan which the concerned officials have an eye on. He observed that the District Rural Development Agency and Regional Rural Banks have left the beneficiary farmers completely in the lurch after granting the assets. They are not generating a sense of responsibility. Trying to pass on responsibility is the usual phenomenon of the programme functionaries.

Bagchee (1987)[43] made an attempt to review the main poverty alleviation programmes covered in the Rural Development sector, in the light of the experience in implementing them during the Sixth Five Year Plan. He believed that these programmes suffer primarily from lack of conceptual clarity and an inadequate understanding of the complex nature of the environment in which these programmes have to be implemented. Greater clarity about objectives and goals of each programme, the norms and other criteria for project selection as well as role specificity of the different level in the organizational structure involved in executing the all programme aspects and more systematic programme planning and designing would go a long way in giving these anti-poverty programmes at least a chance of success in the field.

Tripta Jaiswal (1987)[44] conducted a study in order to explore the socio-economic conditions of the scheduled caste people in the Kalyanpur block of the Kanpur district. She selected Jeora village as a sample. In order to collect primary data about the socio-economic conditions of people, a questionnaire schedule was prepared covering the housing, education, occupation, household incomes, age, health and allied aspects. The survey was conducted with the assistance of National Sample Survey volunteers. The villages consisted of 127 families out of which 106 families belonged to scheduled castes category, 15 families to the backward communities and the remaining to the general castes. She concluded that nearly 60 per cent people live below poverty line. They form the most appropriate target groups of the poverty alleviation programmes and social uplift schemes. Most of them are either marginal workers or unemployed people. She observed that the local feuds and litigation eat away whatever meager resources they have and people remain backward.

Mehta and Bhardwaj (1987)[45] conducted an empirical investigation of 100 households of Kangra and Hamirpur districts of Himachal Pradesh to examine the impact of Integrated Rural Development Programme on economic status of beneficiaries. The main objectives of the study were to analyse the changes in the cropping pattern, income, employment and expenditure of beneficiaries, as well as to work out the changes in expenditure on production and consumption of beneficiaries in the study area. In order to achieve these objectives, 80 beneficiaries were selected by simple random sampling without replacement from two blocks namely, Panchrukhi and Hamirpur of Kangra and Hamirpur district. In addition to this, 20 non-beneficiaries were also chosen by simple random sampling again without replacement, in order to study the changes which have taken place as a result of Integrated Rural Development Programme assistance. The beneficiaries and non-beneficiaries were classified into two categories, namely small and large households on the basis of their gross incomes. The data was then subjected to statistical analysis by employing mathematical models and statistical tools. Analysis of income indicated that the benefits from Integrated Rural Development Programme in Kangra district were being derived in terms of acquiring livestock but in Hamirpur district, the beneficiaries were taking benefits from off-farm sources. Income under beneficiary situation for small and large households was more than under non-beneficiary situation in both the districts. It was observed that employment days for small and large households under beneficiary situation were more than that under non-beneficiary situation in both the districts from off-farm sources which in general were the major sources of employment for beneficiary and non-beneficiary households in the study area. The consumption expenditure under beneficiary situation was more as compared to non-beneficiary situation for small and large households, except for the small beneficiary households of Kangra district. It was also concluded that, in general, expenditure on food was higher as compared to non-food expenditure in case of small households under beneficiary and non-beneficiary situations in both the districts. Higher levels of income, employment and expenditure in case of both small and large households under beneficiary situation in the study area indicated that Integrated Rural Development Programme has produced positive impact on the economic status of its beneficiaries.

Rao and Erappa (1987)[46] in their study on Integrated Rural Development Programme in Karnataka observed that the programme covered only about 5 per cent of poor in Karnataka in 1983-84. He also found that the schemes under Integrated Rural Development Programme appear to have been chosen on the criterion of their adaptability without any prior training and minimal investment rather than on the basis of their likely contribution to rural growth. Integrated Rural Development Programme is implemented in the State every year in a new set of villages but the implementing staff remains so pre-occupied that it is doubtful whether they would be in a position to divert enough time and efforts to monitor objectively the performance of beneficiaries assisted in early years. There seems to be a measure of bias in favour of larger and accessible villages in Integrated Rural Development Programme implementation.

Singh (1987)[47] examined the problems and prospects of poverty alleviation programmes. He observed that although these poverty alleviation programmes contain the basic objective to uplift the socio-economic conditions of the rural poor and the downtrodden, the implementation of these programmes suffer from a large number of problems and bottlenecks. Owing to the lack of suitable and sufficient infrastructure in the rural area, these programmes have not been able to benefit the poorest section of the population upto the level of expectation. He suggested that the adequate regional planning, strong central co-ordination, effective local level organizations, participation of the rural poor in the planning can make these programmes more effective.

Malyadri (1988)[48] in his study of Mallial Block of Karimnagar district of Andhra Pradesh holds that owing to inadequacy of financial assistance, 60 per cent of the borrowers, maintained their animals without shed throughout the year, remaining 40 per cent of beneficiaries built sheds after the purchase of the animals. Special attention has to be paid to feed the breeding stock during pregnancy. Most of the borrowers have not insured their units on account of lack of guidance. Due to lack of training, most of the beneficiaries were ignorant of different diseases and treatments of pigs. Most of the borrowers were troubled for veterinary aid because hospitals were far away from the villages. There was neither a cooperative society nor any other organization of borrowers which could help the beneficiaries to sell their produce at a reasonable rate. Owing to lack of organized marketing system, many a times the borrowers sold out their pigs in their villages itself through middleman at lower price resulting in lower profits.

Chaturvedi *et. al.* (1988)[49] in their study of three states concluded that the Training of Rural Youth for Self-Employment (TRYSEM) beneficiary from Gujarat had his income below poverty-line two and a half years ago before undergoing training in carpentry and acquiring implements. The income generated through this occupation helped him cross the poverty line. This is mainly due to the beneficiary's sincere efforts to go in search of work in and around the village throughout the year.

Desai (1988)[50] stated that out of 1,068 sample households which reported having made repayments of loan installments, 82 per cent said that they had made repayments out of the income derived by them from Integrated Rural Development Programme, whereas 18 per cent reported that they had to manage for the repayments from some other sources. Further, he stated that percentage of sample households reporting overdues was the highest (74 per cent) in desert areas and the lowest (32.6 per cent) in the hill areas, but ranged up to 43 per cent in agriculturally less developed areas. Desai mentioned the reasons for overdues as : (i) return from the schemes not adequate (36 per cent); (ii) income raised from the benefit schemes spent on unforeseen factors like illness, death, marriage and other social obligation (15 per cent); and (iii) repayment of old dues (9 per cent).

Dhillon and Sandhu (1988)[51] in their study on Integrated Rural Development Programme have pointed out number of shortcomings in Rural Development Programme; District Rural Development Agencies do not have staff under their control at block level. Moreover, District Rural Development Agency officials are unable to make frequent visits to beneficiaries in the fields for want of proper conveyance. Further, frequent transfers and vacant posts of key official especially the Project Officers in charge of District Rural Development Agencies, greatly impair the efficiency and effectiveness of the administrative set-up at different levels. Also, inadequacy of banking infrastructure affects credit flow adversely and shortage of staff results in insufficient scrutiny and delayed disposal of loan applications. They also confirm that there prevails corruption and malpractices in the sanctioning of loans and subsidies.

Mohanasundaram (1988)[52] conducted a study in two blocks of Coimbatore district of Tamil Nadu. He suggested some important aspects regarding effective implementation of Integrated Rural Development Programme schemes. He stated that very low perception of the rural poor indicates the dire need for increasing awareness among them about the special schemes meant for their welfare. The lukewarm attitude of the implementation machinery should also be changed. The selection of deserving beneficiaries by conducting household surveys, credit camps and gram sabhas etc., will ensure assisting of right beneficiaries. The major advantages of such exercises are cutting across the dominance of intermediaries and avoidance of leakages. This can be done by the active and also effective coordination among the various village level developmental functionaries. Improving the qualification of the village level workers by way of giving training to them will improve their performance in the rural areas. In a nutshell it can be stated that taking care of the selection of village level workers, their training, supervision, avoiding interference in their working, etc. are some of the steps that need to be considered in order to ensure the effectiveness of implementation of the programmes/schemes.

Rao *et. al.* (1988)[53] in their study on the evaluation of Integrated Rural Development Programme in Warangal District pointed out the deficiencies prevailing in Integrated Rural Development Programme. Their study brings to limelight various deficiencies in the whole chain of Integrated Rural Development Programme in the district which are under financing, providing cash credits by violating the norms, lack of supervision, lack of knowledge on the part of the beneficiaries to utilize the assets, lack of adequate training, the Integrated Rural Development Programme loans not being utilised to the extent of their real objectives.

Hirway (1988)[54] in his study concluded that the Integrated Rural Development Programme emphasizes self employment rather too much. It assumes that the poor and especially the poorest of the poor are capable of self-employment and managing independent enterprises successfully. This assumption is not realistic as many of the poor are illiterates, have low risk capacity, possess little entrepreneurial abilities, and have no or very little assets. Therefore, they are not credit-worthy. They are not capable of managing enterprises independently. Many of them would be better off if they are given wage employment.

Further Integrated Rural Development Programme assumes that the poor need a subsidized income generating asset and when it is given, the needs of the poor are largely satisfied. This assumption also is not fully correct as the asset will perhaps meet a part of their needs. In this sense, Integrated Rural Development Programme is a partial approach which tends to create leakages in the working of the asset schemes and in running of the programme successfully. Finally, Integrated Rural Development Programme assumes that the special arrangements made for the poor will reach them. It is difficult to accept that Integrated Rural Development Programme, which does not attempt to change the prevailing socio-economic system in which it operates, will change the process of percolation of economic programmes in favour of the poor. The planning component of Integrated Rural Development Programme also is found to be weak. First of all there is no systematic approach regarding the allocation of Integrated Rural Development Programme funds among various schemes, various areas and households. There is no provision in Integrated Rural Development Programme which provides for their needs and resources. To allocate specific schemes to the poor households mainly on the basis of their own demands is definitely not a sound way of planning.

Gopal *et. al.* (1989)[55] in their study of Nalgonda district of Andhra Pradesh, discovered misutilization of loan by the beneficiaries. They observed that the loan amount went into domestic consumption. It is natural and logical that the members of target group whose economic conditions are at the level of subsistence cannot invest the amount in the income generating sector as day-to-day consumption needs take precedence over other considerations.

Jose (1989)[56] conducted a study in two blocks of a district of Kerala State, in order to examine the participation of women in Integrated Rural Development Programme. He found that there has been a decline in women's participation in agricultural sector while in the non-agricultural sector there has been an increase. The important finding in respect of work participation is that the marginal increase in total work participation of labourers in Kerala is due to the increase in female work participation in non-agricultural sector. It has been noticed that owing to the operation of Integrated Rural Development Programme, women's employment has increased by 27 per cent and income by 33 per cent in the study region. From this, it may be deducted that rural development activities would, to a certain extent, increase women's economic contribution to the household.

Kulkarni *et. al.* (1989)[57] conducted a study in Bijapur district of Karnataka. They found that different socio-economic factors affect the success or failure of different schemes of Integrated Rural Development Programme. They hold that the success of Integrated Rural Development Programme mainly depends upon the level of education, family size, and ownership of livestock, durable assets and occupational structure. Their study highlights that one of the reasons for poor performance of Integrated Rural Development Programme was the delay in actual sanctioning of loans and releasing of the subsidy amount by the development authorities. They suggested that a single window approach both for subsidy and loan would reduce the time gap and transaction cost of borrowing to the beneficiaries.

Paul (1989)[58] estimated the magnitude of income inequalities of Haryana. The study is based on cross-sectional data of 432 farm, non-farm and labour households. It has been observed that in case of farm households, agriculture constituted the single most important component of household income claiming 68.37 per cent of the total household income of this category. Salaries and livestock with 12.33 and 9.02 per cent shares respectively were the next in order. All other components of income were less significant. In case of non-farm households among the relatively more important components, salaries and business/crafts and professions accounted for 26.59 and 23.21 per cent of the total households income respectively. Agriculture followed by wages has also a significant place and they constituted 19.38 and 15.42 per cent shares respectively. Income generated by house property in this group accounted for 7.56 per cent of the total income. In the case of labour households, wages (agricultural as well as non-agricultural) constituted the single most important component of income, followed by livestock. The former contributing 79.59 per cent of total income and the latter accounted for 13.74 per cent. The contribution of agriculture and other sources was negligible. On the whole, farm households occupied the predominant place with 65.46 per cent share in the total income followed by non-farm (24.70 per cent) and labour households 10.34 per cent. In rural Haryana,

48.74 per cent of the households fell in the lower income groups and their share in the total income was estimated at 18.13 per cent. In contrast, 19.20 per cent of the households figured in the higher income group and they owned 49.69 per cent of the total household income. So far as the income disparities are concerned no significant difference was observed between the farm and non-farm households. The major problem of labour households was not of the economic disparity but of acute general poverty. 93.60 per cent of these households were in the lower income group.

Thakur (1991)[59] conducted an empirical investigation of 137 rural sample households in the low-hill zone areas of Himachal Pradesh in order to examine the socio-economic conditions of the economically weaker-sections with a view to find out the nature, type and magnitude of inter-class as well as the inter-caste-wise socio-economic inequalities as well as to study the extent to which the planned efforts have reduced the disparities in the distribution of income, among these households. She concluded that nearly 65 per cent of the total household consumption expenditure is spent on food-items and the remaining 35 per cent on non-food items. The consumption pattern in this study has been worked out in pursuance of the 'Engel's Law of Consumption' according to which, the percentage of household consumption expenditure on food-items go on decreasing and the percentage expenditure on non-food items (such as fuel, light, clothing, health and education, etc.) go on increasing with an increase in the level of income. The per consumer unit per month saving with the help of 'current account method' has been worked out negative. The per consumer unit per month burden of debt has been estimated Rs. 44.14 and Rs. 37.52 on the marginal and small size of holding. She stated that due to the biased attitude of panchayat pradhans and dishonest administrative staff at the low levels involved in the implementation of Poverty Alleviation Programmes have either knowingly denied the poorest households from the benefits of these programmes or those poor households who have been included under these programmes, they have not been given the benefits according to their needs and requirements.

Mahajan (1991)[60] while studying Integrated Rural Development Programme in Punjab State found that the programme has benefited a number of non-poor families. It was found that the identification of the people below poverty line was not conducted strictly according to the guidelines. Banks and village agencies were not involved at all in the identification of the beneficiaries. Selection of the beneficiaries was not done on the basis of Antyodya principle. Block and district plans have not been drawn as per the guidelines. It was found that the programme had improved the economic conditions of the beneficiaries with which the assets were intact and in good position. He found that about 50 per cent beneficiaries had crossed the poverty line.

While commenting on the causes of failure of anti-poverty programmes, Kanta Ahuja (1991)[61] stated that the programmes have failed mainly due to the cause of leakage, on account of corruption and administrative failure and inefficiency at local level. They have seldom succeeded in creating durable assets because of old material component in such projects and because of poor technical formulation. In spite of indirect indications of unutilized, underemployed labour, mobilization of labour for such employment has been quite inadequate. The programmes have in general, operated as relief cum subsidy programmes rather than as programmes for increasing the productive potential of the community. Their implementation has clearly shown that the rural force is not a lumped mass of under employed workers, who would come forward to work as soon as unskilled work opportunities are created for them. The basic issue in employment policy, therefore, relates to how best to incorporate the development of employment objectives in the local level plans.

Kumar, (1992)[62] assessed the impact of Integrated Rural Development Programme on income and employment of Erode block of Periyar district of Kerala. Out of the total selected beneficiaries 77.50 per cent have generated additional income under the programme. About 13.13 per cent beneficiaries have an additional income upto Rs. 2000; nearly 55.83 per cent have generated between Rs. 2000 to Rs. 4000 and about 8.34 per cent above Rs. 4000 from the assets provided under the programme. Of the total sample respondents, 51-52 per cent have generated

2000-4000 man-hours, and about 3.33 per cent have created above 4000 man hours.

Nambiar (1992)[63] conducted an empirical investigation of 142 sample households in district Palakkad, Kerala to examine the socio-economic status of poor households. A schedule was prepared and data was collected with personal interview method. Besides the data on socio-economic characteristics, income, employment, status and impact of Integrated Rural Development Programme, the author collected data on time disposition by sex to paid and unpaid work, detailed characteristics of employment consumption pattern, assets, indebtedness and housing conditions. Per capita income of Rs. 1280 was considered as the level of cut-off annual income. It was found that problem of destitution was widespread among the labour households. As a strategy of survival, the households resorted to several practices such as cutting down food intake, virtual starvation, high underemployed days, cutting down of pocket expenses and engage family labour in petty jobs to augment household income. It was observed that in the absence of production assets the households were dependent upon physical labour for sustenance and hence poverty phenomenon across households was explained in terms of this exclusive dependence on wage labour. On the impact of poverty intervention programmes the observer made a dismal note. Integrated Rural Development Programme, the core of the intervention programmes was beset with several issues. Low coverage, diversion of assistance to non-poor, low asset formation and disposal of assets were some of them. Even in the case of those assisted households in possession of the assets the income generated was insufficient to bridge the poverty gap. Corruption was endemic in the system and the indifferent attitude of the lower level functionaries involved in the implementation of the programmes towards the poor was most striking. Many poor households also showed little interest in participating in the programme as they were skeptical of a Government scheme involving loan. Their fear was that they might loose their only asset of the tiny piece of land in the event of default in repayment. It was observed that like Integrated Rural Development Programme the accomplishment of other schemes evolved for the poor such as land reforms, social security measures and housing schemes was not different. An attempt was also made to examine the prospects of abolishing poverty by an asset based as well as employment guarantee scheme. From the point of view of the poor the schemes have serious limitations. It was found that the poverty gap varies widely across the households. The other limitation referred to the adaptability of the schemes to individual households.

Singh (1994)[64] conducted an empirical investigation of 400 respondents in Patiala district of Punjab to investigate the impact of District Rural Development Agency (DRDA) on the Socio-Economic conditions of the people. The schemes implemented in different sectors have been taken up for investigation. From the primary sector four schemes viz. dairy, piggery, poultry and sheep/goat-rearing were taken up. From the secondary sector schemes like shoe-making, cycle shop, fruit rehri, etc. were clubbed together. From the tertiary sector two schemes named Kiryana Shop and Mule/Bullock cart/tongas were selected. Regarding the Training of Rural Youth For Self Employment Programme, young people from various trades were interviewed. Out of a total 400 respondents, about one-third felt some increase in their income, on the other hand one-seventh suffered a decrease in their incomes owing to borrowing. In all, only 5 per cent of the respondents held that their standard of living had improved from the pre-assistance level. On the other hand 13 per cent suffered a decline in standard of living because of borrowing. They bemoaned that they could not pay back the loan and were consequently harassed and humiliated by bankers. Moreover, Integrated Rural Development Programme loan could not influence the social position of 82 per cent of the sample respondents; these people do not feel any change in their social status after getting Integrated Rural Development Programme loan. While examining repayment position, it was found that about one-fourth had already repaid the loan while an equal number of the respondents were making the repayment regularly. Repayment position was positively associated with caste position, size of land-holding and education. In an attempt to find out as to whether the beneficiaries used the loan properly or not, it was found that about half of the loanees had used the loan in proper business while other half had used the amount of loan some where else or had failed in their respective business. Regarding subsidy, it was found that the high caste people and people with bigger plots of land expressed more satisfaction than the lower castes and the landless, etc. The data regarding illegal gratification in BDO office pointed out that almost half of the respondents paid some amount as bride. Similar conclusions emerged from the data showing bribe paid to the patwari. Over one-third of the total respondents paid illegal gratification to the veterinary doctor. His main clients were those beneficiaries who took loan for dairy scheme.

So far as the assessment of different schemes is concerned it was found that only dairy, sheep rearing and bullock/mule carts/tonga are successful. Shoe making, retail shop were slightly successful while piggery, poultry were unsuccessful schemes. The analysis of Training of Rural Youth for Self Employment (TRYSEM) gave a mixed result. One-fourth of the respondents called it a successful effort while an equal number of them considered it a failure and over half of them did not respond either ways.

This study suggested that identification of the poor needs serious efforts. Besides the income criterion, potentiality of the loanees in terms of skills and entrepreneurship, for new occupations should be taken seriously for creation of successful models in various enterprises.

Dasgupta (1997)[65] in his study on the Rural development programmes stated that various poverty alleviation programmes are essential for providing supplementary employment to the poor and underemployed. He pointed out that the unabated population growth cuts at the root of all the rural development efforts, and unless this problem is tackled on a war footing, it will be futile exercise to bring about the changes as envisaged.

Ali (1998)[66] conducted a study in Nalgonda district of Andhra Pradesh to analyse the income and employment generated through Integrated Rural Development Programme. He observed that Integrated Rural Development Programme had positive impact on generation of income and employment level of beneficiaries. He also pointed out that the marginal farmers have sold out all their assets created through Integrated Rural Development Programme.

Sandeep Joshi (1999)[67] conducted an empirical analysis of the Impact of Integrated Rural Development Programme on poverty alleviation and employment generation on agriculturist beneficiaries of two blocks Ajagarh and Shahnagar of Panna district of Madhya Pradesh. Total number of 100 beneficiary households were selected for collecting the required information. He found that 18 per cent of the total beneficiaries earned upto Rs. 3000. Nearly 21 per cent earned from Rs. 3001 to 5000, about 19 per cent from 5001-8000, nearly 12 per cent from 8001 to 10,000 and only 1 per cent Rs. 11,000 and above. The beneficiaries whose net household income from all sources other than Integrated Rural Development Programme during last 12 months was upto Rs. 3000 constitutes 9 per cent of the total sample beneficiaries, whereas 16 per cent beneficiaries earned from Rs. 3001 to 5000, 51 per cent from Rs. 5000 to 8000 and 26 per cent from Rs. 8001 to 10,999. This study revealed that there was a positive impact of Integrated Rural Development Programme assistance on the income of the beneficiary households. The study concluded that Integrated Rural Development Programme had enabled the poor peasants of Panna district to improve their lot. Though they had not been able to reap full benefits of the programme, notwithstanding huge investment made by the government the programme had achieved its objectives to some extent.

Mundra *et. al.* (2002)[68] assessed the impact of Training of Rural Youth For Self-Employment (TRYSEM) amongst 300 women beneficiaries belonging to tribal and non-tribal communities of Udaipur and Dugapur districts of Rajasthan. Their study revealed that 70.3 per cent women trainees under Training of Rural Youth for Self-Employment have not yet accepted the trade as a source of self-employment. Mushroom cultivation was not accepted by single women, whereas stitching was accepted by a majority of the trained women. Only 15 per cent women started the job within 6 months after the training, whereas 85 per cent women took more than 6 months to 2 years in starting their own trade. The majority of the tribal could find gainful employment for a period ranging 2 to 6 hours, whereas non-tribal women were utilizing 2 hours per day as gainful employment.

The women beneficiaries could earn Rs. 50 to Rs. 325 per month through engaging themselves in trade in which they were trained. They suggested the need for providing post training facilities such as credit, marketing, raw material to trainees and beneficiaries to start their own job. Co-operatives in the villages must be entrusted to motivate Training of Rural Youth for Self-Employment beneficiaries to do work, facilitate them to get raw material in time at fixed price and to sell their product.

Chopra (2003)[69] conducted a study in Ambala and Gurgaon districts of Haryana during the period 1997-98 to 1999-2000. Out of different sub-schemes, four sub schemes namely, Pair of Bullocks (Agriculture and minor irrigation); Buffalo (Animal Husbandry); Tailoring (Industry, Service and Business); and Jhotta Buggie (Tertiary) were selected. The main objective of the study was to delineate various rural poverty alleviation programmes launched by the Government of India with a view to identify the positive aspects; major shifts in the policy, strategy and approach; and perils and pit falls of these programmes and to highlight their performance in relation to Haryana State. To find out the socio-economic background of the beneficiaries of Integrated Rural Development Programme, and to examine how far their socio-economic conditions satisfy the criterion of below poverty line status. The multi-stage stratified sampling technique was followed and 150 beneficiaries were selected. It was found that 54.67 per cent beneficiaries on an overall basis were below poverty line of Rs. 6400 per annum and the remaining 45.33 per cent were found ineligible for Integrated Rural Development Programme benefits. It was concluded that there were nearly half of the selected beneficiaries of Integrated Rural Development Programme who did not satisfy the income criterion of below poverty line status and were successful in getting themselves identified as the beneficiaries of the programme. The coverage of scheduled caste and scheduled tribe beneficiaries under Integrated Rural Development Programme appeared to be adequate in the selected blocks as 40 per cent beneficiaries belong to this category. However despite the repeated emphasis of the Government the Gram Sabha and the Village Panchayats were not properly involved in the selection of the beneficiaries and 87.37 per cent beneficiaries informed that list of selected beneficiaries was not displayed at Gram Sabha meetings. It was found that 84.67 per cent of beneficiaries received full subsidy 8.67 per cent received only a part of it and 6.66 per cent had not received any subsidy. Repayment of loans was found very poor. About 82.0 per cent beneficiaries expressed their inability in the regular repayment of loans. Nearly 37.33 per cent beneficiaries could not cross the poverty line of Rs. 5530, about 42.00 per cent beneficiaries crossed the poverty line of Rs. 5530 but could not cross the poverty line of Rs. 6760 per annum. There were only 20.67 per cent beneficiaries who crossed the poverty line of Rs. 6760 per annum. Furthermore it was found that even if all the beneficiaries could not cross the determined poverty lines, they have been found significantly better-off after the Integrated Rural Development Programme assistance in both the blocks. However, the study highlighted that there exists certain gaps and inconsistencies in the administrative structure and Integrated Rural Development Programme in relation to co-ordination, supervision monitoring and follow-up of the programme. Most of the Integrated Rural Development Programme beneficiaries had expressed their dissatisfaction or ignorance regarding the identification and selection procedures. Very few of them were repaying loan instalments regularly from the income derived out of the Integrated Rural Development Programme assets, which had been found selectively more in less developed region than the developed one.

The above review of the literature on the impact of Integrated Rural Development Programme and other poverty alleviation programmes clearly showed that the most of the studies conducted by the Government agencies pointed out a positive impact on the levels of living of weaker sections in the rural areas of the country. The poverty alleviation programmes resulted in increased income, employment generation, increase in consumption level, elevation in the overall social status in village community and improved total assets position of the beneficiaries. Some of the studies have also reported wrong identification of beneficiaries and inadequate loan repayment. Whereas most of the studies conducted by the individual researchers, pointed out that the poverty alleviation programme have not been yielding the desired results. Researches have highlighted several loopholes and deficiencies prevailing in the programmes such as wrong policy formulation by the planners, lack of co-ordination, lack of entrepreneurial ability and dynamism on the part of poor, lack of effective implementation of the programme and lack of political will to improve the lot of poor. It has been observed that some of the schemes have led to an increase in income and employment potential of small and marginal farmers and agricultural labourers. Some of the investigators concluded that the procedure for selection of beneficiaries is not systematic and has many loopholes for the acquisition of subsidized loan by non-deserving people. The individual scholars have also noted political interference, lack of will on the part of concerned officers. The researchers have given suggestions for streamlining the procedure of selection of beneficiaries. There is a general consensus that identification may be done with the help of gram panchayat/gram sabha. Most of the researchers observed that the procedure for obtaining loan was cumbersome and time-consuming, amount of loan and subsidy was inadequate and loan repayment was poor. Regarding the phenomenon of bribe, most of the scholars have indicated that poor people are not able to receive their right without paying illegal gratification. So far as participation in the development programme is concerned most of the studies indicated that involvement of the poor in the programme is minimal. Besides other factors, lack of courage and confidence among the poor hampers their involvement in the programme. The results of the studies on the issue of the utilization of loan, indicates that most of the recipients of loan do not use it properly, rather they use it for some other domestic needs.

Notes and References

1. National Productivity Council, Report on Concurrent Evaluation of IRDP Works, District Bhiwani (Haryana), Chandigarh. 1984.
2. Agricultural Finance Corporation Limited, Concurrent Evaluation and Impact Study of IRDP in Rohtak District (Haryana), Bombay, 1984
3. Government of India, (Planning Commission), Evaluation Report on Integrated Rural Development Programme, Programme Evaluation Organisation, New Delhi, May 1985
4. Government of Haryana, (Economic and Statistical Organisation), Evaluation Study of IRDP in Haryana, Chandigarh, Dec. 1987.
5. Government of India, (Planning Commission), Evaluation Report on

Provision of House Sites-*cum*-House Construction : Assistance to the Rural Landless Labour Households, PEO, New Delhi, August, 198.
6. State Bank of Patiala, Financing Under Integrated Rural Development Programme: An Evaluative Study, Patiala, 1987, p. 7.
7. Government of India, Department of Rural Development, Ministry of Agriculture Concurrent Evaluations of IRDP—The Main Findings of the Survey for January 1989 to Sept. 1989, New Delhi, June 1990, pp. 7-10.
8. Government of India, (Planning Commission), Jawahar Rozgar Yojana—A Quick Study for 1991-92, PEO, New Delhi, 1992, pp. 3-61.
9. Government of India, (Planning Commission), Evaluation Study on Employment Assurance Scheme, Programme Evaluation Organisation, New Delhi, April 2000, pp. 1 to 14.
10. Government of India, (The Ministry of Rural Development), All India Report on Concurrent Evaluation of Indira Awas Yojana (1998-99), New Delhi, May, 2001.
11. Government of Himachal Pradesh, Planning Department An Evaluation Study on IRDP in Himachal Pradesh (1992-97), Shimla, 2002, pp. 68-73.
12. D.P. Apte, Fifteen Kolaba Villages, in Planning for TRIBAL Development: (edited), Ranjit Gupta, Ankur Publishers, New Delhi 1976, pp. 176-81.
13. P.N. Sharma, Planning for the Poor, *Kurukshetra*, Vol. 26, No. 19, New Delhi, July 1, 1978, pp 13-21.
14. A.K. Gupta, and B.K. Aggarwal, Socio-Economic Impact of Marginal Farmers and Agricultural Labourers Agencies on the Rural Poor, Annual Research Report, 1980-81, Deptt. of Eco-Sociology, PAU, Ludhiana, 1980, p. 58.
15. Hanumant Yadav and C.S. Mishra, Impact of the Tribal Development Programmes on Employment, Income and Asset Formation in Bastar District of Madhya Pradesh, *Indian Journal of Agricultural Economics*, Vol. XXXV, No. 4, Bombay, October-December 1980, pp. 69-73.
16. Chakradhar Sinha, Jivitesh Kumar Singh, Removal of Poverty and SFDA : A Case Study, Social Change, New Delhi, March, 1981, p. 14.
17. K.V. Sundram, Experience of Area Development Planning in India: Alternative Approaches in Rural Development: National Policies and Experiences (ed.), R.P. Mishra,, Maruzen Asia, Nagoya, Japan, 1981, pp. 158-60.
18. Vasant Deshpandey, Employment Guarantee Scheme: Impact on Poverty and Bondage Among Tribals, Tilak Maharashtra Vidyapeeth, Pune, 1982, pp. 57-66.
19. Abdul Noorbasha, D. Dakashinamurthy, Rich Farmer Grab All Benefits Leaves Poor Farmer in the Lurch, *Yojana*, Vol. 27, No. 13, New Delhi, July 16-31, 1983, p. 23.
20. V. Nayak and S. Prasad, : Levels of Living of Scheduled Caste and Scheduled Tribes, *Economic and Political Weekly*, Vol. 19, No. 30, Bombay, July, 1984, pp. 1205-13.
21. Jaganath Pathy, Tribal Peasantry: Dynamics and Development, Inter-India Publications, New Delhi, 1984, pp. 202-03.
22. C. Parvathamma, Scheduled Castes and Tribes—A Socio-Economic Survey, Ashish Publishing House, New Delhi, 1984.

23. K. Subbarao, Regional Variations in Impact of Anti-Poverty programmes: A Review of Evidence, *Economic and Political Weekly*, Vol. XX, No. 43, October 1985, Bombay, pp. 1830-34.
24. Satyanarayana, and Y.J. Peter, Rural Development : An Appraisal, *Kurukshetra*, Vol. XXXVIII, No. 7, New Delhi, April, 1985, pp. 24-25.
25. M.S. Chandakavate, Tardy Implementation of IRDP, *Yojana*, Vol. 29, No. 19, New Delhi, October 16-31, 1985, p. 19.
26. Rajendra, N. Tewari, Is IRDP lacking thrust? *Yojana*, Vol. 29, No. 20, New Delhi, Nov. 1-15, 1985, pp. 18-19.
27. Naseen, A. Zaidi, Has IRDP helped Alleviate Poverty? *Yojana*, Vol. 229, No. 18, Oct. 1-15, 1985, New Delhi, p. 9.
28. L.C. Jain, B.V. Krishnamurthy and P.M. Tripathi, Grass without Roots : Rural Development Under Government Auspices, Sage Publications, New Delhi, 1985, p. 140-41.
29. G. Ram Reddy and G. Haragopal, Public Policy and the Rural Poor in India, Centre for Economic and Social Studies, Hyderabad, 1985, p. 238.
30. Bharat Dogra, Victims of Poverty Alleviation, *Economic and Political Weekly*, Vol. XXI, No. 28, Bombay, July, 1986, p. 1193.
31. R.K. Khatkar, An impact study of Integrated Rural Development Programmes in Mahendergarh District of Haryana, *Indian Journal of Agricultural Economics*, Vol. 41, No. 4, Bombay, October-December 1986, p. 658.
32. P. Thippaiah, Tackling Rural Poverty, *Yojana*, Vol. 30, No. 22, New Delhi, 1986, p. 15.
33. P. Malyadri, Success of IRDP : Myth or Reality, Khadi Gramodyog, Vol. XXXII, No. 11, Bombay, 1986, p. 11 and 13.
34. Jasbir. K. Singh, and P.C. Deb, People's Participation in Integrated Rural Development Programme, *Guru Nanak Journal of Society*, Vol. 6, No. 2, Amritsar, October. 1986, p. 77.
35. Malkit Kaur, Kusum Aggarwal and Sushil Kharuta, Poverty Alleviation Programmes in Haryana-Need for a new strategy, *Indian Journal of Agricultural Economics*, Vol. 41, No. 4, Bombay, Oct.-Dec., 1986, p. 662.
36. Sibranjan Mishra, Rural Development : A Challenge before IRDP, A Fresh look. *Indian Journal of Agricultural Economics*, Vol. XLI, No. 4, Bombay, Oct.-Dec. 1986, p. 656.
37. S.K. Sharma, Chamar artisans : Industrialization, Skills and Social Mobility, B.R. Publishing House, New Delhi, 1986, pp. 11-162.
38. Kamta Prasad, Planning for Alleviation of Poverty in India : Experience and Lessons, *Social Change*, Vol. 16, No. 2 and 3, New Delhi, June-September 1986, pp. 68-75.
39. Pajula, A.K. Devi, Poverty in Rural Areas : A Study, *Kurukshetra*, Vol. XXXV, Nos. 2-3, Nov.-Dec., 1986, New Delhi, p. 31.
40. Dipankar Gupta, Tribal Development in a West Bengal District, Programmes, Structure and Process, *Economic and Political Weekly*, Vol. XXI, No. 1, Bombay, January 1986, pp. 35-45.
41. S.C. Bose, Planning for Tribal Development : Kerala's experience, *Yojana*, Vol. 30, No. 5, New Delhi, March 16-31, 1986.
42. S.L. Tulsyan, Why Poverty Hangs on? *Yojana*, Vol. 31, No. 17, 16-31, September, 1987, New Delhi, p. 19.

43. Sandeep Bagchee, Poverty Alleviation Programmes in Seventh Plan. *Economic and Political Weekly*, Vol. XXII, No. 4, Bombay, Jan. 24, 1987, p. 146.
44. Km. Tripta Jaiswal, The Socio-Economic Status of Scheduled Caste Population in Kalyanpur Block (Distt. Kanpur Urban)—A Sample study of Jeora village in Schedule Caste and Schedule Tribes in India edited by Dr. B.P. Chaurasia forwarded by Anand Swaroop Jauheri, Chugh Publications, Allahabad, 1990, pp. 179-89.
45. Prakash Mehta and Rattan Chand Bhardwaj, Integrated Rural Development Programme—A Case Study in Himachal Pradesh, B.R. Publishing Corporation, Delhi, 1987, pp. 63-66.
46. V.M. Rao and S. Errapa, IRDP and Rural Diversification—A Study in Karnatka. *Economic and Political Weekly*, Vol. 22, No. 52, Bombay, 1987, pp. A 151-60.
47. R. R. Singh, Poverty Alleviation Problems and Prospects, Khadi Gramodyog, Bombay, December, 1987.
48. Malyadri, Financing Pig Farming: A Study. Kurukshetra, Vol. XXXVII, No. 3, New Delhi, 1988, p. 22.
49. Y.S. Chaturvedi, K.K. Naidu and M.J. Sridhar, Beneficiaries of IRDP in Gujarat, *Kurukshetra*, Vol. XXXVI, No. 12, New Delhi, Sept. 1988, p. 27.
50. Vasant Desai, Rural Development, Vols. I to VI, Himalaya Publishing House, New Delhi, 1988, p. 132 (Vol. II).
51. D.S. Dhillon and N.S. Sandhu, Integrated Rural Development Programme : An Overview, *Kurukshetra*, Vol. XXXVI, No. 12, New Delhi, Sept. 1988, p. 13.
52. V. Mohansundram, How IRDP schemes can be better Implemented?, *Kurukshetra*, Vol. XXXVI, No. 12, New Delhi, Sept. 1988, p. 9.
53. Rao and R. Natrajan, IRDP Assistance in Andhra Pradesh : An Evaluation, *Kurukshetra*, Vol. XXXVI, No. 6, New Delhi, March 1988, p. 29.
54. Indira Hirway, Planning for Poverty Eradication in Rural Areas : An Observation, *Kurukshetra*, Vol. XXXVI, No. 7, New Delhi, April 1988.
55. Hara. G. Gopal, and C.H. Bala Ramulu, Poverty Alleviation Programme : IRDP in an Andhra Pradesh District, *Economic and Political Weekly*, Vol. XXIV, Nos. 35-36. Bombay, 1989, p. 2031.
56. A.M. Jose, IRDP and Employment Generation for Women : A Micro Level Study in Kerala, *Man and Development*, Vol. XI, No. 2, Chandigarh, June, 1989, p. 15.
57. Kulkarni, Rama Chandra Batta and N. Ganesh Kumar, Integrated Rural Development in Bijapur : An Evaluation of Dairy Scheme, *Social Change*, Vol. 19, No. 89, New Delhi, 1989, pp. 7-8.
58. Mohinder Paul, Composition and Distribution of Income Among Rural Households in Haryana, *Margin*, Vol. 21, New Delhi, Jan.-March, 1989, pp. 62-76.
59. Bimla Thakur, Socio-Economic Analysis of Weaker Section : A Rural-Urban Comparative Study in Himachal Pradesh, Daya Publishing House, Delhi, 1991, pp. 77-216.
60. R.K. Mahajan, Integrated Rural Development Programme : A Study of Problems and Prospects in Panjab, Concept Publishing Company, New Delhi., 1999, p. 172.

61. Kanta Ahuja, Agricultural Labour and Rural Employment in M.L. Dantwala (Editor), Indian Agricultural Development Since Independence, II Edition, Oxford and IBH Publishing Company, Pvt. Ltd. Bombay, 1991, pp. 367-98.
62. A.V. Kumar, Impact of IRDP on Income Employment : A Case Study, *Yojana*, Vol. 35, No. 24, New Delhi, 1992, pp. 17-18.
63. A.C.K. Nambiar, Rural Poverty : Problems and Prospects, Ashish Publishing House, Delhi, 1992, pp. 9-124.
64. Sukhdev Singh, IRDP and District Development—Role and Implementation of DRDA Schemes, Deep and Deep Publications, New Delhi, 1994, pp. 71-216.
65. K.R. Dasgupta, Rural Development Programme in India : Concepts and Strategies, *Kurukshetra*, Vol. XLV, No. 11, New Delhi, August 1997.
66. Sayed Ali, Income and Employment Generation Through IRDP : An Analysis, *Kurukshetra*, New Delhi, Vol. 46, No. 10, July 1998.
67. Sandeep Joshi, "IRDP and Poverty Alleviation, Rawat Publication, Jaipur, 1999, pp. 187-194.
68. S.N. Mundra, and K. Kusum, *Indian Journal of Extension Education*, Vol. XXVIII Nos. 1 and 2, 2002.
69. Pravesh, K. Chopra, Political Economy of Rural Poverty Alleviation Measures in India; A Micro Level Study of an Indian State, Wisdom House Academic Books Pvt. Ltd., Panchkula (Haryana), 2003, pp. 292-322.

3

Concepts and Methodology

A large number of studies have been conducted on the socio-economic conditions and characteristics of weaker sections at the national level but a very few attempts have been made in this direction in the State of Haryana. The present study is an attempt to find out that how far the various development and anti-poverty programmes have affected the socio-economic conditions of the weaker-sections in Haryana. This micro-level study will also highlight the problems and shortcomings in the planning, administration and implementation of various programmes for the weaker-sections, which would enlighten the administrators and planners about the reasons for ineffectiveness of various programmes in eradicating poverty.

3.1 OBJECTIVES OF THE PRESENT STUDY

The present study on the impact of anti-poverty programmes on the socio-economic conditions of weaker sections in the rural areas of Haryana, has been taken up for detailed empirical investigation with a view to achieve the following objectives :

(i) to study the income, employment and consumption pattern of the selected households;
(ii) to work out the nature and magnitude of unemployment with the help of 'time', 'income' and 'willingness' criterion among the selected households;
(iii) to analyse the extent of absolute poverty during the pre and post anti-poverty programmes implementation with the help of 'Nutrition Plus Approach';
(iv) to workout the nature and extent of saving and indebtedness among the sample households;
(v) to evaluate the impact of poverty alleviation programmes on the household assets, income, employment and consumption pattern of the selected households, and
(vi) to evolve a set of suggestions for improving the standard of living of the weaker-sections in Haryana.

3.2 SAMPLING PROCEDURE

For the present empirical investigation district Yamunanagar has been selected purposely mainly due to the reason that the area of this district like that of the State as a whole, partly falls in the Shivalik hills and partly in the plain areas due to which the farm and non-farm activities as well as the socio-economic conditions of the weaker sections in the district are more or less the same to that of the State as a whole. Further the inter-district wise percentage of poor varies between 23 to 43 per cent whereas this percentage in Yamunanagar came out 32 per cent. Therefore, both from the topography as well as the percentage of poor point of view this selected district can represent the economic activities as well as the living conditions (poverty) in the State of Haryana as a whole. There are six development blocks in Yamunanagar district viz., Bilaspur, Chhachharauli, Jagadhri, Radaur, Sadhaura and Mustafabad. With the help of multi-stage random sampling a sample of 300 households have been selected from Bilaspur and Sadhaura development blocks. Out of 300 total sample households 108 are landless, 102 marginal, 75 small and 15 fall in the category of medium size of holding group. The required information, in order to achieve the objectives of the present study, has been collected from the above selected 300 households with the help of a schedule by conducting personal interviews of the informants during the year 2003-04.

3.3 METHODS OF ANALYSIS

Both the primary and secondary data has been used in the present study. Secondary data has been collected from the related books, journals and reports. The required primary data has been collected with the help of a schedule by conducting the personal interview of the sample households. The first hand information pertaining to age and sex-wise family composition, source-wise income, employment, consumption, household assets, saving, investment and indebtedness, etc. has been collected from the sample households. The following analytical tools and techniques have been used to workout the results in the present study:

(a) Poverty Index

The value of minimum nutritional requirements of 2400 calories per consumer unit per day in the rural areas as suggested by the Planning Commission and Indian Council of Medical Research[1] at 2000-01 prices before and 2003-04 prices after the implementation of Poverty Alleviation Programmes has been adopted to determine the value of poverty line.

The value of minimum per consumer unit per day consumption basket (both out of home grown stock as well as out of purchases) has been calculated by multiplying the quantities of different food items by their respective actual retail prices prevailing in the sample area during the period of investigation. The total number of males, females and children of varying ages have been converted into 'standard consumption unit' or 'adult man value' by applying the scale of co-efficient suggested by the Indian Council of Medical Research.[2]

The minimum food requirements are necessary but not sufficient for the survival of mankind. Therefore in order to work out the value of 'Poverty line' allowances are also made to the minimum non food requirements by working out the ratio of total non-food expenditure to the total food expenditure.[3]

(b) Employment

The magnitude of unemployment is measured with the help of time, income and willingness criterion. According to time criterion a person may be termed unemployed or under employed if he is gainfully occupied during the year for number of hours or days less than some normal or optimal hours defined as full employment hours. In the present study 8 hours a day, 25 days in a month and 300 days in a year has been adopted as full employment norm to the workers in the rural areas of the study. Persons are inadequately employed not because they devote less time to work but because their earnings from the existing work are not sufficient. All those household workers have been considered unemployed and/or underemployed who earn less income than the value of poverty index, i.e. 317.19 at 2000-01 prices (Rs. 205.20 on food items and Rs. 111.99 on non-food items) before and Rs. 413.01 at 2003-04 prices (i.e. Rs. 263.10 on food and Rs. 149.91 on non-food items) after the implementation of poverty alleviation programmes. According to Raj Krishna, a person may be called unemployed or underemployed according to willingness criterion, "If he is willing to do more work than he is doing at present, he may either be actively searching for more work or be available for more work if it is offered on terms to which he is accustomed." It happened either due to large number of dependents, indebtedness or due to some other economic and social liabilities.[4] Due to differences in the work efficiency of male, female, children and old persons in the present study, the family human labour days have been converted into 'standard mandays' by attaching the proper 'co-efficient of efficiency' i.e. one woman day (WD) has been treated equal to 0.75 manday (MD) and one child day (CD) has been treated equal to one old person day (OD) and both have been considered equal to 0.50 MD.[5]

Thus

1CD = 1OD = 0.50 MD, and
1WD = 0.75 MD

(c) Impact of Anti-poverty Programmes

Impact of anti-poverty programmes on the household assets, income, employment, consumption expenditure as well as on the extent of poverty has been worked out with the help of before and after the implementation of poverty alleviations programmes.

(d) Saving

The magnitude of savings among weaker sections household has been worked out with the help of current account and balance sheet method.[6] According to current account method savings have been worked out by deducting households consumption expenditure from the income reported by the households. Households savings with the help of balance sheet method has been computed as the difference between the changes in physical and financial assets minus changes in liabilities.

$$S = (\Delta P_A + \Delta F_A) - (\Delta L + C_t + C_g)$$

Where ΔP_A = Change in physical assets. (acquisition minus liquidation)

ΔF_A = Change in Financial assets (Increase minus decrease)

ΔL = Change in Liabilities (Increase in borrowings minus increase in lending and repayments)

C_t = Net inflow of capital transfers (inflows minus outflows)

C_g = Net capital gains (gains minus losses)

3.4. DEFINITION OF CONCEPTS

The concepts used in this study are defined as follow:

(A) Weaker-Section

In the discussions regarding the weaker sections; terms such as 'poor', 'disadvantaged', 'economically weak' and 'less privileged' are used interchangeably. But the specific groups to which these descriptions are applied differ from study to study; the reference is to the socially backward groups pursuing economic activities which do not provide reasonable levels of living. The differences in the nomenclatures and their application to specific sections of the population notwithstanding the basic underlying characteristics of the groups described as poor or weak or disadvantaged or the miserably low levels of income and the palpably small productive resources at their command. A considerable body of evidences exists to show that the bulk of the low-income population is concentrated in households engaged in cultivation on small holdings and agricultural labour; these households typically combine other low income rural occupations such as non-agricultural labour, traditional rural arts and crafts, and low grade professions such as barbers, cobblers, tailors, potters, etc. Consideration of these two categories of households as the low-income sections would, therefore, be adequate. Secondly, small landholders and labourers belong overwhelmingly to low social strata composed of relatively low Hindu castes, scheduled castes and tribes and in some cases religious minorities.[7]

In the present study weaker-sections in the rural areas constitute the marginal farmers, small farmers, landless, agricultural labourers, artisans, backward classes, scheduled castes who are either without land or with un-economic size of holdings, having other productive assets which are small in number and/or quantity and less productive in nature, having low paid irregular jobs or no job; and due to high illiteracy and dependency ratio they are unable to earn income even to meet out their minimum requirements from the survival point of view.

(B) Consumption Expenditure

Consumption implies utilization of goods and services to satisfy the human desire and wants. The pattern of consumption varies from place to place and may be influenced by the socio-economic and psychological consideration. But for the purpose of general studies, consumption expenditure implies all expenditure incurred by a household exclusively towards its non-productive domestic consumption, thus, excluding all expenditure towards the enterprise activities of the household transfer payments in kind like loans advanced, charities, gifts and other payments in kind are not considered consumption expenditure. But any consumption out of transfer receipts in kind or free collection is considered for determining total consumption.[8]

(C) Consumption Unit

With the help of food composition tables, the calorie content of diets can be worked out and compared with the suggested requirements; or diet schedules yielding approximately the right amount of calorie can be constructed. In dealing with a group of mixed age and sex composition the "Consumption Units" or "adult man value" in the group is first calculated. The 'Standard Consumption Units' are calculated by assessing the needs of women and children in terms of those of the average man by applying various co-efficients to the different age and sex groups. The standard consumption units are calculated with the help of calorie consumption scale suggested by National Institute of Nutrition.

(D) Engel's Law of Consumption

The proposition of the Engel's law of consumption is—as income increase the expenditure on different items have changing proportions and the proportion diverted to urgent needs decreases, while on luxuries and semi-luxuries increases. Thus, according to Engel's law with given tastes or preferences, the proportion of income spent on food-items diminishes while on non-food items increases with an increase in income.[9]

(E) Demonstration Effect

The consumption standard of low income groups are greatly affected by the consumption standards of high income groups. This phenomenon is called demonstration effect.[10]

(F) Poverty

A family is considered to be living in poverty if its total earning is 'insufficient to obtain the minimum necessities for the maintenance of merely physical efficiency'. In developing countries, areas where incomes are low, absolute poverty is generally reflected mainly in inadequacy of food-intake and the consequent under-nourishment on a mass scale, though the definition of subsistence appropriate to such countries/areas might (in fact should) also include other essential minimum needs such as clothing, housing, fuel light, education and health, etc.[11]

(G) Poverty Index

All those households who even after their best efforts have not been able to earn an income even to meet out their minimum requirements of food and non-food items are termed poor.[12]

(H) Poverty *vs*. Inequality

Poverty as a concept is closely related to inequality. Given the average income level, a higher level of inequality (reflected by the usual measures) will tend to be associated with a high level of poverty. Furthermore, the so-called 'poverty line' may sometimes be drawn in the light of socially accepted 'minimal' standard of living, so that poverty measures, thus defined, may catch an aspect of 'relative' inequality as well.

Poverty line is necessarily defined in relation to social conventions and the contemporary living standards of a particular society.[13]

There are two broad concepts of poverty viz. relative and absolute poverty. Both absolute and relative poverty are closely aligned to inequality in income distribution. Relative Poverty arises entirely as a consequence of an unequal distribution of income irrespective of what the income level or the corresponding state of deprivation of the people at the bottom end of the income scale might be. Absolute Poverty, on the other hand, expresses a collective view on deprivation in its somewhat physical manifestation. Thus, wherever be the line any society chooses to draw to separate deprivation from relative comfort, those on the wrong side of line are defined as poor irrespective of how comfortable or affluent the others may be, the fact that the sense of deprivation among the poor may also depend on how wide is the gap between their income and the income of those who are not poor, is not a consideration relevant to the notion of absolute poverty, though it very much is to be the notion of relative poverty. Any measure of relative poverty is, therefore, inextricably embedded in measures of inequality, whereas, a measure of absolute poverty primarily depends on an exogenously determined standard of poverty line, which represents a socially acceptable minimum level of living.[14]

Poverty has been identical not merely with inequality but also with unemployment. Dandekar and Rath (1971) have defined poverty "an adequate level of employment in terms of its capacity to provide minimum living to the population.[15] In his four-fold classification of unemployment Raj Krishna (1973) identified this approach to unemployment as the income criterion. According to Raj Krishna, a person may be termed unemployed and/or under-employed if:

(i) he is gainfully occupied during the year for a number of hours (or days) less than some normal or optimal hours (or days) defined as full employment hours (or days),

(ii) he earns an income per month/year less than some desirable minimum, and

(iii) he is willing to do more work than he is doing at present, he may either be actively searching for more work or be available for more work, if it is offered on terms to which he is accustomed.[16]

These are termed as time, income and willingness criteria by Raj Krishna and the extent of unemployment is measured in terms of 'idle', 'poor' and 'willing' respectively.

(I) Employment

Workers engaged in gainful activities for a normal period of time on wage or salary basis both in terms of cash and/or kind may be termed as employed. The gainful employment is a situation when all the workers in an economy are in a position to get employment at the existing wage rate/salary according to their skill, ability and qualifications for the optimum number of days in a year.[17]

(J) Unemployment and Underemployment

Unemployment is a situation when persons even after their best possible efforts are not in a position to get work/job at the existing wage rate or even at the low wage rates. Whereas underemployment is a situation when persons are engaged in work/job at a wage rate which is lower according to their qualifications and abilities. All those persons are considered to be underemployed if they are forced to take a job that is not adequately remunerative, or not commensurate with their skill ability and training.[18]

(K) Voluntary Unemployment

Persons are said to be voluntarily unemployed who are searching for specific types of job because of their special educational qualifications or training but they refuse to accept job, which they consider to be below their status.

(L) Productive vs. Necessary Activities

All those household activities (both agricultural and non-agricultural activities) which provide gainful employment to the family human labour and add directly to the household income have been treated productive activities for the purpose of present analysis.[19] All those household activities such as family and social affairs, although involve the human labour days utilization yet these activities neither provide gainful employment to the family human labour nor do they add directly to the household income but the utilization of human labour days in these activities, is necessary from the social obligations as well as survival point of view.[20]

(M) Agricultural Labourer

A person who works on another person's land for wages in money or kind or share basis will be regarded as an agricultural labourer. She or he has no risk in the cultivation, but merely works on another persons' land for wages. An agricultural labourer has no right of lease or contract on land on which she/he works.

(N) Household Industry

Household industry is defined as an industry conducted by one or more members of the household at home or within the village in the rural areas and only within the precincts of the house where the household lives in urban areas. The larger proportion of workers in the household industry should consist of members of the household. The industry should not be run on the scale of a registered factory which would qualify or has to be registered under the Indian Factory Act.[21]

(O) Household Income and Assets

Household income includes current income of all members of the household from all sources. It consists of both farm and non-farm income.[22] All the physical items that the household owns and which has money value is classified as an asset. The assets of the households are those items from which he hopes to get an income or which he keeps to protect his interest.[23] In the present study the household assets have been divided into two categories viz. productive and unproductive assets (i.e. household durables). All the households productive assets (such as land, livestock, poultry, agricultural implements, household industries, commercial vehicles and rented-out buildings, etc.) have been termed as productive assets, which provide gainful employment to the family human labour and directly add to the household income. The household durables constitute those assets which have no direct effect on household income and/or employment, but they indirectly help to raise the efficiency, skill as well as the levels of living of the households which include good housing conditions, electrical appliances, furnishing articles, beddings, etc.

(P) Saving and Investment

The saving of an economic unit is defined as earned surplus or as change in earned net worth during a given period. Saving thus defined can be measured either from the current account or from the balance sheet. In the case of the current account it is measured as the difference between current income of the economic unit and its current expenditure including taxes and capital consumption allowances. This measure of saving corresponds to an estimate of earned surplus. Saving by definition, is also equivalent to the net change in assets and liabilities during a period of time exclusive of all capital gains or losses. Whereas, investment in the economic sense, is defined as net addition to capital stock during a given period. In other words, it includes long-term fixed deposits as well as the acquisition of all types of newly produced capital goods such as buildings, land, livestock, machinery and other equipments and change in the total value of household inventories.

(Q) Indebtedness

Indebtedness includes hereditary debt, short and long-term loans borrowed by the family for various purposes like socio-cultural activities, improvement on land, purchase of land and livestock, construction of house, purchase of other moveable and immoveable assets, crop loan and consumption expenditure, etc. The indebtedness in this study does not include the routine loan or credit outstanding and settled within a month or a shorter period by the family.[24]

(R) Land Holding Groups

In rural areas size of land holdings is one of the important determinants which affect the income, consumption, saving and standard of living of households. Marginal farmers are those having less than 2.5 acres of land (i.e. 0-1 hectare) small farmers with 2.51 to 5.00 acres (i.e. 1-2 hectare) and medium farmers are those having land between 5.1 and 8.00 acres. (i.e. 2-3 hectare).[25]

(S) Net Area Sown

It is the net area sown under crops, the area sown more than once during the year being counted only once.[26]

3.5 LIMITATIONS OF THE PRESENT STUDY

1. This study has been conducted during a particular period of time, hence no comparisons about the conditions and characteristics of weaker-sections can be made with a view to pass on the judgment about the improvement and/or deterioration in their levels of living over a period of time.
2. The present empirical investigation is related to one district of Haryana. Hence due to variations in cropping pattern, differences in non-farm employment opportunities as well as the distribution of assets, the result of this study can not be applied with hundred per cent precision to the State as a whole.

Notes and References

1. Government of India, Draft Fifth Five Year Plan, 1978-83, Vol. II, Planning Commission, New Delhi, 1978, p. 36.
2. C. Gopalan, B.V. Ramashastri and S.C. Bala Subramanian, The Nutritive Value of Indian Foods, The Indian Council of Medical Research, Hyderabad, 1980, p. 10.
3. Government of India, Report of Committee of Experts on Unemployment Estimates, Planning Commission, New Delhi, 1970.
4. Raj Krishna, Unemployment in India (Presidential Address), *Indian Journal of Agricultural Economics*, Vol. 28, No. 5, Bombay, 1973.
5. B.N. Ghosh, Disguised Unemployment in Underdeveloped Countries: With Special Reference to India, Heritage Publishers, New Delhi, 1977, p. 90. Also see Dalip, S. Thakur, Poverty Inequality and Unemployment in Rural India: Some Conçeptual and Methodological Issues in Measurement, B.R. Publishing Corporation, New Delhi, 1985, p. 175.
6. J.P. Bhatti, A Study of Incomes, Savings and Investment Pattern in Agriculturally Progressive Areas of Himachal Pradesh, Kangra District, Agro-Economic Research Centre, Shimla, (Mimeo), 1976, pp. 93-95.
7. Mahendra Desai: Problems of Low Income Sections in Rural Areas, Rural Development for Weaker Sections, Seminar Series-XII, *Indian Society of Agricultural Economics*, Bombay, 1974.
8. This definition has been adopted by N.S.S. organization in various N.S.S. rounds. Also see Bimla Thakur, Socio-Economic Analysis of the Weaker Sections: Rural-Urban Comparative Study in H.P., Daya Publishing House, Delhi, 1991, p. 79.
9. G.B. Bannock, R.F. Bater and R. Rees, The Penguin Dictionary of Economics, Penguin Books Limited, Harmandsworth, Middlesex, England, 1986, p. 145.
10. James, S. Dusenberry, Income, Saving and the Theory of Consumer behaviour, Oxford University Press, New York, 1967, pp. 22-25.
11. A.B. Atkinson, The Economics of Inequality, Oxford University Press, New York, 1975, p. 186.
12. Dalip, S. Thakur, Poverty, Inequality and Unemployment in India; Some Conceptual and Methodological Issues in Measurement, B.R. Publishing Corporation, New Delhi, 1985.
13. Amartya Sen, Poverty Inequality and Unemployment: Some Conceptual Issues in Measurement, in Poverty and Income Distribution, edited, T.N. Srinivasan and P.K. Bardhan, Statistical Publishing Society, Calcutta, 1974, pp. 67-68. Also see A.B. Atkinson, The Economics of Inequality, Oxford University Press, New York, 1975, p. 186.
14. I.Z. Bhatty, Inequality and Poverty in Rural India, in Poverty and Income Distribution in India, (ed.) T.N. Srinivasan and P.K. Bardhan, Statistical Publishing Society, Calcutta, 1974, p. 292.
15. Dandekar, V.M. and Rath, Nilakantha, Poverty in India, Indian School of Political Economy, Bombay, 1971, p. 1.
16. Krishna, Raj, Unemployment in India, *Indian Journal of Agricultural Economics*, Vol. 28, No. 1, 1973, Bombay, pp. 1-6.

17. Dalip Singh Thakur, Poverty, Inequality and Unemployment in India : Some Conceptual and Methodological Issues in Measurement, B.R. Publishing Corporation, New Delhi, 1985, pp. 224-41.
18. Raj Krishna, Unemployment in India, *Indian Journal of Agricultural Economics*, Vol. XXVII, No. 1, Bombay, Jan.-March, 1973, pp. 1-2.
19. Dalip S. Thakur, Poverty Inequality and Unemployment in Rural India : Some Conceptual and Methodological Issues in Measurement, B.R. Publishing Corporation, New Delhi, 1985, pp. 224-41.
20. *Ibid*.
21. Government of Haryana, Census of India 2001, Series 7, Paper-3, Provisional Population Totals (Directorate of Census Operations), Chandigarh, 2001, p. 18.
22. Edward Shapiro, Macro Economic Analysis, Galgotia Publication, New Delhi, 1984, p. 32.
23. Dalip, S. Thakur, Poverty, Inequality and Unemployment in Rural India: Some Conceptual and Methodological Issues in Measurement, B.R. Publishing Corporation, New Delhi, 1985.
24. Bimla Thakur, Socio-Economic Analysis of the Weaker Sections: Rural-Urban Comparative Study in H.P., Daya Publishing House, Delhi, 1991, p. 83.
25. Parvesh, K. Chopra, Political Economy of Rural Poverty Alleviation Measures in India, Wisdom House Academic Books Private Ltd., Panchkula, p. 136.
26. Government of Haryana (Economic and Statistical Orgaisation), Statistical Abstract of Haryana, Chandigarh, 2005, p. 210.

4

Demographic and Socio-economic Profile of the Sample Households

4.1 DEMOGRAPHIC PROFILE OF THE SAMPLE HOUSEHOLDS

Population plays an important role in affecting the income and consumption levels and thereby the living standard of the people. In the present empirical study there are 300 sample households consisting of 1756 males, females and children. Out of the total 300 sample households, 108 households fall in the category of landless, 102 households in the category of marginal farmers having land less than one hectare, 75 households fall in the category of small farmers having land 1-2 hectares, 15 households fall in the category of medium farmers having land 2-3 hectares. The demographic profile of the sample households has been presented in Table 4.1. The age factor has a considerable social significance because it exerts a big influence upon social phenomenon in many ways. Age has an important bearing on the limit, above and below which a person cannot be expected to work for economic benefits. Therefore, the age composition of a society sets limits to the availability of working

TABLE 4.1
Age and Sex-wise Family Composition among Sample Households

Sl. No.	*Age Group*	*Landless*	*Marginal Holdings*	*Small Holdings*	*Medium Holdings*	*All Holdings*
1	0-9 years					
	Male	82	71	43	8	204
	Female	64	55	33	6	158
	Total	146	126	76	14	362
2	9-15 years					
	Male	40	38	24	10	112
	Female	28	22	17	8	75
	Total	68	60	41	18	187
3	15-59 years					
	Male	182	177	160	37	556
	Female	178	170	145	31	524
	Total	360	347	305	68	1080
4	59-65 years					
	Male	9	14	17	3	43
	Female	7	8	14	3	32
	Total	16	22	31	6	75
5	65 years and above					
	Male	5	10	12	1	28
	Female	6	7	9	2	24
	Total	11	17	21	3	52
6	Total Population					
	Male	318	310	256	59	943
	Female	283	262	218	50	813
	Total	601	572	474	109	1756
7	Sex Ratio per thousand	890	845	852	847	862
8	Total Standard Mandays	436	417	353.25	80.75	1287
9	Per household average standard mandays	4.03	4.08	4.71	5.38	4.55

force and hence it also sets a limit to the economic gains which can be reaped by particular social groups.

The distribution of the sample population according to different age groups has been presented in Table 4.1 where the population has been divided into five groups, i.e. below 9 years, 9-15 years, 15 to 59 years, 59 to 65 years and above 65 years. This has been done with a view of having better insight of the age composition in detail as well as in order to convert the working/sample population of different sex and varying ages into standard mandays by attaching co-efficient of efficiency. The first group includes infants who are not supposed to do any manual work. The next age group includes the family members between 9-15 years who are supposed to study, but it has been observed that persons in this age group too help substantially in fields as well as in other light household activities such as rearing of children, bringing water and fuel, looking after cattle, etc. The persons falling in the age group of 15 to 59 years are actively available for gainful economic activities and therefore, this group forms the main working force. The family members falling in the age group of 59 to 65 years also help in fields and light household activities, whereas, the family members above 65 yeas of age have been termed as dependents. Table 4.1 reveals that out of total population of 1756 persons, 943 are males and 813 are females. This table further shows that the age-wise composition of the total sample population consists of 362 infants below 9 years, 187 fall in the age group of 9 to 15 years, 1080 persons fall in the age group of 15-59 years (out of which 556 are males and 524 are females), 75 persons fall in the age group of 59-65 years and 52 persons are above 65 years of age. Out of total sample population of 1756 persons, 601 fall among the landless households, 572 fall on the marginal size of holdings, 474 on the small size of holdings and the remaining 109 persons fall on the medium size of holding groups.

On an average there are 862 females per one thousand males in the present sample area of district Yamunanagar. The females ratio per thousand males has been worked out 890, 845, 852 and 847 among the landless, marginal, small and medium size of holdings respectively. Due to the differences in the efficiency of male, female, children and old persons, standard mandays have been worked out in the present study by attaching the 'proper co-efficient of efficiency'. The standard mandays have been worked out 436.0, 417.0, 353.25 and 80.75 among the landless, marginal, small and medium size of holdings respectively. Among all the households together the standard mandays came out 1287.0 as is evident from Table 4.1

Total Number of Standard Consumer Units among the Sample Households

The size and composition of family is the main determinant of the household consumption expenditure. A large number of studies have been conducted on rural poverty, but most of these studies have either underestimated or overestimated the magnitude of rural poverty by taking into account the total number of family members as such, without making allowances to their age and sex. Besides many other factors, the difference in age and sex largely affect the required nutrition norms in order to keep a person in a normal health and efficient working position. Therefore, in the present study, in order to avoid the underestimation and/or overestimation of poverty the family members of varying age and sex among the different holding groups have been converted into 'standard consumer units' by applying the scale of coefficient suggested by the Nutrition Experts. The total number of 'standard consumer units' of the sample households have been presented in Table 4.2. The total number of males, females and children of varying ages have been converted into 'standard consumer units' or 'adult man value' by applying the scale of coefficient suggested by the Indian Council of Medical Research. This table clearly reveals that the total number of 'standard consumer units' of the total 300 sample households have been worked out 1959. Out of the total consumer units, i.e. 1959 among all the sample households, the landless, marginal, small and medium sized holdings accounted for 655.3, 633.9, 548.6 and 121.2 consumer units respectively.

4.2 SOCIO-ECONOMIC PROFILE OF THE SAMPLE HOUSEHOLDS

The average size of holding, average family size, percentage of dependents, per household per day available

TABLE 4.2

Number of Standard Consumer Units among the Sample Households

Sl. No.	Age Group	Scale	Landless		Marginal Farmers		Small Farmers		Medium Farmers		All Farmers	
			No. of persons	Standards consumer Units	No. of persons	Standards consumer Units	No. of persons	Standards consumer Units	No. of persons	Standards consumer Units	No. of persons	Standards consumer Units
	(1)	(2)	(3)	(4)	(5)	(6)	(7)	(8)	(9)	(10)	(11)	(12)
1.	0-3 years	0.4	46	18.4	41	16.4	31	12.4	6	2.4	124	49.6
2.	3-5 years	0.5	40	20	35	17.5	20	10	3	1.5	98	49
3.	5-7 years	0.6	38	22.8	33	19.8	16	9.6	3	1.8	90	54
4.	7-9 years	0.7	22	15.4	17	11.9	9	6.3	2	1.4	50	35
5.	9-12 years	0.8	44	35.2	38	30.4	26	20.8	13	10.4	121	96.8
6.	12-21 years	1	61	61	58	58	44	44	22	22	185	185
7.	21-59 years											
	Male	1.6	166	265.6	161	257.6	147	235.2	28	44.8	502	803
	Female	1.2	157	188.4	150	180	129	154.8	23	27.6	459	550.8
8.	Above 59 years											
	Male	1.2	14	16.8	24	28.8	29	34.8	4	4.8	71	85.2
	Female	1.9	13	11.7	15	13.5	23	20.7	5	4.5	56	50.4
9.	Total number of persons/ Consumer Units		601	665.3	572	633.9	474	548.6	109	121.2	1756	1959

standard mandays, per household per day standard consumer units and the literacy percentage among all the households has been presented in Table 4.3 which clearly indicates that average size of holding comes out 0.64, 1.40, 2.49 hectares on the marginal, small and medium size of holding groups. Among all the holdings together the average size of holding comes out 1.51 hectares. The average size of family has been worked out 5.56, 5.60, 6.32 and 7.26 among the landless, marginal, small and medium size of holdings respectively. The average size of family among all the sample households together came out 6.18. The percentage of family work force has been worked out 59.91, 60.67, 64.35 and 62.39 per cent among landless, marginal, small and medium size of holdings respectively. Among all the households together the percentage of family work force came out 61.83 per cent. The percentage of dependents among the households has been worked out 40.09, 39.33, 35.65 and 37.61 per cent among landless, marginal, small and medium farmers respectively. Among all the households together this percentage came out 38.17 per cent.

Literacy is an important indicator of the levels of living. In the sample as a whole 66.28 per cent are literate, out of which 70.20 per cent are males and 61.74 per cent are females. The literacy percentage is the highest on the medium size of holdings (i.e. 76.14%) and it decreases to 71.30, 66.78 and 60.06 per cent on small, marginal and landless households respectively. It happened mainly due to the reason that the households falling comparatively on the larger size of holdings have sound and regular sources of income, hence they can afford to make investment on the education of their wards. Contrary to it households falling on the smaller holdings and among the landless, due to their uneconomic size of holdings and meager and irregular sources of household income can not afford to bear the expenses of the education of their children i.e. mainly for the higher education. Further whatever education facilities the Government have provided in the sample area are availed by the poor households mainly upto the primary or middle level by getting assistance from the Government in the form of fee concession, free books and dresses, etc. The literacy percentage among women increases with an increase in the size of holdings which has been worked out 55.47, 62.59, 66.51 and

TABLE 4.3

Average Size of Holding, Average Family Size, Percentage of Family Work Force, Percentage of Dependents. Number of Standards Mondays, Number of Consumer Units and Literacy Percentage among Sample Households

Sl. No.	Particulars	Landless	Marginal Holdings	Small Holdings	Medium Holdings	All Holdings
	(1)	(2)	(3)	(4)	(5)	(6)
1.	Total No. of Households	108	102	75	15	300
2.	Total No. of Family Members	601	572	474	109	1756
3.	Average Size of Holding (in hectares)	—	0.64	1.4	2.49	1.51
4.	Average size of family	5.56	5.6	6.32	7.26	6.18
5.	Percentage of Family Work Force	360	347	305	68	1080
		(59.91)	(60.67)	(64.35)	(62.39)	(61.83)
6.	Percentage of Dependents	241	225	169	41	676
		(40.09)	(39.33)	(35.65)	(37.61)	(38.17)
7.	No. of Consumer Units	655.3	633.9	548.6	121.2	1959
8.	No. of Per Household Consumer Units	6.06	6.21	7.31	8.08	6.91
9.	Total Standard Mandays	436	417	353.25	80.75	1287
10.	Per Household per day Standard Mandays	4.03	4.08	4.71	5.38	4.55
11.	Literacy Percentage					
	Male	204	218	193	47	662
		(64.15)	(70.32)	(75.39)	(79.66)	(70.20)
	Female	157	164	145	36	502
		(55.47)	(62.59)	(66.51)	(72.00	(61.74)
	Total	361	382	338	83	1164
		(60.06)	(66.78)	(71.30)	(76.14)	(66.28)

Note : Figures in parenthesis indicate percentage.

72.00 per cent among landless, marginal, small and medium size of holdings respectively. The percentage of literacy among males also shows an increasing tendency with an increase in the size of holdings which came out 64.15, 70.32, 75.39 and 79.66 per cent among the landless, marginal, small and medium size of holdings respectively.

5

Pattern of Household Assets and Income of the Sample Households

The quantity and quality of household productive assets determine the level of gainful employment, income and thereby the levels of living of the family. This chapter deals with the analysis of land ownership, land use pattern and the source wise value of household assets such as land, livestock, buildings, agricultural implements, machinery and other household durables.

5.1 DISTRIBUTION PATTERN OF HOUSEHOLD ASSETS

This section deals with the land use pattern as well as the distribution pattern of household assets among the sample households.

5.1. A. Land Use Pattern

It has been proved by many studies that in the rural areas the variations in the levels of living is high due to uneven distribution of productive resources, mainly land. The distribution of land is such that only a small proportion of the total land is owned by the majority of the marginal and small farmers. Consequently, these holdings swell the rank of non-viable units to produce sufficient output in order to support the cultivator and his family with reasonable comforts and also to provide gainful employment to the family human labour. Further, some of the households do not own any land at all and are entirely dependent on the agricultural as well as non-agricultural wage employment of their family human labour. The land use pattern of the sample households has been presented in Table 5.1 which clearly indicates that the per household average area operated in the case of marginal, small and medium farmers has been worked out 0.69, 1.52, 2.80 hectares respectively, whereas among all the holdings together the average operated area came out 1.67 hectares. In the total cultivated area the percentage of leased-in land increased from 7.24 per cent on the marginal size of holdings to 9.86 per cent on small size of holdings and to 14.28 per cent on medium size of holdings. Among all the holdings together per household total leased—in area come out 11.97 per cent. The percentage of leased-out land on marginal size of holdings is zero. This is attributed to the fact that due to very small size of holdings the marginal farmers can not afford to lease out their land and cultivate their land on their own. The percentage of leased out land increases as the size of holding increases. It increased from 1.97 per cent on the small size of holdings to 3.21 per cent on the medium size of holdings.

The percentage of uncultivated area is higher on the marginal size of holdings, i.e. 17.39 per cent which decreases to 15.79 per cent and further to 13.57 per cent on small and medium size of holdings respectively. The high percentage of uncultivated area on marginal size of holdings is mainly due to the reason that either the land is barren and/or uncultivable as there is no source of irrigation or the land is a part of the river. The low percentage of uncultivated land on the small size of holdings is mainly due to the lack of alternative regular sources of household income and further the small and medium farmers with large number of dependents can not afford to keep their own cultivable land uncultivated.

5.1.B. Source-wise Value of Land

Land is the main productive asset in the rural areas of

TABLE 5.1

Land Use Pattern Among the Selected Households

(Area in Hectares)

Sl. No.	Holding Group	Total Area Owned			Area Leased-Out	Area Leased-In	Total Area Operated	Total Area Sown	Total Uncultivated Area
		Cultivated	Uncultivated	Total					
	(1)	(2)	(3)	(4)	(5)	(6)	(7)	(8)	(9)
1.	Landless	—	—	—	—	—	—	—	—
2	Marginal Holdings	0.52 (75.36)	0.12 (17.39)	0.64 (92.75)	0 0.00	0.05 (7.24)	0.69 (100.00)	0.57 (82.60)	0.12 (17.39)
3	Small Holding	1.16 (76.31)	0.24 (15.79)	1.4 (92.10)	0.03 (1.97)	0.15 (9.86)	1.52 (100.00)	1.28 (84.21)	0.24 (15.79)
4	Medium Holdings	2.11 (75.35)	0.38 (13.57)	2.49 (88.92)	0.09 (3.21)	0.4 (14.28)	2.8 (100.00)	2.42 (86.42)	0.38 (13.57)
5	All Holdings	1.26 (75.45)	0.25 (14.97)	1.51 (90.42)	0.04 (2.39)	0.2 (11.97)	1.67 (100.00)	1.42 (85.03)	0.25 (14.97)

Note : Figure in the parenthesis indicate the percentage to total operated area.

Haryana which provides direct employment to the family labour force and contributes a major share in the total household income. The source-wise value of land among different holding groups has been presented in Table 5.2. On the marginal size of holdings the value of inherited land is lowest (i.e. 97.82 per cent) which increased to 98.02 per cent and 98.90 per cent on small and medium size of holdings respectively. Among all the households together this percentage comes to 98.52 per cent. The value of land purchased out of own savings constitutes 2.18 per cent on marginal size of holdings as against 1.98 per cent and 1.00 per cent on small and medium size of holdings respectively. Among all the households together this percentage come out 1.48 per cent. These results clearly indicate that the value of land purchased out of own savings is higher on marginal size of holdings.

TABLE 5.2
Source-wise Value of Household Assets in the Rural Area : Land

(*Value in Rs.*)

Source	*landless*	*Marginal Holdings*	*Small Holdings*	*Medium Holdings*	*All Holdings*
Inherited	—	95873.03 (97.82)	330752.13 (98.02)	611053.33 (98.90)	345892.83 (98.52)
Out of Own Savings	—	2136.76 (2.18)	6681.33 (1.98)	6780 (1.10)	5199.36 (1.48)
Total	—	98009.79 (100.00)	337,433.46 (100.00)	617833.33 (100.00)	351092.19 (100.00)

Note : Figure in the parenthesis denote percentage to column total.

It indicates that weakest households prefer to make investment on the purchase of land as it provides direct employment to their family labour force on one hand and adds directly and immediately to the household income in near future without any much time lag on the other, whereas, the better-off households can afford to make long-run investments such as in education which increases their household income at some future date. The results of source-wise value of land in case of all households indicates that inheritance remained the major source of land followed by land purchased out of own savings.

5.1.C. Source-wise Value of Livestock

In the rural areas, agriculture and allied pursuits are the mainstay of the people. The animal husbandry is one of the important sub-sectors of agricultural economy and plays a significant role in the rural economy by providing gainful employment particularly to the small, marginal farmers, women and agricultural landless labourers. This sector also provides milk, eggs, meat, hides and skin, dung, bones etc. Haryana is the milk pail of India and is famous for its breed of 'Hariana Cows' and 'Murrah' buffaloes. The cattle in the study area mainly depend on the crop residues abundantly available in the area. Area being a sugarcane belt, sugarcane residue called 'gola' in local dialect is freely available as fodder for the cattle. Buffaloes and cows are of healthy nature and quite productive. The source-wise value of livestock has been presented in Table 5.3 which indicates that the value of livestock purchased out of own savings among landless, marginal, small and medium size of holdings is highest, followed by value of livestock received under the Government schemes and livestock purchased out of loans. But among landless and marginal

TABLE 5.3

Source-wise Per Household Average Value of Household Assets: Livestock

(*Value in Rs.*)

Source	*landless*	*Marginal Holdings*	*Small Holdings*	*Medium Holdings*	*All Holdings*
Own Saving	2549.63 (53.75)	5374.16 (58.89)	7227.66 (70.25)	9371.66 (75.92)	6130.77 (67.18)
Out of Loan	282.4 (5.95)	975.49 (10.69)	1284.66 (12.49)	1783.33 (14.44)	1081.38 (11.85)
Government Scheme	1911.47 (40.30)	2776.08 (30.42)	1775.33 (17.26)	1190 (9.64)	1913.22 (20.97)
Total	4743.5 (100.00)	9125.73 (100.00)	10287.65 (100.00)	12344.99 (100.00)	9125.37 (100.00)

Note : Figures in the parenthesis denote percentage to column total.

farmers the value of livestock received under Government schemes is quite high (i.e. 40.30 per cent for landless and 30.42 per cent among marginal farmers) as compared to the value of livestock received under Government schemes on small size of holdings and on medium size of holdings (i.e. 17.26 per cent among small and 9.64 per cent among medium farmers).

As a result of it, among landless households and on marginal size of holdings the value of livestock purchased out of own savings and out of loans is less, i.e. 53.75 per cent and 5.95 per cent among landless and 58.89 per cent and 10.69 per cent among marginal farmers as compared to the value of livestock purchased by the small and medium farmers out of own savings and out of loans which constitute 70.25 per cent and 12.49 per cent on small size of holdings and 75.92 per cent and 14.44 per cent on medium size of holdings. The value of livestock among all the households together indicates that the percentage value of livestock purchased out of own savings is the highest (i.e. 67.18%) followed by the value of livestock received under the Government schemes (i.e. 20.97 per cent) and the livestock purchased out of loans (i.e. 11.85 per cent).

5.1.D. Source-wise Value of Agriculture Implements

The agricultural implements (i.e. both human as well as bullock drawn implements) used by the marginal farmers are of traditional types which are either made locally or purchased from the nearby market, whereas the small and medium farmers use modern type of agricultural implements. Some of the small and medium farmers also get their lands ploughed by hiring tractors. Use of tractor on hire basis for ploughing is common among all the holding groups particularly among small and medium farmers. The percentage of human drawn implements shows a decreasing tendency with an increase in the size of holding, while bullock drawn implements shows an increasing tendency with an increase in the size of holding. It happened mainly due to the reason that larger size of holding groups are engaged more in agricultural activities while smaller size of holdings are engaged less in agricultural activities and more in wage work.

The source-wise value of agricultural implements among the different holdings have been presented in Table 5.4 which

TABLE 5.4

Source-wise Per Household Average Value of Household Assets : Agricultural Implements, Machinery and Transport Equipments

(*Value in Rs.*)

Sl. No.	*Items*	*landless*	*Marginal Holdings*	*Small Holdings*	*Medium Holdings*	*All Holdings*
1.	**Agricultural Implements out of own savings**					
	(a) Human Drawn	84.51 (100.00)	164.01 (61.83)	238.06 (59.18)	285.66 (48.61)	193.06 (57.64)
	(b) Bullock Drawn	—	101.27 (38.17)	164.2 (40.82)	302 (51.39)	141.8 (42.36)
	Total	84.51 (100.00)	265.28 (100.00)	402.26 (100.00)	587.66 (100.00)	334.92 (100.00)
2.	**Machineries***					
	1. Own Savings	29.86 (5.23)	76.12 (7.28)	381.38 (16.92)	538.62 (19.57)	256.49 (15.49)
	2. Under Government Scheme	241.17 (42.24)	226.02 (21.61)	209.56 (9.30)	175.45 (6.37)	213.05 (12.87)
	3. Gifted	299.93 (52.53)	743.72 (71.11)	1663.04 (73.78)	2038.69 (74.06)	1186.34 (71.64)
	4. Total (1 to 3)	570.96 (100.00)	1045.84 (100.00)	2253.98 (100.00)	2752.76 (100.00)	1655.88 (100.00)
3.	**Transport Equipments****	116 (100.00)	503.18 (100.00)	13546.01 (100.00)	33580.8 (100.00)	119336.49 (100.00)

Note : Figures in parenthesis denote percentage to column total.

* Machineries include sewing machine, weaving machine, ban making machine, fodder cutting machine, etc.

** Transport equipment includes motor cycle/scooter, bicycle, jeep, car, khachar rehra, bughi-jhota, etc.

indicates that the value of human drawn agricultural Implements out of own savings, among landless-households and on marginal size of holdings is higher (i.e. 100 per cent among landless and 61.83 per cent among marginal farmers) as compared to the value of the human drawn agricultural implements on small and medium size of holdings (i.e. 59.18 per cent and 48.61 per cent) whereas contrary to it, the value of bullock drawn agricultural implements out of own savings among landless households is nil and on marginal size of holdings is low (i.e. 38.17 per cent) as compared to the value of bullock drawn agricultural implements on small and medium size of holdings (i.e. 40.82 per cent on small and 51.39 per cent on medium size of holdings) among all the households together the value of human and bullock drawn agricultural implements out of own savings have been worked out 57.64 per cent and 42.36 per cent respectively.

The source-wise pattern of machineries among the sample households has been presented in the Table 5.4. It is clear from this table that the percentage value of machineries (i.e. sewing, weaving and ban making machines, etc.) out of own savings shows an increasing tendency with an increase in the size of holdings. The percentage value of these machines has been worked out 5.23, 7.28, 16.92 and 19.57 among the landless, marginal, small and medium size of holdings respectively. Among all the households together this percentage came out 15.49 per cent, whereas, the percentage value of machineries received under Government programmes is comparatively higher among the landless households (i.e. 42.24%) and it shows a decreasing tendency with an increase in the size of holdings i.e. to 21.61, 9.30 and 6.37 per cent on the marginal, small and medium size of holdings respectively. It happened mainly due to the reason that the households falling on the smaller size of holdings and the landless households were entitled under various Anti-Poverty Programmes to receive these machines in order to supplement their meagre household income, whereas, the households falling on the larger holdings groups have the maximum percentage share of machineries by way of dowry. The percentage value of machineries received by way of dowry has been worked out 52.23, 71.11, 73.78 and 74.06 per cent among landless, marginal, small and medium size of holding respectively. Whereas among all the households together this percentage value came out 71.64 per cent. This clearly indicates that dowry system is prevailing among the rural people of district Yamunanagar. The landless and marginal households are having bicycles. Some of them are also having Khachar Rehras and Bughi- Jhotas which these households have received under Poverty Alleviation Programmes. Khachar Rehras and Bughi Jhotas are mainly used for transportation of their products like Ban, Dari, Khes, Shoes, Baskets, etc. to the weekly local markets being held in different small towns in the district. These weekly markets are termed as 'Peeth' in the local dialect. The small and medium size of holding groups possess all sorts of luxury items and transport means including motor cycles, scooters etc. To transport their agriculture produce small and medium farmers make use of Jhota Bughi, tractor trolleys, etc.

5.1.E. Source-wise Value of Buildings

The value of buildings among the landless, marginal, small and medium holding groups which includes the space used for residential purposes, household industries, cowsheds, shops, stores etc. have been presented in Table 5.5. Most of the landless and marginal households live in Kuccha houses. They keep their cattle in mud cattle-sheds and the cattle sheds made of straw. A fraction of the landless households have also been provided

TABLE 5.5
Source-wise Per Household Average Value of Household Assets : Buildings

(Value in Rs.)

Source	*landless*	*Marginal Holdings*	*Small Holdings*	*Medium Holdings*	*All Holdings*
Inherited	33314.81 (67.36)	66441.17 (76.02)	92595 (78.12)	125284 (82.10)	79408.74 (78.43)
Out of Own Saving	1256.48 (2.54)	4168.62 (4.77)	15446 (13.03)	22126.99 (14.50)	10749.52 (10.62)
Government Scheme	14887.95 (30.10)	13785.29 (15.77)	10488.33 (8.85)	5188 (3.40)	11087.39 (10.95)
Total Value	49459.24 (100.00)	87395.08 (100.00)	118529.33 (100.00)	152599.99 (100.00)	101245.65 (100.00)

Note : Figure in the parenthesis denote percentage to column total.

with small houses under Indira Awas Yojana. Majority of the small and medium farmers have pucca houses to live in. They have proper cattle sheds also. Table 5.5 clearly indicates that among the landless and marginal size of holding groups the value of inherited buildings is the highest i.e. 67.36 per cent and 76.02 per cent respectively followed by the value of buildings constructed under Government Scheme i.e. 30.10 per cent and 15.77 per cent but the value of buildings constructed out of own savings is lower i.e. 2.54 per cent and 4.77 per cent among the landless and marginal farmers respectively. On the small and medium size of holdings groups the value of inherited buildings is the highest i.e. 78.12 per cent and 82.10 per cent respectively but the value of buildings constructed out of own savings is low, i.e. 13.03 and 14.50 per cent on the small and medium size of holdings. The value of buildings constructed under Government scheme is 8.85 and 3.40 per cent. The source-wise value of buildings of all the holdings together indicates that the value of inherited buildings is the highest i.e. 78.43 per cent followed by the value of buildings constructed by the assistance received under Government schemes and out of own savings i.e. 10.95 per cent and 10.62 per cent respectively.

5.1.F. Source-wise Value of Household Durables

The source-wise value of household durables which includes furnishing articles, electrical appliances, utensils, beddings, etc. have been presented in Table 5.6, which shows that among landless households, the value of inherited household durables is highest i.e. 50.36 per cent followed by the value of household durables purchased out of own savings, i.e. 22.33 per cent gifted household durables, i.e. 18.21 per cent, household durables purchased out of loans, i.e. 9.00 per cent. On marginal size of holdings the value of inherited household durables is highest i.e. 38.77% followed by the value of household durables purchased out of own savings i.e. 30.24%, gifted household durables i.e. 20.10% and household durables purchased out of loans i.e. 10.89%. On small size of holdings the value of household durables purchased out of own savings is highest i.e. 34.36% followed by the value of durables received by way of dowry i.e. 33.40% and inherited households i.e. 32.24%. Similarly on medium size of holdings the value of household durables received by way of dowry is the highest i.e. 37.30% followed by the household durables purchased out of own savings i.e. 36.57% and inherited durables i.e. 26.13%. The farmers falling on the small and medium size of holdings have not purchased any household durable out of loans, whereas the value of household durables purchased out of loans among landless and marginal farmers constitutes 9.00 per cent and 10.89 per cent. The inter-class source wise comparison of the

TABLE 5.6

Source-wise per Household Average Value of Household Assets : Household Durables*

(*Value in Rs.*)

Source	*landless*	*Marginal Holdings*	*Small Holdings*	*Medium Holdings*	*All Holdings*
Inherited	5094.35 (50.36)	7612.77 (38.77)	9619.06 (32.24)	10592 (26.13)	8229.54 (32.88)
Out of Own Savings	2258.19 (22.33)	5937.05 (30.24)	10248.86 (34.36)	14828.33 (36.57)	8310.1 (33.24)
Out of Loan	910.83 (9.00)	2137.35 (10.89)	—	—	762.04 (3.04)
Gifted	1841.94 (18.21)	3945.58 (20.10)	9966.07 (33.40)	15120.33 (37.30)	7718.48 (30.84)
Total	10115.31 (100.00)	19631.98 (100.00)	29834.99 (100.00)	40538.66 (100.00)	25028.16 (100.00)

Note : Figure in the parenthesis denote percentage to column total.
* Household durables includes—furnishing articles, electrical appliances, utensils, beddings, etc.

household durables clearly indicates the fact that the dowry system prevailed more among better-off households, because the value of gifted household durables is high i.e. 33.40% and 37.30% on small and medium size of holding respectively. Whereas among landless and marginal size of holdings the value of gifted household durables is 18.21 per cent and 20.10 per cent respectively. This is mainly due to the reason that higher holding groups can afford to give dowry in marriage ceremonies due to their sound and regular sources of household income. These results clearly indicate the prevalence of dowry system among the sample households in Yamunanagar district.

5.1.G Total Value of All Household Assets

The size of holdings wise value of all household assets have been presented in Table 5.7 which clearly reveals that among landless households value of buildings constitutes the highest percentage value to the total households assets (i.e. 75.98%) followed by household durables (i.e. 15.55%), livestock (i.e. 7.29%), Machinery i.e. (0.88%). Transport equipments (i.e. 0.17%) and agriculture implements (i.e. 0.13%). On the marginal

TABLE 5.7
Source-wise Per Household Average Value of Household Assets

(Values in Rs.)

Source	*landless*	*Marginal Holdings*	*Small Holdings*	*Medium Holdings*	*All Holdings*
Land		98009.79 (45.38)	3,37,433.46 (65.87)	6,17,833.33 (71.82)	263319.14 (63.70)
Livestock	4743.5 (7.29)	9125.73 (4.23)	10287.65 (2.01)	12344.99 (1.44)	9125.46 (2.21)
Agricultural Implements	84.51 (0.13)	265.28 (0.12)	402.26 (0.08)	587.66 (0.07)	334.92 (0.08)
Machinery*	570.96 (0.88)	1045.84 (0.48)	2253.98 (0.44)	2752.76 (0.32)	1655.88 (0.40)
Transport Equipments	116 (0.17)	503.18 (0.23)	13546.01 (2.64)	33580.8 (3.90)	11936.49 (2.89)
Buildings	49459.24 (24.67)	87395.08 (75.98)	118529.33 (40.47)	152599.99 (23.14)	101995.91 (17.74)
Household Durables	10115.31 (15.55)	19631.98 (9.09)	29834.99 (5.82)	40538.66 (4.71)	25030.23 (6.05)
Total	65089.52 (100.00)	2,15,976.88 (100.00)	512237.68 (100.00)	860238.19 (100.00)	413398.03 (100.00)

Note : Figures in Parenthesis denote the percentages to column total.
* Include sewing, weaving, ban making machines, etc.

size of holdings land constitutes the highest percentage value to the total household assets (i.e. 45.38%) followed by the value of buildings (40.47%), household durable (i.e. 9.09%), livestock (i.e. 4.23%), machinery (i.e. 0.48%), transport equipments (i.e. 0.23%) and Agricultural implements (i.e. 0.12%). Similarly on small size of holdings land constitutes highest percentage value to the total household assets (i.e. 65.87%) followed by the value of buildings (i.e. 23.14%) household durables (i.e. 5.82%), livestock (i.e. 2.01%), transport equipment (i.e. 2.64%), machinery (0.44%) agricultural implements (i.e. 0.08%).

On the medium size of holdings also land constitutes the highest percentage value of household assets (i.e. 71.82%) followed by the percentage value of buildings (i.e. 17.74%), household durables (i.e. 4.71%), transport equipments (i.e. 3.90%), livestock (i.e. 1.44%), machinery (i.e. 0.32%) and agricultural implements (i.e. 0.07%). The percentage value of livestock although shows a decreasing tendency with an increase in the size of holding but the value of livestock in absolute terms indicates an increasing tendency, which clearly shows that the poorest benefited the least and the least poor benefited the most.

5.1.H. Value of Productive Assets and Household Durables Among the Sample Households

The value of all household assets (i.e. both productive assets and households durables) has been presented in Table 5.8.

TABLE 5.8
Average Per Household Value of Productive Assets and Household Durables among The Sample Households

(Value in Rs.)

Sl. No.	Items	landless	Marginal Holdings	Small Holdings	Medium Holdings	All Holdings
A.	**Productive Assets**					
1.	Land	—	98009.79 (45.38)	3,37,433.46 (65.87)	6,17,833.33 (71.82)	263319.14 (63.70)
2.	Livestock	4743.5 (7.29)	9125.73 (4.23)	10287.65 (2.01)	12344.99 (1.44)	9125.46 (2.21)
3.	Agricultural Implements	84.5 (0.13)	265.28 (0.12)	402.26 (0.08)	587.66 (0.07)	334.92 (0.08)
4.	Machinery*	570.96 (0.88)	1045.84 (0.48)	2253.98 (0.44)	2752.76 (0.32)	1655.88 (0.40)
5.	Other Productive Assets**	116 (0.17)	503.18 (0.23)	13546.01 (2.64)	33580.8 (3.90)	11936.49 (2.89)
6.	Sub-Total of (1 to 5) Productive Assets	5514.97 (8.47)	108949.82 (50.45)	363923.36 (71.04)	667099.54 (77.55)	286371.89 (69.27)
B.	**Household Durables**	10115.31 (15.53)	19631.98 (9.09)	29834.99 (5.82)	40538.66 (4.71)	25030.23 (6.05)
C.	**Buildings**	49459.24 (76.04)	87395.08 (40.47)	118529.33 (23.14)	152599.99 (17.74)	101995.91 (24.67)
D.	**Sub-Total of B and C**	59574.55 (91.53)	107027.06 (49.55)	148364.32 (28.96)	193138.65 (22.45)	127026.84 (30.73)
	Grand Total	65089.52 (100.00)	215976.88 (100.00)	512287.68 (100.00)	860238.19 (100.00)	413398.03 (100.00)

Note : Figures in parenthesis denote the percentages to the column total.
* Includes sewing machines, weaving machines, ban making machines, etc.
** Includes the transport equipments used for commercial purposes, etc.

This Table clearly shows that the percentage value of land to the total value of household assets has been worked out 45.38, 65.87 and 71.82 per cent among marginal, small and medium holdings respectively. Among all the holdings together this percentage value came out 63.70 per cent. Land is the major productive asset in the area under study due to the reason that this area is a sugarcane dominating belt of Haryana and most of the land is put under commercial crops like rice, sugarcane, sunflower, eucalyptus trees, etc. by the small and medium farmers.

The percentage value of live stock to the total value of household assets is marginally higher among landless and marginal size of holdings (i.e. 7.29% and 4.23%) and it decreases with an increase in the size of holdings. The increase in the value of livestock among landless and on marginal size of holdings occurred mainly due to the reason that the landless and smaller size of holding groups have received milch buffaloes under the Anti-Poverty Programmes on subsidized rates in order to supplement their meagre household income.

The percentage value of agricultural implements has been worked out 0.13, 0.12, 0.08, 0.07 per cent among landless, marginal, small and medium size of holdings respectively. The percentage value of machineries (i.e. sewing, weaving, ban-making etc.) came out 0.88, 0.48, 0.44 and 0.32 per cent among the landless, marginal, small and medium size of holdings respectively, whereas the percentage value of other productive assets come out 0.17, 0.23, 2.64 and 3.90 among the landless, marginal, small and medium size of holdings respectively. The percentage value of agricultural implements and machineries shows a decreasing tendency with an increase in the size of holdings but the value of these agricultural implements and machinery in absolute terms shows an increasing tendency with an increase in the size of holdings. The percentage value of other productive assets is the highest on medium size of holdings and shows a decreasing tendency with a decrease in the size of holdings. It happened mainly due to the reason that the landless and smaller holding groups have received loans, training and instruments for establishing household industries under the Anti-Poverty Programmes, whereas, the larger holdings groups due to their sound and regular sources of household income can afford to make investment in vehicles for commercial purposes. Land, Livestock, agricultural implements, machineries used in household cottage industries and transport equipments have been treated as the productive assets in the present study. The percentage value of these productive assets together has been worked out 8.47, 50.45, 71.04 and 77.55 among landless, marginal, small and medium size of holdings respectively which shows an increasing tendency with an increase in the size of holdings. Among all the holding groups together the percentage value of these productive assets came out 69.27 per cent.

The percentage value of household durables i.e. furnishing articles, electrical appliances, utensils and beddings, etc. to the total value of household assets also varies sharply from one size of holding group to the other. The variation in the distribution of these durables necessarily indicate the variations in the levels of living of the sample households but have a negligible direct effect on the pattern of household income and employment. The percentage value of buildings to the total value of household assets has been worked out 76.04, 40.47, 23.14 and 17.74 per cent among landless, marginal, small and medium size of holdings respectively. It happened mainly due to the reason that the households falling among landless and on smaller size of holdings groups due to their meagre sources of household income and due to their uneconomic size of holdings have received houses under Anti-Poverty Programmes (i.e. Indira Awas Yojana). These houses are used by the sample households entirely for their residential purposes.

The percentage value of household durables and buildings together to the total value of household assets has been worked out 91.53, 49.55, 28.96 and 22.45 per cent among the landless, marginal, small and medium size of holdings respectively. Among all the household together this percentage came out 30.73. Though the value of household durables and buildings together in percentage terms indicates a decreasing tendency with an increase in the size of holdings, but in absolute terms the per household combined value of household durables and buildings indicates an increasing tendency with an increase in the size of holdings, which has been worked out Rs. 59, 574.55, 1,07,027.06, 1,48,364.32 and 1,93,138.65 among the landless, marginal, small and medium size of holdings respectively, which is evident from Table 5.8.

Thus, the above distribution pattern of household assets shows that there exists an unequal distribution of these assets among the different categories of households. In case of all households together the percentage value of land to the total value of household assets is the highest i.e. 63.70 per cent.

The percentage value of land shows an increasing tendency with an increase in the size of holdings. The second major household assets is the buildings which accounts for 24.67 per cent. The percentage value of total productive assets come out 69.27 per cent, and the percentage value of household durables and buildings come out 30.73 per cent among all households together.

5.2 PATTERN OF HOUSEHOLD INCOME

This section deals with the pattern of household income among the sample households of district Yamunanagar.

5.2.A. Pattern of Household Agricultural Income

In the rural areas of Haryana, agriculture, animal husbandry and cottage industries are the major sources of household income.

The size of holding-wise comparative amount of agricultural income received by way of leasing out land farm output, agricultural wages, income from livestock, forestry and fishery have been presented in Table 5.9. The size of holding wise receipts of agricultural income clearly indicate that as landless households have no land, the percentage contribution of farm income to the total household income is zero. Therefore, the agricultural income among the landless households includes mainly income from hired-out labour, income from livestock, fishery and forestry activities. Among landless households income from livestock constitutes the highest percentage of their agricultural income (i.e. 41.90%) followed by the wages received by way of the hired out family human labour (i.e. 39.22%) and income from fisheries and forestry (i.e. 18.88%). Among the landless households percentage of the income received from livestock is highest because these households have received

TABLE 5.9

Per Household Average Value of Agricultural Income Among the Selected Households

(*Qty: Qtls, Value in Rs.*)

Holding Group	*Value of Farm Output**		*Wages in kind received by Agri-hired out labour*		*Receipts on leased out land*		*Farm income*	*Livestock*	*Fisheries and Forestry*	*Total Farm Income*
	Qty.	*Value*	*Qty.*	*Value*	*Qty.*	*Value*				
(1)	(2)	(3)	(4)	(5)	(6)	(7)	(8)	(9)	(10)	(11)
Landless	—	—	1.88	1222.00 (39.22)	—	—	1222.00 (39.22)	1305.32 (41.90)	588.19 (18.88)	3115.51 (100.00)
Marginal Holdings	5.98	3887.00 (58.40)	0.9	585.00 (8.79)	—	—	4470.00 (67.19)	1811.00 (27.22)	471.70 (7.09)	6652.70 (100.00)
Small Holdings	13.97	9080.50 (67.69)	—	—	—	118.00 (0.88)	9198.50 (68.67)	3755.06 (27.99)	460.86 (3.44)	13414.42 (100.00)
Medium Holdings	36.78	23907.00 (71.35)	—	—	—	465.40 (1.39)	24372.40 (72.74)	8723.39 (26.04)	409.62 (1.22)	33505.41 (100.00)
All Holdings	14.18	9218.62 (65.18)	0.66	432.25 (3.05)	—	146.19 (1.03)	9815.72 (69.27)	3913.69 (27.61)	442.59 (3.12)	14318.19 (100.00)

Note : Figures in the parenthesis indicates the percentage to the column total.
*Value of Farm output includes both income and by products.

cattle under Anti-Poverty Programmes. On the marginal size of holding group the highest percentage of agricultural income has been contributed by the farm output (i.e. 58.40%) followed by income from livestock (i.e. 27.22%), wages received by way of the hired-out family human labour (i.e. 8.79%) and income from fisheries and forestry (i.e. 7.09%). On the small size of holding groups the highest percentage of agricultural income has been contributed by farm output (i.e. 67.69%) followed by the income from livestock (i.e. 27.99%), forestry and fishery (i.e. 3.44%) and income received by way of leasing out their land (i.e. 0.88%). Similarly on the medium size of holding group also the highest percentage of agricultural income has been contributed by farm output (i.e. 71.35%) followed by the income from livestock (i.e. 26.04%), income received by way of leasing-out their land (i.e. 1.39%) and income from fisheries and forestry (i.e. 1.22%).

5.2.B. Pattern of Household Non-Agricultural Income

The pattern of household non-agricultural income has been presented in Table 5.10. The percentage share of income derived from services to the total non-agricultural income has been worked out 18.95, 23.61, 30.47 and 38.26 per cent among the landless, marginal, small and medium size of holdings respectively. Whereas among all the holding groups together this percentage came out 30.13 per cent. Thus, the percentage share of household income from services, shows an increasing tendency with an increase in the size of holdings. This happened mainly due to the higher literacy percentage among the larger size of holding groups. The percentage share of income from business activities shows an increasing tendency with an increase in the size of holdings. This is attributed to the fact that larger size of holding groups due to their sound and regular sources of income can afford to make investment in business activities out of their own savings.

The percentage share of income derived from wage work to the total household non-agricultural income is highest among landless households (i.e. 49.57%) followed by marginal (i.e. 43.82%), small (i.e. 32.18%) and medium farmers (i.e. 16.64%). The percentage share of income from wage work shows a decreasing tendency with an increase in the size of holdings. This happened mainly due to the reason that the smaller

TABLE 5.10
Average per Household Annual Non-Agricultural Income among the Selected Household

(*Value in Rs.*)

Sl. No.	*Source-wise Income*	*Landless*	*Marginal Farmers*	*Small Farmers*	*Medium Farmers*	*All Households*
1.	Service	3696.6 (18.95)	4882.5 (23.61)	8482.44 (30.47)	16164.83 (38.26)	8306.59 (30.13)
2.	Business	1819.44 (9.33)	2363.95 (11.43)	4159.6 (14.94)	8973.71 (21.24)	4329.17 (15.70)
3.	Wages	9671.34 (49.57)	9063.18 (43.82)	8958.7 (32.18)	7031.81 (16.64)	8681.25 (31.49)
4.	Household Industries	2945.64 (15.10)	2567.46 (12.41)	2855.53 (10.26)	3148 (7.45)	2879.15 (10.44)
5.	Pension	565.6 (2.90)	749.69 (3.62)	1391.06 (5.00)	2958.36 (7.00)	1416.17 (5.14)
6.	Income of Spouse	475.1 (2.43)	601.34 (2.91)	1186.26 (4.26)	2238.76 (5.30)	1125.36 (4.08)
7.	Other Income*	334.81 (1.72)	455.14 (2.20)	804.42 (2.89)	1737.09 (4.11)	832.86 (3.02)
8.	Total Non-Agri-Income	19508.53 (100.00)	20683.26 (100.00)	27838.01 (100.00)	42252.56 (100.00)	27570.55 (100.00)

Note : Figures in parenthesis denote the percentage to the column totals.
* Other income includes income from religious work, contract, income from vehicles for commercial use, mason work, grazing other's cattle etc.

holding groups as well as the landless households due to the lack of regular gainful employment on their own farms, high percentage of illiteracy and dependency, meagre income and high burden of debt repayment can not afford to remain unemployed even during the peak agricultural season and offered their services for the wage work, irrespective of the nature of work as well as the wage rate paid to them, whereas contrary to it the households falling on the larger holding groups due to high literacy percentage, regular and sound sources of income, availability of regular gainful employment on their own farm do not prefer to work on wage basis. They are willing to get specific white collar jobs, whereas the households falling comparatively on the smaller size of holdings and among landless households can not afford to remain unemployed, hence they lay their hands on any type of work.

The percentage share of income derived from household industries is the highest among landless households (i.e. 15.10%) as compared to marginal (i.e. 12.41%), small (i.e. 10.26%) and medium size of holdings group (i.e. 7.45%). Among all the holding groups together this percentage came out 10.44 per cent. The percentage share of income from household industries shows a decreasing tendency with an increase in the size of holdings. This happened mainly on account of the fact that the households falling among the landless and on the smaller size of holding groups have received loans on subsidized rates, training as well as instruments (specially weaving, ban making and shoe-making machines) under the 'Anti-Poverty Programmes' in order to supplement their meagre household income.

The percentage share of income from pension to the total household non-agricultural income has been worked out 2.90, 3.62, 5.00 and 7.00 per cent among the landless, marginal, small and medium size of holdings respectively. Similarly income of spouse also shows an increasing tendency with an increase in the size of holdings. The percentage share of income from the spouse's income is lowest among landless (i.e. 2.43%) and is increasing with the increase in the size of holdings i.e. 2.91, 4.26 and 5.30 on marginal, small and medium size of holding groups respectively. The percentage share of income from other sources (i.e. income from religious work, commercial vehicles, mason work, grazing other's cattle etc.) shows an increasing tendency with an increase in the size of holdings i.e. 1.72, 2.20, 2.89 and 4.11 per cent among landless, marginal, small and medium size of holdings respectively. Among all the households together the percentage of income from these sources come out 3.2 per cent.

5.2.C. Pattern of Household Agricultural and Non-Agricultural Income

The pattern of household total income (i.e. both from agricultural and non-agricultural sources) has been presented in Table 5.11. This Table clearly reveals that the percentage share of farm income is highest on medium size of holding groups (i.e. 32.17%) as compared to small (i.e. 22.30%), marginal (i.e.

TABLE 5.11
Per Household Average Annual Agricultural and Non-Agricultural Income Among the Selected Households

(Value in Rs.)

Sl. No.	*Source-wise Income*	*Landless*	*Marginal Holdings*	*Small Holdings*	*Medium Holdings*	*All Holdings*
I. Agricultural Income						
1.	Farm Income	1222 (5.40)	4470 (16.36)	9198.5 (22.30)	24372.4 (32.17)	9815.72 (23.50)
2.	Livestock	1305.32 (5.77)	1811 (6.63)	3755.06 (9.10)	8723.39 (11.51)	3898.69 (9.33)
3.	Forestry, Fishery and Poultry	588.19 (2.60)	471.7 (1.73)	460.86 (1.12)	409.62 (0.54)	482.59 (1.16)
4.	Total Agricultural Income (1 to 3)	3115.51 (13.77)	6652.7 (24.31)	13414.42 (32.52)	33505.41 (44.22)	14197 (33.99)
II. Non-Agricultural Income						
5.	Services	3696.6 (16.34)	4882.5 (17.86)	8482.44 (20.56)	16164.83 (21.34)	8306.59 (19.89)
6.	Business	1819.44 (8.04)	2363.95 (8.65)	4159.6 (10.08)	8973.71 (11.85)	4329.17 (10.37)
7.	Wage Work	9671.34 (42.74)	9063.18 (34.25)	8958.7 (21.72)	7031.81 (9.28)	8681.25 (20.78)
8.	Household Industry	2945.64 (13.02)	2567.46 (8.30)	2855.53 (6.92)	3148 (4.16)	2879.15 (6.89)
9.	Pension	565.6 (2.50)	749.69 (2.74)	1391.53 (3.37)	2958.36 (3.91)	1416.17 (3.39)
10.	Income of Spouse	475.1 (2.10)	601.34 (2.20)	1186.26 (2.88)	2238.76 (2.95)	1125.36 (2.70)
11.	Other Income*	334.81 (1.49)	455.14 (1.67)	804.42 (1.95)	1737.09 (2.29)	832.86 (1.99)
12.	Total Non-Agricultural Income (5 to 11)	19508.53 (86.23)	20683.26 (75.67)	27838.01 (67.48)	42252.56 (55.78)	27570.55 (66.05)
13.	Total Income (I & II)	22624.04 (100.00)	27335.96 (100.00)	41252.43 (100.00)	75757.97 (100.00)	41767.55 (100.00)

Note : Figures in parenthesis indicates the percentages to column total.
* Includes income from religious work, contract and vehicles work, grazing other's cattle, etc.

16.36%) and landless households (i.e. 5.40%). Among all the households together this percentage came out 23.50 per cent. This happened mainly due to the reason that the households falling on the medium and small size of holding groups make intensive use of their land which is comparatively more fertile, whereas, contrary to it, the households falling on the marginal size of holdings due to their uneconomic size of holdings which is generally infertile and barren can not produce food grains even to meet out their domestic needs. Among the landless household the percentage share of income earned from agriculture is the lowest. This is mainly due to the reason that as these households do not possess any land of their own, this income totally comes by way of hiring out their labour in agricultural sector.

The percentage share of household income earned by way of livestock activities is the lowest among the landless households (i.e. 5.77%) and is increasing with an increase in the size of holdings (i.e. 6.63, 9.10 and 11.51 per cent on the marginal, small and medium size of holding groups respectively. This is due to the reason that most of the cattle kept by landless and marginal farmers, have been received under Anti-Poverty Programmes which are ill nourished, weak and less productive. Hence, even after selling most of the available livestock products in order to supplement their meagre household income, the percentage share of livestock income to the total household income on the smaller holding groups remained low as compared to the livestock income earned by the households falling on the larger holding groups who can afford to keep more cattle which are healthy and more productive. The percentage share of agricultural income from forestry, fisheries and poultry etc. to the total household income shows a decreasing tendency with an increase in the size of holdings.

The percentage share of Agricultural income to the total household income has been worked out 13.77, 24.31, 32.52 and 44.22 per cent among landless, marginal, small and medium size of holdings respectively. Whereas among all the holdings together this percentage came out 33.99. The percentage share of agricultural income to the total household income shows an increasing tendency with an increase in the size of holdings. It happened mainly due to the scattered, uneconomic size of holdings, lack of fertilizers, manures, irrigation facilities, inferior quality of seeds, untimely and less intensive ploughing operation by the hired in bullock labour, lack of modern inputs used by the households falling on smaller holding groups as compared to the households falling on the larger size of holdings.

The percentage share of household income earned from services to the total household income has been worked out 16.34, 17.86, 20.56 and 21.34 per cent among the landless, marginal, small and medium size of holding respectively. The percentage share of household income from services to the total household income shows an increasing tendency with an increase in the size of holding. This happened mainly on account of the higher literacy percentage among the households falling on the larger size of holding.

The percentage share of household income earned from business activities to the total household income is the highest on the medium size of holdings (i.e. 11.85%) as compared to the small (i.e. 10.08%), marginal (i.e. 8.65%) and the landless households (i.e. 8.04%). This percentage share is highest on larger size of holdings, mainly on account of the fact that the households falling on the larger size of holding groups due to their sound and regular sources of income can afford to make investment in business activities out of their own savings. Whereas the household on the smaller size of holdings and the landless households have received loans under self-employment scheme to start their business.

The percentage share of household income earned from wage work to the total household income has been worked out 42.74, 34.25, 21.72 and 9.28 per cent among the landless, marginal, small and medium size of holdings respectively. Among all the holdings together this percentage come out 20.78 per cent. The percentage share of household income from wage work is the highest among landless households and shows a decreasing tendency with an increase in the size of holding. It happened mainly an account of the fact that landless households as they do not possess any land of their own have to go for wage work nearby, mainly in road construction, sugarcane crushers, rice shellers etc. Similarly the marginal and small farmers also on account of their meagre household farm income and lack of gainful employment opportunities on their own farms, prefer to go for wage work. These households (landless, marginal and small) due to their meagre household income, high dependency ratio higher debt burden can not afford to remain without work and as a result of it, they lay their hands on any wage work irrespective to the nature of work as well as the wage rate given to them. On the medium size of holding, the percentage share of income to the total household income, is low mainly due to the reason that these households on their large size of holdings, get gainful work throughout the full agricultural year and therefore, they do not prefer to work on wage basis.

The Table further reveals that the percentage share of household income earned from household industries which include mainly tailoring, weaving, shoe-making, ban-making, basket making, flour mills etc, is comparatively high among the households falling among the landless household (i.e. 13.02%) followed by the marginal (i.e. 8.30%), small (i.e. 6.92%) and medium size of holdings (i.e. 4.16%). The higher percentage share of the household income from household industries among the landless, marginal and small size of holdings is mainly due to the financial assistance and skill formation provided under Anti-Poverty Programmes as well as to supplement the meagre household income of these poor household. Most of the households falling among the landless, marginal and small size of holdings are provided with financial assistance, skill formation and instruments mainly for the expansion of their traditional cottage industries (i.e. mainly weaving and shoe-making industries) with a view to raise their household income, whereas, the households falling on the medium size of holding have established their traditional cottage industries (weaving, wooden furniture, building material, steel utensils etc.) by utilising own resources in the rural areas.

The percentage share of income derived from pension to the total household income has been worked out 2.50, 2.74, 3.37 and 3.91 per cent among landless, marginal, small and medium size of holdings respectively, whereas the percentage share of income from spouse's income came out 2.10, 2.20, 2.88 and 2.95 per cent among landless, marginal, small and medium size of holding respectively. The percentage share of household income earned from other non-agricultural activities (i.e. mainly from religious work, commercial vehicles, mason etc.) have been worked out 1.49, 1.67,1.95 and 2.29 per cent among the landless, marginal, small and medium size of holdings respectively. Among all the households together this percentage of income came out 1.99 per cent. The percentage share of household income from other sources shows an increasing tendency with an increase in the size of holdings, mainly due to the reason that the households falling on the medium size of holdings can afford to invest in vehicles for commercial purposes as well as in other productive activities as compared to smaller size of holding groups and the landless households.

Thus, the percentage share of household non-agricultural income to the total household income has been worked out 86.23, 75.67, 67.48 and 55.78 per cent among the landless marginal, small and medium size of holdings respectively, whereas among all the holdings, together this percentage come out 66.05 per cent. The percentage share of household non-agricultural income to the total household income shows a decreasing tendency with an increase in the size of holdings. It occurred mainly due to fertile lands, production of commercial crops like sugarcane, on the larger size of holding whereas the households falling on the smaller size of holding groups and among landless households due to uneconomic size of holdings, meagre household income, high dependency ratio and higher burden of debt repayment, generally supplement their meagre household agricultural income mainly by way of wage work as well as through other non-agricultural sources of household income.

6

Pattern of Human Labour Utilization and the Extent of Unemployment among the Sample Households

This chapter deals with the pattern of human labour utilization in agricultural and non agricultural activities, in both the productive and necessary activities as well as the extent of unemployment among the sample households.

6.1 PATTERN OF HUMAN LABOUR UTILIZATION

6.1.A. Pattern of Human Labour Utilization in Agricultural Activities

In the present study agricultural employment includes mainly human labour days utilized in crop production, mandays used with bullock labour, looking after livestock and human days used in fisheries, poultry and forestry. The percentage distribution of the mandays (adult workers) in crop production to the total mandays used in agricultural activities have been presented in Table 6.1. This Table clearly reveals that the percentage of mandays spent in crop production is 27.11,

TABLE 6.1
Per Household Average Number of Human Labour Days Utilization in Agricultural Activities

(Standard Mandays Per Year)

Sl. No.	Activity	Landless Holdings	Marginal Holdings	Small Holdings	Medium Holdings	All Holdings
I.	**Human Labour Days used in Crop production**					
	(a) Family Human Labour Days	—	135.72 (37.14)	323.95 (54.35)	526.74 (63.18)	246.6 (48.57)
	(b) Hired-in Labour Days	—	—	0.12 (0.02)	5.5 (0.66)	1.4 (0.27)
	(c) Hired-out Labour Days	63.81 (27.11)	1.86 (0.51)	—	—	16.41 (3.23)
	Sub-Total of I	63.81 (27.11)	137.58 (37.65)	324.07 (54.37)	532.24 (63.84)	264.41 (52.08)
II.	**Human Days used with bullocks**					
	(a) Family Human Labour Days	—	2.74 (0.75)	9.65 (1.62)	28.01 (3.36)	10.1 (1.99)
	(b) Hired-in Human Labour Days	—	8.11 (2.22)	7.33 (1.23)	8 (0.96)	5.86 (1.15)
	(c) Hired-out Human Labour Days	—	2.26 (0.62)	9 (1.51)	17.34 (2.08)	7.14 (1.40)
	Sub-Total of II	— (3.59)	13.11 (4.36)	25.98 (6.40)	53.35 (4.55)	23.1
III.	Total Mandays used in Crop production (I + II)	63.81 (27.11)	150.69 (41.23)	350.05 (58.74)	585.59 (70.23)	287.51 (56.64)
IV.	Human Days used in Looking after Cattle	160.33 (68.12)	205.99 (56.37)	238.6 (40.03)	242.19 (29.05)	237.77 (46.84)
V.	Human Labour days used in Fisheries, and Poultry	7.34 (3.12)	5.22 (1.43)	5.72 (0.96)	6 (0.72)	6.07 (1.20)
VI.	Human Labour used in Forestry	3.89 (1.65)	3.54 (0.97)	1.6 (0.27)	—	2.25 (0.44)
VII.	Total mandays used in Agriculture	235.37 (100.00)	365.44 (100.00)	595.97 (100.00)	833.78 (100.00)	507.62 (100.00)

Note : Figures in the parenthesis show percentage to column total.

37.65, 54.37 and 63.84 per cent among the landless, marginal, small and medium size of holdings respectively. Among all the households together this percentage come out 52.08 per cent. The percentage of mandays spent in crop production shows an increasing tendency with an increase in the size of holding. The percentage of hired-in human labour shows an increasing tendency with an increase in the size of holdings. There is no hired-in human labour days among landless and marginal households, whereas, the percentage of mandays hired-out come out 27.11 and 0.51 per cent among the landless and marginal size of holdings respectively, which indicates a decreasing tendency with an increase in the size of holdings. The percentage of hired-out human labour mandays shows a decreasing tendency with an increase in the size of holdings, mainly due to the reason that the landless households, as they do not have any land of their own, can not afford to remain unemployed and therefore, in order to supplement their meagre household income they work as agricultural labourer on higher size of holdings. Similarly in case of marginal farmers due to their uneconomic size of holdings, the family human labour are either disguisedly underemployed and/or disguisedly unemployed as they are not necessarily required on their own farms throughout the full agricultural year. Hence, in order to supplement their household income they work on wage basis on other's farms. The percentage of hired-out human labour days is zero both on the small and medium size of holdings. Contrary to it, the percentage of hired-in human labour mandays indicates an increasing tendency with an increase in the size of holdings. It is mainly due to the reason that on the comparatively larger size of holdings the supply of family human labour is less to the demand for labour mainly during the peak harvesting season of agricultural crops.

The percentage of mandays used with bullock labour during the ploughing, harvesting and threshing operations come out 3.59, 4.36 and 6.40 per cent on the marginal, small and medium size of holding groups respectively. The percentage of human labour mandays spent in livestock activities to the total mandays spent in agricultural activities has been worked out 68.12, 56.37, 40.03 and 29.05 per cent among the landless, marginal, small and medium size of holdings respectively, whereas, among all the holdings together this percentage come out 46.84. The percentage of mandays spent in looking after cattle is the highest among the landless households followed by marginal, small and medium size of holdings. This happened mainly due to the reason that the landless households as well as the households falling on the smaller size of holding groups due to either no land of their own or due to uneconomic size of holdings can not afford to feed cattle (which have been received mainly under Government schemes) at the cattle shed and therefore, they leave the cattle for grazing for most of the time during the day.

The percentage of mandays spent in fisheries and poultry has been worked out 3.12, 1.43, 0.96 and 0.72 per cent among the landless, marginal, small and medium size of holdings respectively which shows a decreasing tendency with an increase in the size of holding. Similarly the percentage of mandays spent in collecting the forest products also shows a decreasing tendency with an increase in the size of holdings, this percentage come out 1.65, 0.97 and 0.27 per cent among the landless, marginal small and medium size of holdings respectively. Among all the holdings together this percentage come out 0.44 per cent.

These results indicate that the small and medium farmers having comparatively larger size of holdings spent more human labour days in crop production which is more productive and spent less percentage of labour days in looking after the cattle. Whereas the marginal farmers with too little land and landless households with no land of their own spent less percentage of human labour days in crop production and more in looking after the cattle. Further the landless households, marginal and small farmers have also utilized human labour days in activities like forestry, fisheries and poultry with a view to supplement their meagre household income, whereas on medium size of holding no human labour days have been utilized in activities like forestry. On all the holding groups together the percentage of human labour days spent in crop production (i.e. 52.08 per cent) is higher to the percentage of human labour days utilized in looking after the cattle (i.e. 46.84 per cent) followed by the human labour days utilized with bullock labour (i.e. 4.55%), fisheries and poultry (1.20%) and forestry (i.e. 0.44%).

6.1.B. Pattern of Human Labour Utilization in Productive and Necessary Activities

Pattern of human labour days utilization both in productive activities (i.e. crop production, livestock activities, business, wages, industries, services etc.) as well as necessary activities (i.e. family and social affairs) have been presented in Table 6.2. It is clear from this Table that the percentage of mandays spent in crop production to the total mandays utilized in different activities is the lowest among landless, households (i.e. 7.99%) as compared to marginal (i.e. 16.67%), small (i.e. 28.32%) and medium size of holdings (i.e. 39.50%). Among all the holdings together this percentage come out 26.02 per cent. The percentage of mandays spent in crop production shows an increasing tendency with an increase in the size of holdings. It happened mainly due to the reason that the landless households as well as the households falling on the smaller size of holdings groups keep themselves busy in more remunerative regular jobs outside agriculture, whereas, the households falling on the medium size of holding group due to gainful employment on their own economic size of holdings devote maximum time in agriculture.

The percentage of human labour mandays spent in livestock activities is the highest on the marginal size of holdings (i.e. 22.78%) as compared to landless (i.e. 20.10%), small (19.30%) and medium (i.e. 16.34%). This happened mainly due to the reason that the landless households as well as the households falling on the smaller size of holdings due to their uneconomic size of holdings can not afford to feed the cattle (which have been received by them mainly under Government Schemes) at the cattle-shed and therefore, they leave them for grazing for most of the time during the day. Further, it is observed that during the busy agricultural periods, less mandays are spent per household in looking after the cattle, whereas during the lean agricultural seasons, the farmers spent most of their time for looking after the cattle.

The percentage of mandays spent in fisheries, forestry and poultry shows a decreasing tendency with an increase in the size of holdings, i.e. 1.41, 0.97, 0.59 and 0.40 per cent among the landless, marginal, small and medium size of holdings

TABLE 6.2
Per Household Family Labour Utilization in Agricultural Activities, Non-Agricultural Activities, Social and Family Affairs

(Standard mandays per year)

Sl. No.	*Activities*	*Landless*	*Marginal Holdings*	*Small Holdings*	*Medium Holdings*	*All Holdings*
A.	**Agricultural Activities**					
1	Crop Production	63.81 (7.99)	150.69 (16.67)	350.05 (28.32)	585.59 (39.50)	287.53 (26.02)
2	Livestock	160.33 (20.10)	205.99 (22.78)	238.6 (19.30)	242.19 (16.34)	211.77 (19.16)
3	Fisheries, Poultry and Forestry	11.23 (1.41)	8.76 (0.97)	7.32 (0.59)	6.00 (0.40)	8.32 (0.75)
	Sub-Total (1 to 3)	235.37 (29.50)	365.44 (40.42)	595.97 (48.21)	833.78 (56.25)	507.62 (45.93)
B.	**Non-Agriculture Activities**					
1	Business	20.83 (2.61)	33.51 (3.70)	78.72 (6.37)	132.06 (8.90)	66.28 (6.00)
2	Wages	236.59 (29.65)	203.97 (22.52)	190.80 (15.43)	129.86 (8.76)	190.30 (17.22)
3	Household Industry	43.89 (5.50)	36.38 (4.02)	34.21 (2.76)	29.94 (2.00)	36.10 (3.27)
4	Service	20.10 (2.52)	31.16 (3.44)	81.93 (6.62)	125.40 (8.45)	64.64 (5.85)
5	Others	9.89 (1.24)	14.67 (1.62)	34.96 (2.83)	48.12 (3.23)	26.91 (2.43)
	Sub-Total B (1 to 5)	331.3 (41.52)	319.69 (35.36)	420.62 (34.03)	465.38 (31.39)	384.23 (34.77)
C.	**Family Affairs**					
	1. Family Affairs	208.1 (26.08)	191.41 (21.17)	181.22 (14.90)	135.12 (9.11)	178.96 (16.19)
	2. Social Affairs	23.14 (2.90)	27.57 (3.05)	38.32 (3.10)	48.17 (3.25)	34.30 (3.10)
	Sub-Total C (1+2)	231.24 (28.98)	218.98 (24.22)	219.54 (17.76)	183.29 (12.36)	213.26 (19.30)
	Grand Total of Labour Days utilized (A+B+C)	797.91 (100.00)	904.11 (100.00)	1236.13 (100.00)	1482.45 (100.00)	1105.11 (100.00)

Note : Figures in the parenthesis denote percentage to column total.

respectively. The percentage of mandays spent in all agricultural activities to the total mandays utilized in all the activities come out 29.50, 40.42, 48.21 and 56.25 per cent among the landless, marginal, small and medium size of holdings respectively, whereas, among all the holdings together this percentage come out 45.93 per cent.

The percentage of mandays spent in business activities is highest among the medium households (i.e. 8.90%) as compared to the small (i.e. 6.37%), marginal (03.70%) and landless households (i.e. 2.61%). The percentage of mandays spent in business activities by the medium households is highest mainly on account of the fact that the households falling on medium size of holdings due to their sound and regular sources of income as well as due to higher literacy percentages can afford to make investment in business activities. Contrary to it, most of the households among the landless households and on marginal size of holdings due to their meager income, higher illiteracy, uneconomic size of holdings are not prepared to take risk by taking Government loans for business activities which are advanced by Government agencies, against the security of their land and/or houses.

The percentage of mandays spent in wage work is the highest among the landless households (i.e. 29.65%) as compared to marginal (i.e. 22.52%), small (i.e. 15.43%) and medium size of holdings (i.e. 8.76%). Among all holdings together this percentage come out 17.22 per cent. This happened mainly due to higher dependency ratio, uneconomic size of holdings and meagre household income, due to which they can not afford to remain unemployed during the lean agricultural season and/or even during the peak agricultural season, when they are not necessarily required on their own uneconomic size of holdings, whereas on the medium size of holdings due to their higher percentage of literacy, sound and regular sources of household income and social status they consider wage work below their status.

The percentage of mandays spent in household industries is the highest among the landless households (i.e. 5.50%) and it decreases with increase in the size of holdings i.e. to 4.02, 2.76 and 2.00 per cent on marginal, small and medium size of holdings respectively. This happened mainly due to the reason that landless households and the smaller holdings groups have received loans on subsidized rates, training as well as instruments under the Anti-Poverty Programmes to start their household industries i.e. mainly weaving, spinning, ban-making and shoe-making industries in order to supplement their meagre household income.

The percentage of mandays spent in services is the lowest among the landless households (i.e. 2.52%) as compared to marginal (i.e. 3.44%), small (i.e. 6.62%) and medium size of holdings (i.e. 8.45%). Among all holdings together this percentage came out 5.85 per cent. The percentage of mandays spent in services, shows an increasing tendency with an increase in the size of holdings. This happened mainly on account of the higher literacy percentage among the households falling on the larger size of holdings as compared to landless and smaller size of holdings.

The percentage of mandays spent in other activities, has been worked out 1.24, 1.62, 2.83 and 3.23 per cent among the landless, marginal, small and medium size of holdings respectively, whereas, among all the holdings together this percentage come out 2.43 per cent. The percentage of mandays spent in all the non-agricultural activities such as business, wage work, household industries, services and other activities come out 41.42, 35.36, 34.03 and 31.39 per cent among the landless, marginal, small and medium size of holdings respectively. Among all the holdings together this percentage came out 34.77 per cent.

The percentage of mandays spent in family affairs has been worked out 26.08, 21.17, 14.90 and 9.11 per cent among the landless, marginal, small and medium size of holdings respectively. The percentage of mandays spent in social affairs has been worked out 2.90, 3.05, 3.10 and 3.25 per cent among the landless, marginal, small and medium size of holdings respectively. The percentage of mandays spent in necessary activities to the total mandays spent in all the activities, has been worked out 28.98, 24.22, 17.76 and 12.36 per cent among the landless, marginal, small and medium size of holdings respectively. Whereas among all the holding groups together this percentage come out 19.30. Thus, the percentage distribution of mandays spent in different activities by the sample households shows that the major proportion of mandays is spent in agricultural activities followed by non-agricultural and necessary activities.

6.2. EXTENT OF UNEMPLOYMENT

The per household unemployment mandays, percentage of mandays willing for additional work, percentage of voluntary unemployed mandays as well as the extent of unemployment according to time, willingness and income criterion has been presented in Table 6.3.

6.2.A. Time Criterion

According to Time Criterion, a person may be termed unemployed or underemployed, if he is gainfully occupied during the year for a number of days less than some normal or optimal days defined as full employment days. The Table 6.3 clearly indicates that the total numbers of available mandays per household has been worked out 1209, 1224, 1413 and 1614 among the landless, marginal, small, medium size of holdings respectively. Among all the holdings together the total mandays available came out 1365. The percentage of mandays utilized in all the agricultural, non-agricultural and necessary activities (i.e. in both productive and necessary activities) during the year has been worked out 66.00, 73.87, 87.48 and 91.85 per cent among the landless marginal, small and medium size of holdings respectively. Among all the households together this percentage of mandays utilized in all these activities came out 80.96 per cent. Hence the percentage of unemployed mandays to the full employment norms, i.e. 8 hours a day 25 days in a month or 300 days in a year according to Time Criterion, has been worked out 34.00, 26.13, 12.52 and 8.27 per cent among the landless, marginal, small and medium size of holdings respectively. Among all the holdings together this percentage of unemployed mandays according to Time Criterion came out 19.04 percent.

6.2.B. Willingness Criterion

A person may be called unemployed or underemployed according to willingness criterion, if he is willing to do more

TABLE 6.3
Percentage of Unemployed Mandays Time, Willingness and Income Criterion

(Standard Mandays)

Sl. No.	*Activities*	*Landless*	*Marginal Holdings*	*Small Holdings*	*Medium Holdings*	*All Holdings*
1.	Total Available Mandays (Annual)	1209 (100.00)	1224 (100.00)	1413 (100.00)	1614 (100.00)	1365 (100.00)
2.	Total Employed Mandays	797.91 (66.00)	904.11 (73.87)	1236.13 (87.48)	1482.45 (91.85)	1105.11 (80.96)
3.	No. of Annual Unemployed Mandays (Time Criterion)	411.09 (34.00)	319.89 (26.13)	176.87 (12.52)	131.55 (8.27)	259.89 (19.04)
4.	No. of Annual Mandays available for additional work (Willingness Criterion)	464.49 (38.42)	355.39 (28.30)	201.17 (14.23)	109.65 (6.79)	282.67 (20.70)
5.	Type of work required by households (%)					
	(i) Farm work	46.18	43.74	22.66	6.66	29.81
	(ii) Non-farm Work	53.82	56.26	77.34	93.34	70.19
6.	Wage rate acceptable (Rs. Per day)					
	(i) Within the Village	50	60	75	100	63.75
	(ii) Outside Village	70	80	90	150	90
7.	No. of voluntary unemployed mandays	—	—	—	21.9 (1.35)	5.47 (0.40)
8.	Willingness for over employment (3+4)	53.4 (4.41)	35.5 (2.90)	24.3 (1.71)	—	28.3 (2.07)
9.	Unemployed mandays (Income or Poverty Criterion)	276.8 (42.24)	230.5 (36.36)	145.4 (26.50)	—	652.3 (33.29)

Note : Figures in the parenthesis denote percentage to column total.

work than he is doing at present, he may either be actively searching for more work or be available for more work, if it is offered on terms to which he is accustomed. The percentage of mandays available/willing for additional work to the total available mandays, has been worked out 38.42, 28.30, 14.23 and 6.79 per cent among the landless, marginal, small and medium size of holdings respectively. Among all the households together the percentage of mandays willing for additional work to the total available mandays came out 20.70 per cent. Thus, the percentage of mandays willing for additional work shows a decreasing tendency with an increase in the size of holdings.

The percentage of available mandays willing for farm work (casual and/or seasonal farm work) has been worked out 46.18, 43.74, 22.66 and 6.66 present among the landless, marginal, small and medium size of holdings respectively. The percentage of mandays willing for non-farm work to the total available mandays has been worked out 53.82, 56.26, 77.34 and 93.34 percent among the landless, marginal, small and medium size of holdings respectively. The landless households are willing to work at a daily wage rate of Rs. 50 within the village and at a daily wage rate of Rs. 70 outside the village. The marginal farmers are willing to work at a daily wage rate of Rs. 60 within the village and at Rs. 80 outside the village. Similarly, small farmers are ready to work at a daily wage rate of Rs. 75 within the village and at Rs. 90 per day outside the village whereas the medium farmers are willing to work at a daily wage rate of Rs. 100 within the village and at Rs. 150 per day outside the village.

Thus it is clear from Table 6.3 that the percentage of mandays willing for farm work shows a decreasing tendency with an increase in the size of holdings, whereas, the percentage of mandays willing for non-farm work shows an increasing tendency with an increase in the size of holdings. It happened mainly on account of the higher illiteracy and higher dependency percentage, uneconomic size of holdings, where all the family workers are not required on their farm throughout the year and even during the peak agricultural seasons, whereas, on the medium size of holdings, where all family members are gainfully employed on their own farm, the percentage of mandays willing for non-farm work particularly services, is the highest on the larger size of holdings mainly due to the higher literacy percentage as compared to the smaller size of holdings as well as to the landless households. Due to the higher literacy percentage and regular sources of income the households falling on the medium size of holdings are interested to get white collar jobs. As a result of it the percentage of voluntary unemployed mandays has been worked out 1.35 per cent on the medium size of holdings where as, contrary to it the percentage of mandays willing for over employment came out 4.41, 2.90 and 1.71 among landless, marginal and small size holdings respectively. The landless workers and those falling on the smaller size of holdings are willing to work for longer hours mainly due to the higher dependency ratio, meagre household income and higher burden of debt repayment. Among all the households together the percentage of mandays willing for over-employment came out 2.07 per cent. This clearly confirms the fact that the smallest suffers the most, the least small suffers the least from involuntary unemployment according to Willingness Criterion.

6.2.C. Income Criterion

The workers are inadequately employed not because they devote less time to work but because their earnings from the existing work are not sufficient to meet out the basic needs of their family members. This point of view is strongly stated by Dandekar and Rath in their study 'Poverty in India' (1972). They stated that, an inadequate level of employment be defined in terms of its capacity to provide minimum living to the population.[1] In the context of employment, under-nutrition is of crucial importance as it affects the ability to work and the efficiency of work. According to Raj Krishna, a person may be called unemployed and/or underemployed if, he earns an income per year/month less than some desirable minimum.[2] The number of underemployed workers earning less than the minimum desirable monthly income has been presented in Table 6.3. In the present study the minimum desirable level of per month income in order to meet out the minimum food and non-food requirements of a person at 2003-2004 local prices prevailing in the study area has been worked out Rs. 413.01 [as is evident from Table 7.4 (b)]

The number of underemployed workers who are earning less than the minimum desirable income, is the highest among the landless households (i.e. 42.24%) as compared to marginal (i.e. 36.36%) and small size of holdings (i.e. 26.50%). Thus the percentage of underemployed among the landless and on smaller size of holding groups exists mainly due to high ratio of dependency, low literacy percentage, uneconomic size of holdings and higher burden of debt repayments etc. Whereas, the households falling on the medium size of holding groups due to their sound and regular sources of household income, higher literacy percentage as well as the availability of gainful employment on their own farms, do not suffer from underemployment according to 'Income Criterion'.

Notes and References

1. V.M. Dandekar and Nilakantha Rath, Poverty in India, *Indian School of Political Economy*, Bombay, 1971, p. 2.
2. Raj Krishna, Unemployment in India, *Indian Journal of Agricultural Economics*, Vol. XXVIII, No. 1, Bombay, January-March, 1973, pp. 1-2.

7

Pattern of Household Consumption Expenditure among the Sample Households

This chapter deals with the pattern of household consumption expenditure on food and non-food items, as well as the value of poverty index before and after the implementation of Poverty Alleviation Programmes.

7.1 PATTERN OF HOUSEHOLD CONSUMPTION EXPENDITURE ON FOOD ITEMS AMONG THE SAMPLE HOUSEHOLDS BEFORE AND AFTER IMPLEMENTATION OF POVERTY ALLEVIATION PROGRAMMES

The pattern of household consumption expenditure on food items among the sample households falling on the different size of holdings before and after the implementation of Poverty Alleviation Programmes has been presented in Table 7.1 (a) and 7.1 (b). The Table 7.1 (a) clearly reveals the percentage amount of money spent on cereals to that of total household

TABLE 7.1 (a)

Distribution Pattern of Per Consumer Unit Per Month Consumption Expenditure on Food Items among the Sample Households before the Implèmentation of Poverty Alleviation Programmes

(Values in Rs.)

Sl. No.	*Items*	*Landless*	*Marginal Holdings*	*Small Holdings*	*Medium Holdings*	*All Holdings*
1.	Cereals	108.90 (61.84)	109.80 (56.57)	111.90 (51.59)	114.87 (45.22)	111.37 (53.03)
2.	Pulses	4.50 (2.56)	6.60 (3.41)	8.10 (3.73)	12.00 (4.74)	7.80 (3.71)
3.	Vegetables	16.80 (9.54)	19.20 (9.89)	23.70 (10.93)	27.60 (10.91)	21.83. (10.40)
4.	Milk	20.40 (11.58)	24.60 (12.67)	27.60 (12.72)	35.40 (14.00)	27.00 (12.86)
5.	Meat, Fish and Eggs	2.70 (1.53)	3.90 (2.01)	5.40 (2.49)	8.10 (3.20)	5.02 (2.39)
6.	Oil and Fats	15.00 (8.53)	19.80 (10.20)	27.00 (12.45)	'36.00 (14.24)	24.45 (11.64)
7.	Sugar and Gur	3.30 (1.87)	3.90 (2.01)	4.50 (2.08)	7.50 (2.97)	4.80 (2.29)
8.	Fruits	0.90 (0.52)	2.10 (1.08)	2.70 (1.24)	3.00 (1.19)	2.17 (1.03)
9.	Others*	3.60 (2.04)	4.20 (2.16)	6.00 (2.77)	8.43 (3.33)	5.55 (2.65)
	Total (1 to 9)	176.10 (100.00)	194.10 (100.00)	216.90 (100.00)	252.90 (100.00)	210.00 (100.00)

Note : Figures in the parentheses denote the percentage to column total.
* Includes expenditure on salt, spices, biscuits, etc.

food expenditure before the implementation of Poverty Alleviation Programme which came out 61.84, 56.57, 51.59 and 45.22 per cent among the landless, marginal, small and medium size of holdings respectively, whereas, among all the holdings together this percentage came out 53.03 per cent. After the implementation of Poverty Alleviation Programmes this percentage came out 61.31, 55.08, 49.51 and 42.80 per cent among landless, marginal, small and medium holdings respectively, as clear from Table 7.1 (b). Among all the holdings together this percentage came out 51.13 per cent. Thus, the

TABLE 7.1 (b)

Distribution Pattern of per Consumer Unit per month Consumption Expenditure on Food Items among the Sample Households after the Implementation of Poverty Alleviation Programmes

(Values in Rs.)

Sl. No.	*Items*	*Landless*	*Marginal Holdings*	*Small Holdings*	*Medium Holdings*	*All Holdings*
1.	Cereals	140.40 (61.31)	142.04 (55.08	144.98 (49.51)	147.65 (42.80	143.77 (51.13)
2.	Pulses	8.10 (3.54)	9.90 (3.84)	12.50 (4.27)	17.50 (5.07)	12.00 (4.27)
3.	Vegetables	21.90 (9.56)	26.00 (10.08)	30.50 (10.42)	35.50 (10.29)	28.47 (10.12)
4.	Milk	26.10 (11.40)	31.40 (12.18)	36.80 (12.57)	45.80 (13.27)	35.02 (12.46)
5.	Meat, Fish and Eggs	3.60 (1.57)	5.40 (2.09)	8.00 (2.73)	14.40 (4.17)	7.85 (2.79)
6.	Oil and Fats	18.90 (8.25)	28.60 (11.09)	39.70 (13.56)	53.60 (15.54)	35.20 (12.52)
7.	Sugar and Gur	5.40 (2.36)	6.30 (2.44)	7.90 (2.70)	11.20 (3.25)	7.70 (2.74)
8.	Fruits	1.80 (0.79)	3.00 (1.16)	5.40 (1.84)	7.90 (2.29)	4.52 (1.61)
9.	Others*	2.80 (1.22)	5.26 (2.04)	7.02 (2.40)	11.45 (3.32)	6.63 (2.36)
	Total (1 to 9)	229.00 (100.00)	257.90 (100.00)	292.80 (100.00)	345.00 (100.00)	281.16 (100.00)

Note : Figures in the parenthesis denote the percentage of column total.
* Include expenditure on salt, spices, biscuits, etc.

percentage amount of expenditure on cereals shows a decreasing tendency with an increase in the size of holding. It is also clear from Tables 7.1 (a) and 7.1 (b) that the percentage expenditure on cereals is high before the implementation of Poverty Alleviation Programmes as compared to the expenditure incurred after the implementation of Poverty Alleviation Programmes. Thus, the percentage amount of expenditure on cereals shows a decreasing tendency with an increase in the size of holdings. The percentage expenditure on pulses to total household food expenditure before the implementation of Poverty Alleviation Programmes has been worked out 2.56, 3.41, 3.73 and 4.74 percentage among the landless, marginal, small and medium size of holdings respectively which increased to 3.54, 3.84, 4.27 and 5.07 per cent after the implementation of Poverty Alleviation Programmes among the landless, marginal, small and medium size of holdings respectively. The percentage expenditure on vegetables (i.e. on leafy, root and other vegetables) came out 9.54, 9.89, 10.93 and 10.91 per cent before the implementation of Poverty Alleviation Programmes which changed to 9.56, 10.08, 10.42 and 10.29 per cent after the Poverty Alleviation Programme among the landless, marginal, small and medium size of holding group respectively. The percentage expenditure on milk and milk products to the total household food expenditure has been worked out 11.58, 12.67, 12.72, 14.00 per cent before implementation of Poverty Alleviation Programmes which came out 11.40, 12.18, 12.57 and 13.27 per cent after the implementation of Poverty Alleviation Programmes among the landless, marginal, small & medium holdings respectively. The percentage expenditure on meat, eggs, fish came out 1.53, 2.01, 2.49, 3.20 per cent before which has changed to 1.57, 2.09, 2.73 and 4.17 per cent after the implementation of Poverty Alleviation Programmes among the landless, marginal, small and medium holdings respectively. The percentage expenditure on oil and fats also shows an increasing tendency both before and after the implementation of Poverty Alleviation Programmes with an increase in the size of holdings. This percentage has been worked out 8.53, 10.20, 12.45, 14.24 per cent before and came out 8.25, 11.09, 13.56 and 15.54 per cent after the implementation of Poverty Alleviation Programmes among the landless, marginal, small and medium size of holdings respectively. The percentage expenditure on sugar and gur to the total household expenditure on food items has been worked out 1.87, 2.01, 2.08, 2.97 per cent before and 2.36, 2.44, 2.70, 3.25 per cent after the implementation of Poverty Alleviation Programmes among the landless, marginal, small and medium holdings respectively. The percentage expenditure on fruits came out 0.52, 1.08, 1.24 and 1.19 per cent before and increased to 0.79, 1.16, 1.84 and 2.29 per cent after the implementation of

Poverty Alleviation Programmes among the landless, marginal, small and medium size of holdings respectively. The percentage expenditure on other food items (i.e. salt, species, bread, biscuits, tea etc.) to the total household expenditure on food items has been worked out 2.04, 2.16, 2.77 and 3.33 per cent before which came out 1.22, 2.04, 2.40 and 3.32 percent after the implementation of Poverty Alleviation Programmes, among the landless marginal, small and medium size of holdings respectively. Thus from Tables 7.1 (a) and 7.1 (b) it can be concluded that the smaller holding groups allocated the major part of their total food expenditure on cereals, mainly due to their low income and higher percentage of dependents and a very little is left to meet out the requirements of other food-items, whereas, contrary to it, the households falling on the larger holding groups spent comparatively low percentage of their total household, food expenditure on cereals and a higher share is left to meet out the requirements of other nutritive food-items such as milk, meat, vegetables, fruits, etc.

7.2 PATTERN OF HOUSEHOLD CONSUMPTION EXPENDITURE ON NON-FOOD ITEMS AMONG THE SAMPLE HOUSEHOLDS BEFORE AND AFTER THE IMPLEMENTATION OF POVERTY ALLEVIATION PROGRAMMES

The Minimum food requirement is 'necessary', but not 'sufficient' for the survival of mankind. Therefore, certain amount of household expenditure for meeting out the minimum non-food requirements is equally important for the survival of mankind. In this study due consideration has been given to the non- food items such as fuel, light, clothing, footwear, health, education, etc. No specific norms comparable to minimum calorie requirements, has so far been suggested by any Government agency or individual scholar for non-food items. Due to the variation in topography, climatic conditions, nature, type and intensity of economic activities carried out, the minimum non-food requirements also varies from country to country and even from region to region within the country. The pattern of per household per month consumption expenditure on non-food items has been presented in Tables 7.2 (a) and 7.2 (b). These Tables clearly indicate that the percentage share

TABLE 7.2 (a)

Distribution Pattern of Per Consumer Unit Per Month Consumption Expenditure on Non-Food Items among the Sample Households before the Implementation of Poverty Alleviation Programmes

(*Value in Rs.*)

Sl. No.	*Items*	*Landless*	*Marginal Holdings*	*Small Holdings*	*Medium Holdings*	*All Holdings*
1.	Fuel & Light	8.05	10.9	13.1	21.02	13.26
		(9.78)	(10.98)	(11.22)	(13.12)	(11.56)
2.	Clothing	37.12	36.68	39.07	41.87	38.68
		(45.07)	(36.92)	(33.48)	(26.12)	(33.74)
3.	Footwear	6.79	9.26	11.34	16.76	11.03
		(8.24)	(9.32)	(9.71)	(10.46)	(9.62)
4.	Education	8.47	10.94	14.21	22.86	14.12
		(10.28)	(11.00)	(12.18)	(14.26)	(12.31)
5.	Health	2.27	4.61	6.26	11.37	6.12
		(2.76)	(4.64)	(5.37)	(7.09)	(5.44)
6.	Amusement, Fair and Festivals	2.89	4.32	6.32	9.44	5.74
		(3.51)	(4.35)	(5.42)	(5.89)	(5.33)
7.	Toilet requisites	5.31	6.02	6.72	7.19	6.31
		(6.45)	(6.05)	(5.76)	(4.49)	(5.50)
8.	Conveyance	4.49	5.82	7.36	11.21	7.22
		(5.45)	(5.86)	(6.31)	(7.00)	(6.29)
9.	Intoxicants	1.82	2.86	3.76	5.64	3.52
		(2.21)	(2.87)	(3.22)	(3.52)	(3.07)
10.	Others expenses*	5.15	7.97	8.54	12.91	8.64
		(6.25)	(8.01)	(7.32)	(8.05)	(7.53)
	Total (1 to 10)	82.36	99.38	116.68	160.27	114.64
		(100.00)	(100.00)	(100.00)	(100.00)	(100.00)

Note : Figures in parenthesis denote the percentage to column total.
* Includes payments made to tailors, lawyers, patwaries, potters etc.

on fuel and light in the total non food consumption expenditure accounts for 9.78, 10.98, 11.22, 13.12 per cent before and 9.86, 11.08, 11.05, 12.67 per cent after the implementation of Poverty Alleviation Programme among the landless, marginal, small and medium size of holdings respectively, whereas among all holdings together this percentage came out 11.56 per cent before

TABLE 7.2 (b)

Distribution Pattern of Per Consumer Unit Per Month Consumption Expenditure on Non-Food Items among the Sample Households after the Implementation of Poverty Alleviation Programmes

(Value in Rs.)

Sl. No.	*Items*	*Landless*	*Marginal Holdings*	*Small Holdings*	*Medium Holdings*	*All Holdings*
1.	Fuel & Light	10.83	14.86	18.20	29.46	18.33
		(9.86)	(11.08)	(11.05)	(12.67)	(11.44)
2.	Clothing	47.68	50.74	55.79	64.89	54.77
		(43.44)	(37.83)	(33.88)	(27.91)	(34.19)
3.	Footwear	9.54	12.60	16.13	24.78	15.76
		(8.69)	(9.39)	(9.80)	(10.66)	(9.84)
4.	Education	11.58	16.25	21.89	35.42	21.28
		(10.55)	(12.11)	(13.29)	(15.23)	(13.28)
5.	Health	4.56	7.24	10.30	15.13	9.30
		(4.15)	(5.40)	(6.26)	(6.51)	(5.80)
6.	Amusement,	5.34	6.48	9.03	13.86	8.67
	Fair and Festivals	(4.86)	(4.83)	(5.49)	(5.96)	(5.41)
7.	Toilet requisites	5.78	6.66	7.53	8.46	7.10
		(5.27)	(4.96)	(4.57)	(3.64)	(4.43)
8.	Conveyance	6.52	8.59	11.83	19.52	11.61
		(5.94)	(6.40)	(7.18)	(8.40)	(7.25)
9.	Intoxicants	2.61	2.95	3.35	4.57	3.37
		(2.38)	(2.20)	(2.03)	(1.97)	(2.10)
10.	Others expenses*	5.33	7.78	10.62	16.39	10.03
		(4.86)	(5.80)	(6.45)	(7.05)	(6.26)
	Total (1 to 10)	109.77	134.15	164.67	232.48	160.22
		(100.00)	(100.00)	(100.00)	(100.00)	(100.00)

Note : Figures in parenthesis denote the percentage to column total.
* Includes the expenditure on salt, spices, biscuits etc.

and 11.44 per cent after the Poverty Alleviation Programmes. The percentage expenditure on clothing has been worked out 45.07, 36.92, 33.48, 26.12 per cent before and 43.44, 37.83, 33.88, 27.91 per cent after the implementation of Poverty Alleviation Programmes among the landless, marginal, small, medium holdings respectively, whereas among all the holdings together this percentage expenditure came out 33.74 per cent before and 34.19 per cent after the Poverty Alleviation Programmes.

The percentage expenditure on footwear to the total expenditure on non-food items has been worked out 8.24, 9.32, 9.71, 10.46 per cent before and 8.69, 9.39, 9.80, 10.66 per cent after the implementation of Poverty Alleviation Programmes among the landless, marginal, small and medium holdings respectively. Among all the holdings together this percentage came out 9.62 per cent before and 9.84 after the implementation of Poverty Alleviation Programmes. The percentage expenditure on education to the total non-food expenditure has been worked out 10.28, 11.00, 12.18 and 14.26 per cent before and 10.55, 12.11, 13.29 and 15.23 per cent after the implementation of Poverty Alleviation Programmes among the landless, marginal, small and medium holdings respectively. The percentage expenditure on health to the total expenditure on non food items has been worked out 2.76, 4.64, 5.37, 7.09 per cent before and 4.15, 5.40, 6.26, 6.51 after the implementation of Poverty Alleviation Programmes among landless, marginal, small and medium size of holdings respectively.

The percentage expenditure on amusement, fair and festival etc. to the total non-food expenditure has been worked out 3.51, 4.35, 5.42, 5.89 per cent before and 4.86, 4.83, 5.49, 5.96 after the implementation of Poverty Alleviation Programmes among the landless, marginal, small and medium holdings respectively. Among all the households this percentage expenditure came out 5.33 per cent before and 5.41 per cent after the implementation of programmes. The percentage expenditure on toilet and requisites has been worked out 6.45, 6.05, 5.76, 4.49 per cent before and 5.27, 4.96, 4.57, 3.64 per cent after the implementation of Poverty Alleviation Programmes among the landless, marginal, small and medium size of holding groups respectively. The percentage expenditure on conveyance to the total non-food expenditure came out 5.45, 5.86, 6.31,7.00 per cent before and 5.94, 6.40, 7.18, 8.40 per cent after the implementation of Poverty Alleviation Programmes, among landless, marginal, small and medium holdings respectively. The percentage expenditure on intoxicants to the total holdings expenditure on non-food items came out 2.21, 2.87, 3.22, 3.52 per cent before and 2.38, 2.20, 2.03, 1.97 per cent after the implementation of Poverty Alleviation Programme among the landless, marginal, small and medium size of holdings respectively. The percentage expenditure on other items to the total non-food expenditure has been worked out 6.25, 8.01, 7.32, 8.05 per cent before and 4.86, 5.80, 6.45, 7.05 per cent after the implementation of Poverty Alleviation Programme among the landless, marginal, small and medium holdings respectively. Among all the holding groups this percentage came out 7.53 per cent before and 6.26 per cent after the implementation of Poverty Alleviation Programmes.

7.3 PATTERN OF HOUSEHOLD TOTAL CONSUMPTION EXPENDITURE ON FOOD AND NON-FOOD ITEMS AMONG THE SAMPLE HOUSEHOLDS BEFORE AND AFTER THE IMPLEMENTATION OF POVERTY ALLEVIATION PROGRAMMES

Pattern of consumption expenditure on both food and non-food items before and after the implementation of Poverty Alleviation Programmes among the sample households has been presented in Tables 7.3 (a) and 7.3 (b). These Tables clearly indicate that the percentage expenditure on food items both before and after the implementation of Poverty Alleviation Programmes is highest among the landless households i.e. 68.13 per cent before and 67.60 per cent after the implementations of Poverty Alleviation Programmes. It shows a decreasing tendency with an increase in the size of holdings i.e. 66.14, 65.02, 61.21 per cent before and 65.78, 64.00 and 59.74 after the Poverty Alleviation Programmes on marginal, small and medium size of holding groups respectively. Among all the holding groups together the percentage share of expenditure on food items came out 64.69 per cent before and 63.70 per cent after the implementation of Poverty Alleviation Programmes. Contrary to it, the expenditure on non-food items to the total consumption expenditure has been worked out 31.87, 33.86, 34.98, 38.79 per cent before and 32.40, 34.22, 36.00, 40.26 per cent after the Poverty Alleviation Programmes among landless, marginal, small and medium size of holdings respectively. Among all the holdings together this percentage expenditure came out 35.31 per cent before and 36.30 after the

TABLE 7.3 (a)
Distribution Pattern of Per Consumer Unit Per Month Consumption Expenditure on Food Items and Non-Food Items among the Sample Households before the Implementation of Poverty Alleviation Programmes

(Value in Rs.)

Sl. No.	*Items*	*Landless*	*Marginal Holdings*	*Small Holdings*	*Medium Holdings*	*All Holdings*
	(1)	(2)	(3)	(4)	(5)	(6)
1.	Cereals	108.9 (42.13)	109.8 (37.41)	111.9 (33.55)	114.87 (27.80)	111.37 (34.30)
2.	Pulses	4.5 (1.74)	6.6 (2.25)	8.1 (2.43)	12 (2.90)	7.8 (2.40)
3.	Vegetables	16.8 (6.50)	19.2 (6.54)	23.7 (7.10)	27.6 (6.68)	21.83 (6.72)
4.	Milk and Products	20.4 (7.89)	24.6 (8.38)	27.6 (8.27)	35.4 (8.57)	27 (8.32)
5.	Meat, Fish and Eggs	2.7 (1.04)	3.9 (1.33)	5.4 (1.62)	8.1 (1.96)	5.02 (1.55)
6.	Oil and Fats	15 (5.80)	19.8 (6.75)	27 (8.09)	36 (8.71)	24.45 (7.53)
7.	Sugar and Gur	3.3 (1.28)	3.9 (1.33)	4.5 (1.35)	7.5 (1.82)	4.8 (1.48)
8.	Fruits	0.9 (0.35)	2.1 (0.72)	2.7 (0.81)	3 (0.73)	2.18 (0.67)
9.	Others*	3.6 (1.39)	4.2 (1.43)	6 (1.80)	8.43 (2.04)	5.55 (1.71)
10.	Total (1 to 9)	176.1 (68.13)	194.1 (66.14)	216.9 (65.02)	252.9 (61.21)	210 (64.69)
11.	Fuel and Light	8.05 (3.11)	10.9 (3.71)	13.1 (3.93)	21.02 (5.09)	13.26 (4.08)
12.	Clothing	37.12 (14.36)	36.68 (12.50)	39.07 (11.71)	41.87 (10.13)	38.68 (11.91)
13.	Footwear	6.79 (2.63)	9.26 (3.16)	11.34 (3.40)	16.76 (4.06)	11.03 (3.40)
14.	Education	8.47 (3.28)	10.94 (3.73)	14.21 (4 26)	22.86 (5.53)	14.12 (4.35)
15.	Health	2.27 (0.88)	4.61 (1.57)	6.26 (1.88)	11.37 (2.75)	6.12 (1.89)
16.	Amusement, Fair and Festivals	2.89 (1.12)	4.32 (1.47)	6.32 (1.89)	9.44 (2.28)	5.74 (1.77)

(Contd.)

TABLE 7.3 (a)

(1)	(2)	(3)	(4)	(5)	(6)
17. Toilet requisites	5.31 (2.05)	6.02 (2.05)	6.72 (2.01)	7.19 (1.74)	6.31 (1.94)
18. Conveyance	4.49 (1.70)	5.82 (1.98)	7.36 (2.21')	11.21 (2.71)	7.22 (2.22)
19. Intoxicants	1.82 (0.70)	2.86 (0.97)	3.76 (1.13)	5.64 (1.36)	3.52 (1.08)
20. Other expenses**	5.15 (1.99)	7.97 (2.72)	8.54 (2.56)	12.91 (3.12)	8.64 (2.66)
21. Sub-Total (11 to 20)	82.36 (31.87)	99.38 (33.86)	116.68 (34.98)	160.27 (38.79)	114.64 (35.31)
22. Grand Total (10 to 21)	258.46 (100.00)	293.48 (100.00)	333.58 (100.00)	413.17 (100.00)	324.64 (100.00)

Note : Figures in parenthesis denotes percentage to columns total.

* Includes expenditure on salt, spices, biscuits, etc.

** Includes payments made to tailors, lawyers, patwaries, potters etc.

TABLE 7.3 (b)

Distribution Pattern of Per Consumer Unit Per Month Consumption Expenditure on Food and Non-Food Items among the Sample Households after the Implementation of Poverty Alleviation Programmes

(Value in Rs.)

Sl. No.	Items	Landless	Marginal Holdings	Small Holdings	Medium Holdings	All Holdings
	(1)	(2)	(3)	(4)	(5)	(6)
1.	Cereals	140.40 (41.44)	142.04 (36.23)	144.98 (31.69)	147.65 (25.57)	143.77 (32.58)
2.	Pulses	8.10 (2.39)	9.90 (2.52)	12.50 (2.73)	17.50 (3.03)	12.00 (2.72)
3.	Vegetables	21.90 (6.46)	26.00 (6.63)	30.50 (6.67)	35.50 (6.14)	28.47 (6.45)
4.	Milk and Products	26.10 (7.70)	31.40 (8.00)	36.80 (8.04)	45.80 (7.93)	35.02 (7.94)
5.	Meat, Fish and Eggs	3.60 (1.06)	5.40 (1.38)	8.00 (1.75)	14.40 (2.49)	7.85 (1.78)

(Contd.)

TABLE 7.3 (b)

(1)	(2)	(3)	(4)	(5)	(6)
6. Oil and Fats	18.90 (5.58)	28.60 7.29	39.70 (8.68)	53.60 (9.28)	35.20 (7.98)
7. Sugar and Gur	5.40 (1.59)	6.30 (1.61)	7.90 (1.73)	11.20 (1.94)	7.70 (1.75)
'8. Fruits	1.80 (0.53)	3.00 (0.76)	5.40 (1.18)	7.90 (1.37)	4.52 (1.02)
9. Others*	2.80 (0.83)	5.26 (1.34)	7.02 (1.53)	11.45 (1.98)	6.63 (1.50)
10. Total (1 to 9)	229.00 (67.60)	257.90 (65.78)	292.80 (64.00)	345.00 (59.74)	281.17 (63.70)
11. Fuel and Light	10.83 (3.20)	13.86 (3.53)	18.20 (3.98)	29.46 (5.10)	18.33 (4.15)
12. Clothing	47.68 (14.07)	50.74 (12.92)	55.79 (12.19)	64.89 (11.24)	54.77 (12.41)
13. Footwear	9.54 .(2.82)	12.60 (3.21)	16.13 (3.52)	24.78 (4.29)	15.76 (3.57)
14. Education	11.58 (3.42)	16.25 (4.14)	21.89 (4.78)	35.42 (6.13)	21.28 (4.82)
15. Health	4.56 (1.35)	7.24 (1.85)	10.30 (2.25)	15.13 (2.62)	9.30 (2.11)
16. Amusement, air and festivals	5.34 (1.58)	6.48 (1.65)	9.03 (1.97)	13.86 (2.40)	8.67 (1.96)
17. Toilet requisites	5.78 (1.71)	6.66 (1.69)	7.53 (1.65)	8.46 (1.46)	7.10 (1.61)
18. Conveyance	6.52 (1.92)	8.59 (2.19)	11.83 (2.58)	19.52 (3.38)	11.61 (2.63)
19. Intoxicants	2.61 (0.77)	2.95 (0.75)	3.35 (0.73)	4.57 (0.79)	3.37 (0.76)
20. Other expenses**	5.33 (1.57)	7.78 (1.98)	10.62 (2.32)	16.39 (2.84)	10.03 (2.27)
21. Sub-Total (11 to 20)	109.77 (32.40)	134.15 (34.22)	164.67 (36.00)	232.48 (40.26)	160.22 (36.30)
22. Grand Total 10 to 21)	338.77 (100.00)	392.05 (100.00)	457.47 (100.00)	577.48 (100.00)	441.38 (100.00)

Note : Figures in parenthesis denotes percentage to columns total.

* Includes expenditure on salt, spices, biscuits, etc.

** Includes payments made to tailors lawyers, potters etc.

implementation of Poverty Alleviation Programmes. The percentage expenditure on non-food items to the total household consumption expenditure shows an increasing tendency with an increase in the size of holdings among the sample households. Thus the empirical results of the present study have supported the Engel's Law of Consumption, which states that as the income increases, the percentage expenditure on food items decreases and the percentage expenditure on non-food items increases.

7.4 COMPOSITION OF RECOMMENDED AND ACTUAL AVERAGE DIET AMONG THE SAMPLE HOUSEHOLDS BEFORE AND AFTER THE IMPLEMENTATION OF POVERTY ALLEVIATION PROGRAMMES

The composition of per consumer unit per day recommended average diet as has been suggested by the Nutrition Experts as well as the composition of per capita per day actual consumptions of food items both before and after the implementation of Poverty Alleviation Programmes both in quantity as well as value terms has been presented in Tables 7.4 (a) 7.4 (b) and 7.5 (a) 7.5 (b). The Tables 7.4 (a) and 7.4 (b) reveal the value of recommended diet at the local prevailing prices in the study area at the time of survey. The value of per consumer unit per day diet before the implementation of Poverty Alleviation Programmes at 2000-01 local prices prevailing in the sample areas has been worked out Rs. 6.84.

The per consumer unit per month value of the recommended diet come out Rs. 317.19. The ratio of total non-food expenditure to the total food expenditure has been worked out 54.58 per cent, which account for Rs. 111.99 per consumer unit per month for meeting out the minimum non-food requirements. Thus by taking into account the value of both the food and non-food items the value of poverty index came out Rs. 317.19 (i.e. Rs. 205.20 on food items and Rs. 111.99 on non-food items).

The value of recommended diet after the implementation of Poverty Alleviation Programmes at the local prevailing prices has been presented in Table 7.4 (b). The value of per consumer unit per day diet at 2003-04 local prices prevailing in the sample area has been worked out Rs. 8.77.

The per consumer unit per month value of the recommended diet come out Rs. 413.01. The ratio of total non food expenditure to the total food expenditure has been worked out 56.98 per cent, which account for Rs. 149.91 per consumer unit per month for meeting out the minimum non-food requirements. Thus by taking into account the value of both the food and non food items the value of poverty index came out Rs. 413.01 (i.e. Rs. 263.10 on food items and Rs. 149.91 on non-food items).

The actual composition of per consumer unit per day diet before the implementation of Poverty Alleviation Programmes has been presented in Table 7.5 (a) which clearly reveals that the per consumer unit, per day average consumption of cereals came out 519, 524 and 534 gms among the landless, marginal and small holdings respectively which fall short of the recommended diet of 540 grams of these items, whereas on the medium size of holding the per consumer unit per day actual consumption of cereals came out 547 gms which is higher to the recommended diet.

The per capita per day actual consumption of pulses has been worked out 6, 9, 11, 16 gms among landless, marginal,

TABLE 7.4 (a)

Value of Per Consumer Unit Per Day Recommended Diet among the Sample Households (Quantity in Grams) at 2000-01 Prices before the Implementation of Poverty Alleviation Programmes

Sl. No.	*Items*	*Quantity (gms.)*	*Value (Rs.)*
1.	Cereals	540	3.78
2.	Pulses	12	0.30
3.	Vegetables	99	0.79
4.	Milk	80	0.80
5.	Meat, Fish and Eggs	5	0.22
6.	Oil and Fats	15	0.75
7.	Sugar and Gur	13	0.13
8.	Fruits	5	0.07
	Total		6.84

small and medium size of holdings respectively. Among all the households groups together the per capita per day actual consumption of pulses came out 11 gms as against the recommended per capita per day consumption of pulses, i.e. 12 gms.

The per consumer unit per day required consumption expenditure on food items = Rs. 6.84

The per consumer unit per month required consumption expenditure on food items = Rs. 6.84 x 30 = Rs. 205.20

The ratio of non-food expenditure to food expenditure came out i.e. 54.58 per cent i.e Rs. 111.99

Thus the value of poverty index = 205.20 + 111.99 = 317.19

TABLE 7.4 (b)

Value of Per Consumer Unit Per Day Recommended Diet among the Sample Households (Quantity in Grams) at 2002-03 Prices after the Implementation of Poverty Alleviation Programmes

Sl. No.	*Items*	*Quantity (gms.)*	*Value (Rs.)*
1.	Cereals	540	4.81
2.	Pulses	12	0.36
3.	Vegetables	99	0.99
4.	Milk	80	0.96
5.	Meat, Fish and Eggs	5	0.30
6.	Oil and Fats	15	1.05
7.	Sugar and Gur	13	0.20
8.	Fruits	5	0.10
	Total	---	8.77

The per consumer unit per day required consumption expenditure on food items = Rs. 8.77

The per consumer unit per month required consumption expenditure on food items = Rs. 8.77 x 30 = Rs. 263.10

The ratio of non-food expenditure to food expenditure came out 56.98 per cent i.e. Rs. 149.91

Thus the value of poverty index = 263.10 + 149.91 = 413.01

TABLE 7.5 (a)

Composition of Per Consumer Unit Per Day Actual Average Diet before the Implementation of Poverty Alleviation Programmes

(Quantity in gms.)

Sl. No.	*Items*	*Landless*	*Marginal Holdings*	*Small Holdings*	*Medium Holdings*	*All Holdings*
1.	Cereals	519	524	534	547	531
2.	Pulses	6	9	11	16	11
3.	Vegetables	70	81	99	115	91
4.	Milk and Products	68	82	92	118	90
5.	Meat, Fish and Eggs	2	3	4	6	4
6.	Oil and Fats	10	11	15	20	14
7.	Sugar and Gur	11	13	15	25	16
8.	Fruits	2	5	6	7	5

TABLE 7.5 (b)

Composition of Per Consumer Unit Per Day Actual Average Diet after the Implementation of Poverty Alleviation Programmes

(Qty. in gms.)

Sl. No.	*Items*	*Landless*	*Marginal Holdings*	*Small Holdings*	*Medium Holdings*	*All Holdings*
1.	Cereals	526	532	543	553	538
2.	Pulses	9	11	14	19	13
3.	Vegetables	73	86	101	118	94
4.	Milk and Products	72	87	102	127	97
5.	Meat, Fish and Eggs	2	3	4	8	4
6.	Oil and Fats	9	14	19	25	17
7.	Sugar and Gur	12	14	17	25	17
8.	Fruits	3	5	9	13	7

TABLE 7.6 (a)

Consumption Pattern of Per Consumer Unit Per Day Actual Consumption of Food Items among the Sample Households before the Implementation of Poverty Alleviation Programmes (At 2000-01 Prices)

(*Qty. in gms.*)

Sl. No.	*Items*	*Landless*	*Marginal Holdings*	*Small Holdings*	*Medium Holdings*	*All Holdings*
1.	Cereals	3.63	3.66	3.73	3.83	3.71
2.	Pulses	0.15	0.22	0.27	0.40	0.26
3.	Vegetables	0.56	0.64	0.79	0.92	0.72
4.	Milk	0.68	0.82	0.92	1.18	0.90
5.	Meat, Fish and Eggs	0.09	0.13	0.18	0.27	0.16
6.	Oil and Fats	0.50	0.66	0.90	1.20	0.81
7.	Sugar and Gur	0.11	0.13	0.15	0.25	0.16
8.	Fruits	0.03	0.07	0.09	0.10	0.07
9.	Others	0.12	0.14	0.20	0.28	0.19
	Total (1 to 9)	5.87	6.47	7.23	8.43	6.98

TABLE 7.6 (b)

Distribution Pattern of Per Consumer Unit Per Day Actual Consumption of Food Items among the Sample Households after the Implementation of Poverty Alleviation Programmes (At 2003-04 Prices)

(*Value in Rs.*)

Sl. No.	*Items*	*Landless*	*Marginal Holdings*	*Small Holdings*	*Medium Holdings*	*All Holdings*
1.	Cereals	4.68	4.74	4.83	4.92	4.79
2.	Pulses	0.27	0.33	0.41	0.58	0.39
3.	Vegetables	0.73	0.86	1.01	1.18	0.94
4.	Milk and Products	0.87	1.04	1.22	1.52	1.16
5.	Meat, Fish and Eggs	0.12	0.24	0.32	0.48	0.29
6.	Oil and Fats	0.63	0.89	1.26	1.78	1.14
7.	Sugar and Gur	0.18	0.21	0.26	0.37	0.25
8.	Fruits	0.06	0.10	0.18	0.26	0.15
9.	Others	0.09	0.17	0.23	0.38	0.22
	Total (1 to 9)	7.63	8.58	9.72	11.47	9.33

The per capita per day actual consumption of vegetables has been worked out 70, 81, 99, 115 grams among the landless, marginal, small and medium size of holdings respectively. Among all the household groups together the per capita per day actual consumption of vegetables came out 91 gms whereas, the recommended per capita per day consumption of vegetables is 99 grams.

The per capita per day actual consumption of milk and products has been worked out 68, 82, 92 and 118 grams among the landless, marginal, small and medium size of holdings respectively, whereas among all the holding groups together the per capita per day actual consumption of milk came out 90 grams against the recommended quantity of 80 grams.

The per capita per day actual consumption of meat, fish and eggs has been worked out 2, 3, 4 and 6 grams among the landless, marginal, small and medium size of holdings respectively. Among all the holding groups together the per capita per day actual consumption of meat, fish and eggs came out 4 grams against the recommended quantity of 5 grams.

The per capita per day actual consumption of oil and fats has been worked out 10, 11, 15 and 20 grams among the landless, marginal, small and medium size of holdings respectively. Among all the holding groups together the per capita per day actual consumption of oil, fats came out 14 grams against the recommended quantity of 15 grams. The per capita per day actual consumption of sugar and gur has been worked out 11, 13, 15 and 25 grams among the landless, marginal, small and medium size of holdings respectively. Among all the holding groups together the per capita per day consumption of sugar and gur came out 16 grams against the recommended quantity of 13 grams.

The per consumer unit actual consumption of fruits has been worked out 2, 5, 6 and 7 grams among the landless, marginal, small and medium size of holdings respectively. Among all the holdings together the per consumer unit per day actual consumption of fresh fruits came out 5 grams which is equal to the recommended quantity of 5 grams.

The actual composition of per consumer unit per day diet after the implementation of Poverty Alleviation Programmes has been presented in Table 7.5 (b) which clearly reveals that the per consumer unit, per day average consumption of cereals is 526, 532 gms among the landless and marginal households respectively which falls short of the recommended diet of 540 grams, whereas on the small and medium size of holding the per consumer unit per day actual consumption of cereals came out 543 and 553 gms which is higher to the recommended diet.

The per capita per day actual consumption of pulses has been worked out 9, 11, 14 and 19 gms among landless, marginal, small and medium size of holdings respectively. Among all the holdings together the per capita per day actual consumption of pulses came out 13 gms as against the recommended per capita per day consumption of pulses, i.e. 12 gms.

The per capita per day actual consumption of vegetables has been worked out 73, 86, 101 and 118 grams among the landless, marginal, small and medium size of holdings respectively. Among all the holding groups together the per capita per day actual consumption of vegetables came out 94 gms, whereas the recommended per capita per day consumption of vegetables is 99 grams.

The per capita per day actual consumption of milk products has been worked out 72, 87, 102 and 127 grams among the landless, marginal, small and medium size of holdings respectively, whereas among all the households together the per capita per day actual consumption of milk come out 97 grams against the recommended quantity of 80 grams.

The per capita per day actual consumption of meat, fish and eggs has been worked out 2, 3, 4 and 8 grams among the landless, marginal, small and medium size of holdings respectively. Among all the holding groups together the per capita per day actual consumption of meat, fish and eggs came out 4 grams against the recommended quantity of 5 grams.

The per capita per day actual consumption of oil and fats has been worked out 9, 14, 19 and 25 grams among the landless, marginal small and medium size of holdings respectively. Among all the household groups together the per capita per day actual consumption of oil and fats came out 17 grams against the recommended quantity of 15 gms. The per capita per day actual consumption of sugar and gur has been worked out 12, 14, 17 and 25 grams among the landless, marginal, small and medium size of holdings respectively. Among all the holding groups together the per capita per day consumption of sugar and gur come out 17 grams against the recommended quantity of 13 grams.

The per consumer unit actual consumption of fruits has been worked out 3, 5, 9 and 13 grams among the landless, marginal, small and medium size of holdings respectively. Among all the households together the per consumer unit per day actual consumption of fresh fruits came out 7 grams against the recommended quantity of 5 grams.

The value of per consumer unit per day actual consumption of food items among the households before the implementation of Poverty Alleviation Programmes has been presented in Table 7.6 (a) which indicates that the value of per consumer unit per day actual consumption of food items at 2000-01 local prices prevailing in the study area came out Rs. 5.87 for landless households, Rs. 6.47 on marginal size of holding which increases to Rs. 7.23 on the small size of holding group and to 8.43 on the medium size of holding group. On all the holding groups together the value of per consumer per day consumption basket of food items turned out Rs. 6.98. This Table clearly indicates that the per consumer unit per day consumption expenditure on food items go on increasing with an increase in the size of holdings.

The value of per consumer unit per day actual consumption of food items among the households after the implementation of Poverty Alleviation Programmes has been presented in Table 7.6 (b) which indicates that the value of per consumer unit per day actual consumption of food items at 2003-04 local prices prevailing in the study area came out Rs. 7.63, 8.58, 9.72 and Rs. 11.47 among the landless, marginal, small and medium size of holdings respectively. On all the holding groups together the value of per consumer per day consumption basket of food items turned out Rs. 9.33. This Table also reveals the fact that the per consumer unit per day consumption expenditure on food items goes on increasing with an increase in the size of holdings.

7.5 VALUE OF POVERTY INDEX AND THE EXTENT OF POVERTY : A NUTRITION APPROACH

The value of average daily diet composition as suggested by the Indian Council of Medical Research, which provides 2400 calories per consumer unit per day, has been adopted for determining the value of poverty line in the present study. The quantities of food items consumed by each household during the month preceding the survey, have been divided by the number of respective household standard consumer units in order to arrive at the per consumer unit per month consumption of food items. The value of per consumer unit per month consumption basket has been calculated by multiplying the quantities of different food items by their respective prices prevailing in the study area during the period of investigation. The value of per consumer unit per month food items to meet out the minimum calorie requirements (i.e. 2400 calories) before the implementation of Poverty Alleviation Programmes has been worked out Rs. 205.20 at 2000-01 local prices prevailing in the study area. The per consumer unit per month actual consumption expenditure on food items has been worked out Rs. 176.10, 194.10, 216.90 and 252.90 among the landless, marginal, small and medium holdings respectively. Among all the households together the value of per consumer unit per month consumption expenditure on food items came out Rs. 210.00 which is evident from Table 7.7 (a), whereas the value of per consumer unit per month food items to meet out the minimum calories requirements (i.e 2400 calories) after the implementation of Poverty Alleviation Programmes has been worked out Rs. 263.10. The per consumer unit per month actual consumption expenditure on food items has been worked out Rs. 229.00, 257.90, 292.80 and 345.00 among the landless, marginal, small and medium holdings respectively. Among all the holdings together the value of per consumer unit per month consumption expenditure on food items came out Rs. 281.17 which is clear from Table 7.7 (b).

By adopting Rs. 205.20 as the value of poverty index the percentage of poor among landless, marginal, small and medium size of holdings has been worked out 38.19, 30.11, 28.78 and 7.92 per cent. Whereas the overall percentage of poor

TABLE 7.7 (a)

Per Consumer Unit Per Month Consumption Expenditure on Food and Non-Food Items among The Sample Households Before the Implementation of Poverty Alleviation Programmes (At 2000-01 prices)

(Values in Rs.)

Sl. No.	*Items*	*Landless*	*Marginal Holdings*	*Small Holdings*	*Medium Holdings*	*All Holdings*
1.	Food items	176.10	194.10	216.90	252.90	210.00
2.	Non-food Items	82.36	99.38	116.68	160.27	114.64
3.	Food and non-food items	258.46	293.48	333.58	413.17	324.64
4.	Percentage expenditure on food items	68.13	66.14	65.02	61.21	64.69
5.	Percentage expenditure on non-food items	31.87	33.86	34.98	38.79	35.31
6.	Percentage expenditure of non-food to food items	46.76	51.20	53.79	63.37	54.58

TABLE 7.7 (b)

Per Consumer Unit Per Month Consumption Expenditure on Food and Non-Food Items among the Sample Households after the Implementation of Poverty Alleviation Programmes (At 2003-04 prices)

(Value in Rs.)

Sl. No.	*Items*	*Landless*	*Marginal Holdings*	*Small Holdings*	*Medium Holdings*	*All Holdings*
1.	Food items	229.00	257.90	292.80	345.00	281.17
2.	Non-food Items	109.77	134.15	164.67	232.48	160.22
3.	Food items and non-food items	338.77	392.05	4578.47	577.48	441.38
4.	Percentage expenditure on food items	67.60	65.78	64.00	59.74	63.70
5.	Percentage expenditure on non-food items	32.40	34.22	36.00	40.25	36.30
6.	Percentage expenditure on non-food to food items	47.93	52.01	56.23	67.38	56.98

among all the households together came out 31.07 per cent before the implementation of Poverty Alleviation Programmes. Table 7.8 (a) clearly reveals that the percentage of poor is the highest among the landless followed by marginal, small and medium holdings. By adopting Rs. 263.10 as the value of poverty index after the implementation of Poverty Alleviation

TABLE 7.8 (a)
Percentage of Poor by Size of Holdings on the Basis of Per Consumer Unit Per Month Food Expenditure at 2000-01 Prices before Implementation of Poverty Alleviation Programmes

Sl. No.	*Items*	*Landless*	*Marginal Holdings*	*Small Holdings*	*Medium Holdings*	*All Holdings*
1.	Total no. of persons	655.30	633.90	548.60	121.20	1959.00
2.	No. of poor persons	250.30	190.90	157.90	9.6	608.7
3.	Percentage of poor	38.19	30.11	28.78	7.92	31.07

TABLE 7.8 (b)
Percentage of Poor by Size of Holdings on the Basis of Per Consumer Unit Per Month Food Expenditure at 2003-04 Prices after Implementation of Poverty Alleviation Programmes

Sl. No.	*Items*	*Landless*	*Marginal Holdings*	*Small Holdings*	*Medium Holdings*	*All Holdings*
1.	Total no. of persons	655.30	633.90	548.60	121.20	1959.00
2.	No. of poor persons	238.8	178.2	137.8	—	554.8
3.	Percentage of poor	36.44	28.11	25.11	—	28.32

Programmes, the percentage of poor among the landless, marginal and small size of holdings has been worked out 36.44, 28.11, 25.11 per cent respectively. The overall percentage of poor among all the holding groups together came out 28.32 per cent after the implementation of Poverty Alleviation Programmes. The Tables 7.8 (a) and 7.8 (b) clearly reveals that the percentage of poor is the highest among landless households followed by marginal, small and medium size of holdings. It is important to mention here that among the landless, marginal and small households due to high percentage of illiteracy and dependency, meagre household income, lack of gainful employment, uneconomic size of holding and high burden of debt repayment, the percentage of poor is the highest. But contrary to it among the medium size of holding group the percentage of poor is quite low before the implementation of Poverty Alleviation Programmes and is reduced to zero after the implementation of the programmes mainly due to the increased percentage of literacy, low percentage of dependency, higher gainful employment opportunities and sound and regular sources of household income among them.

7.6 VALUE OF POVERTY INDEX AND THE EXTENT OF POVERTY : A NUTRITION PLUS APPROACH

The minimum food requirement is 'necessary' but not 'sufficient' for the existence of mankind. A certain minimum amount of non-food items is equally important for the survival of human beings. In the present study due consideration is given to the non-food items such as light, clothing, footwear, health, education, etc. No specific norms comparable to 'minimum calorie requirement' has so far been suggested by any Government agency or individual scholars for non-food items. Due to variation in the topography, climatic conditions, nature, type and intensity of economic activities carried out, the minimum non-food requirement also varies from country to country and even from region to region within the country. Therefore, in the present study in order to find out the value of poverty index the value of 'minimum non-food requirement' has been worked out by calculating the ratio of total non-food expenditure to food expenditure for the poor. This percentage of non-food expenditure to the minimum food expenditure before the implementation of Poverty Alleviation Programmes came out 46.76, 51.20, 53.79 and 63.37 per cent among the landless, marginal, small and medium farmers respectively. Among all the holdings together this percentage has been worked out 54.58 per cent. Thus the ratio of non-food expenditure to the minimum food expenditure for the poor came out 54.58 per cent before the implementation of Poverty Alleviation Programmes.

The addition of Rs. 111.99 (i.e. 54.58%) as the minimum expenditure on non-food items in the per month value of the food items providing minimum calorie requirements (i.e. 2400 calories per capita per day) determines the value of poverty index in the present study. Thus the value of both minimum food and non-food requirements (i.e. Nutrition Plus Approach), came out Rs. 317.19 (i.e. the value of per capita per month minimum food items Rs. 205.20 plus the value of per capita per month minimum non-food items Rs. 111.99) which is evident from the Table 7.4 (a)

This percentage of non-food expenditure to the minimum food expenditure after the Poverty Alleviation Programmes came out 47.93, 52.01, 56.23 and 67.38 percent among the landless, marginal, small and medium holdings respectively. Among all the holdings together this percentage has been worked out 56.98 per cent. Thus the ratio of non-food expenditure to the minimum food expenditure for the poor came out 56.98 per cent after the implementation of Poverty Alleviation Programmes. The addition of Rs. 149.91 (i.e. 56.98 per cent) as the minimum expenditure on non-food items in the per month value of the food items providing minimum calories requirements (i.e. 2400 calories per capita per day) determines the value of poverty index in the present study. Thus the value of both minimum food and non-food requirements (i.e. Nutrition Plus Approach), came out Rs. 413.01 (i.e. the value of per capita per month minimum food items Rs. 263.10 plus the value of per capita per month minimum non-food items Rs. 149.91) which is evident from the Table 7.4 (b).

TABLE 7.9 (a)

Percentage of Poor by Size of Holdings on The Basis of Per Consumer Unit Per Month Food and Non-Food Expenditure at 2000-01 Prices before Implementation of Poverty Alleviation Programmes

Sl. No.	*Items*	*Landless*	*Marginal Holdings*	*Small Holdings*	*Medium Holdings*	*All Holdings*
1.	Total no. of persons	655.3	633.9	548.6	121.2	1959.0
2.	No. of poor persons	303.9	263.2	171.7	14.2	753.0
3.	Percentage of poor	46.37	41.52	31.29	11.71	38.43

TABLE 7.9 (b)

Percentage of Poor by Size of Holdings on the Basis of Per Consumer Unit Per Month Food and Non-Food Expenditure at 2003-04 Prices after Implementation of Poverty Alleviation Programmes

Sl. No.	*Items*	*Landless*	*Marginal Holdings*	*Small Holdings*	*Medium Holdings*	*All Holdings*
1.	Total no. of persons	655.3	633.9	548.6	121.2	1959.0
2.	No. of poor persons	276.8	230.5	145.4	—	652.3
3.	Percentage of poor	42.24	36.36	26.50	—	33.29

The Tables 7.9 (a) and 7.9 (b) clearly show that by providing due allowances to the non-food items the percentage of poor among landless, marginal, small and medium size of holdings has been worked out 46.37, 41.52, 31.29 and 11.71 respectively before and 42.24, 36.36 and 26.50 per cent among landless, marginal and small size of holdings respectively after the implementation of Poverty Alleviation Programmes.

8

Nature and Extent of Household Savings, Indebtedness and Impact of Anti-poverty Programmes on the Assets, Income, Employment and Consumption

In general the surplus of household income over consumption expenditure results in household savings, which if invested in productive activities, further multiplies the household income. But contrary to it, if the household income falls short of consumption expenditure, it results in household indebtedness which is further multiplied by the high rate of interest, and hence the households fall in the 'debt trap' and thereby in the 'vicious circle of poverty'. The welfare State like that of ours then came forward with income and employment generating programmes for the poor with a view to lift them above the poverty line by raising their income and thereby taking them out of the 'debt trap' as well as the 'vicious circle of poverty'.

This chapter deals with the extent of household savings

(which has been worked out with the help of Current Account Method and Balance Sheet Method) nature, extent, sources and purpose of household indebtedness, impact of Anti-Poverty Programmes on household assets, income, employment, and consumption level of the sample households.

8.1 METHOD OF ESTIMATING HOUSEHOLD SAVINGS

The size of holding-wise savings of the household have been estimated with the help of two methods: (i) by Current Account Method (i.e. by deducting household consumption expenditure from the income reported by the households), and (ii) By Balance Sheet Method. In the asset account of Balance Sheet Method, savings have been computed as the difference between changes in physical and financial assets minus changes in liabilities. Symbolically, gross savings of the households under Balance Sheet Method may be expressed as:

$$S = (\Delta PA + \Delta FA) - (\Delta L + C_t + Cg)$$

where

ΔPA = change in physical assets (acquisitions minus liquidations)

ΔFA = change in Financial assets (Increase minus decrease)

ΔL = change in liabilities (Increase in borrowings minus increase in lending and repayments)

Ct = Net inflow of capital transfers (inflow minus outflow)

Cg = Net capital gains (gains minus losses)

8.2 NATURE AND EXTENT OF HOUSEHOLD SAVINGS: CURRENT ACCOUNT METHOD

According to the Current Account Method per capita per month savings have been worked out by deducting the per capita per month consumption expenditure (i.e. both on food and non-food items) from the per capita per month total income. Table 8.1 clearly indicates that among the landless and marginal size of holdings the per capita per month income falls short of per capita per month consumption expenditure and as a result of it the per capita per month savings turned out negative. The extent of per capita per month negative savings is higher among landless households and lower among the marginal size of holdings. The deficit of income over consumption expenditure is met out by these households by way of taking loans from the local money-lenders as well as by

TABLE 8.1
Per month Household Savings : Current Account Method

(*Value in Rs.*)

Holding Group	*Per consumer unit per month income*	*Per consumer unit per month expenditure*	*Per consumer unit per month savings month*	*Per consumer unit per month burden of debt*
Landless	311.11	338.77	(-) 27.66	122.88
Marginal Holdings	366.83	392.05	(-) 25.22	105.91
Small Holdings	470.27	457.47	(+) 12.8	67.88
Medium Holdings	781.33	577.48	(+) 203.85	54.60
All Holdings	445.42	441.38	40.94	84.65

purchasing day to day consumption items on credit basis. On small and medium size of holdings per capita per month income is higher than the per capita per month consumption expenditure, and as a result of it per capita per month savings turned out positive. The extent of per capita per month savings is higher on medium size of holdings and lower on small size of holdings.

8.3 NATURE AND EXTENT OF HOUSEHOLD SAVINGS: BALANCE SHEET METHOD

The size of holding-wise changes in household physical assets (i.e. acquisitions minus liquidations), changes in financial assets (i.e. increase minus decrease), change in liabilities (i.e. increase in borrowings minus increase in lending and repayments), net inflow of capital transfer (i.e. inflow minus outflow), and net capital gains (i.e. gains minus losses), have been presented in Table 8.2, which clearly indicates that the per household per month savings among landless households and on marginal size of holdings turned out negative i.e (-) Rs. 100.80 and (-) Rs. 60.03. The extent of per capita per

TABLE 8.2
Per Month Household Savings : Balance Sheet Method

Holding Group	ΔPA	ΔFA	$\Delta PA + \Delta FA$	ΔL	Ct	Cg	$\Delta L + Ct + Cg$	$(\Delta PA + \Delta FA)$[5] $(\Delta L + Ct + Cg)$
(1)	(2)	(3)	(4)	(5)	(6)	(7)	(8)	(9)
Landless	261.18	6.94	268.12	94.16	134.62	140.14	368.92	– 100.80
Marginal Holdings	664.48	16.82	681.13	188.52	298.46	254.18	731.16	– 60.03
Small Holdings	918.24	373.62	1291.86	384.62	401.24	326.26	1112.12	179.74
Medium Holdings	1882.42	963.24	2845.66	628.20	735.35	520.82	1884.37	961.29
All Holdings	931.58	340.15	1271.69	323.87	392.41	310.35	1026.63	245.06

Note : ΔPA = Change in Physical assets (acquisitions minus liquidations).
ΔFA = Change in Financial assets (increase minus decrease).
ΔL = Change in Liabilities (increase in borrowings minus increase in lending and repayment).
Ct = Net inflow of capital transfers (inflow minus outflow).
Cg = Net Capital Gains (gains minus losses).

month negative savings is higher among landless households and lower on marginal size of holdings. Whereas on small and medium size of holdings the per capita per month savings have been worked out Rs. 179.94 and Rs. 961.29 respectively, which clearly indicate an increasing tendency in the per household per month savings with an increase in the size of holdings.

8.4 NATURE AND EXTENT OF INDEBTEDNESS AMONG THE SAMPLE HOUSEHOLDS

The source-wise amount and percentage of loans taken by the households falling on different holding groups have been presented in Table 8.3 which clearly indicates that the main sources of borrowings are : banks, co-operative societies, Government schemes under the Poverty Alleviation Programmes, village money-lenders, friends and relatives. Generally the loans taken from the money-lenders have been used by the debtors mainly for unproductive purposes such as for the treatment of illness, consumption purposes, celebrations of birth, death and marriage ceremonies and partly for productive purposes such as purchase of cattle, training and education of children. The loans received under the Anti Poverty Programmes have been used mainly for productive purposes such as purchase of livestock, starting self-employment activities like repair shops and household industries, purchase of cattle. The loans taken from banks and co-operative societies at low rate of interest have been used partly for the construction of cow sheds, repair of residential houses, improvement of land and mainly to pay back the outstanding loans of money lenders. Table 8.3 indicates that the landless and marginal households have received the highest percentage of loans, i.e., 66.44 and 52.31 per cent through the Government Scheme under the Anti-Poverty Programmes, which is advanced at a low rate of interest along with subsidies and have been used by the beneficiaries for productive purposes. The second major source of loan is village money-lenders which constitutes 29.35 and 22.62 per cent among the landless households and on marginal size of holdings respectively. The loans taken from money-lenders at a very high rate of interest have been used mainly for unproductive

TABLE 8.3
Pattern of Household Borrowings among the Sample Households

(Value in Rs.)

Sl. No.	*Sources of Loan*	*Landless*	*Marginal Holdings*	*Small Holdings*	*Medium Holdings*	*All Holdings*
	(1)	*(2)*	*(3)*	*(4)*	*(5)*	*(6)*
I	**Outstanding Loans at the time of Survey**					
	1. Banks	370.27 (4.21)	920.88 (11.71)	1728.33 (29.75)	1522 (30.24)	1135.37 (16.66)
	2. Cooperative Society	126.57 (1.43)	636.76 (8.14)	1925 (33.14)	1826.66 (36.29)	1078.74 (15.83)
	3. Govt. Schemes	5626.85 (63.98)	4399.50 (56.23)	1042.66 (17.95)	705.33 (14.02)	2943.58 (43.19)
	4. Money Lender	2522.22 (28.68)	1739.21 (22.23)	904.66 (15.58)	751.66 (14.93)	1479.43 (21.71)
	5. Others	149.56 (1.70)	126.47 (1.61)	208.00 (3.58)	227.00 (4.51)	177.75 (2.61)
	Total	8795.47 (100.00)	7822.82 (100.00)	5808.65 (100.00)	5032.65 (100.00)	6814.87 (100.00)
II.	**Loan taken during 2003-04**					
	1. Banks	—	120.10 (8.74)	128.53 (9.20)	153.00 (9.17)	100.40 (5.88)
	2. Cooperative Society	—	238.62 (17.36)	353.4 (25.31)	376.66 (22.58)	242.17 (14.19)
	3. Govt. Schemes	1524.3 (63.58)	335.04 (24.37)	311.33 (22.30)	—	540.16 (31.65)
	4. Money Lender	721.06 (30.08)	425.00 (30.91)	402.00 (28.79)	633.33 (37.97)	545.34 (31.96)
	5. Others	152.08 (6.34)	225.98 (18.62)	201.13 (14.40)	505.00 (30.28)	278.54 (16.32)
	Total	2397.44 (100.00)	1374.74 (100.00)	1396.39 (100.00)	1667.99 (100.00)	1706.61 (100.00)
III.	**Amount of Loan paid back**					
	1. Banks	206.43 (9.15)	101.42 (7.77)	141.04 (11.28)	351.00 (24.96)	199.97 (12.86)
	2. Cooperative Society	110.23 (4.88)	108.23 (8.29)	154.55 (12.36)	278.00 (19.77)	162.75 (10.47)

(Contd.)

TABLE 8.3 (Contd.)

(1)	(2)	(3)	(4)	(5)	(6)
3. Govt. Schemes	1213.93 (53.79)	606.22 (46.44)	514.53 (41.15)	452.33 (32.16)	696.75 (44.82)
4. Money Lender	620.97 (27.51)	379.16 (29.05)	322.00 (25.75)	325.00 (23.11)	411.78 (26.49)
5. Others	105.09 (4.66)	110.19 (8.45)	118.26 (9.46)	—	83.38 (5.36)
Total	2256.65 (100.00)	1305.22 (100.00)	1250.38 (100.00)	1406.33 (100.00)	1554.64 (100.00)
IV. Balance of Loan					
1. Banks	163.84 (1.83)	939.56 (11.90)	1715.82 (28.81)	1324.00 (25.00)	1035.80 (14.76)
2. Cooperatives Society	16.34 (0.18)	767.15 (9.72)	2123.85 (35.66)	1925.32 (36.37)	1208.16 (17.21)
3. Govt. Schemes	5937.22 (66.44)	4128.32 (52.31)	839.46 (14.10)	253.00 (4.78)	2789.50 (39.74)
4. Money Lender	2622.31 (29.35)	1785.05 (22.62)	984.66 (16.54)	1059.99 (20.02)	1613.00 (22.98)
5. Others	196.55 (2.20)	272.26 (3.45)	290.87 (4.89)	732.00 (13.83)	372.92 (5.31)
Total	8936.26 (100.00)	7892.34 (100.00)	5954.66 (100.00)	5294.31 (100.00)	7019.39 (100.00)
Per Capita Burden of debt	1474.63	1270.90	814.59	655.23	1015.83

Note : Figures in the Parenthesis indicate the percentage to the column wise.

purposes by the households. The percentage of loans taken from banks is 1.83 and 11.90 per cent among landless and marginal households respectively while from co-operative societies it is 0.18 per cent and 9.72 per cent respectively. The percentage of loans taken from the banks and co-operative societies is less because the procedure of taking loans from banks and co-operative societies is complicated and time-consuming. As a result of it, people avoid these sources of loans. Loans taken from friends and relatives constitute 2.20 and 3.45 per cent among landless and marginal farmers respectively. On the small and medium size of holding groups co-operative societies constitute the highest percentage i.e. 35.66 and 36.37 per cent respectively. This is mainly due to the reason that there is a good network of co-operative societies in Haryana which provide loans to farmers against securities of their lands. Banks constitutes the second major source i.e. 28.81 and 25.00 per cent on small and medium size of holding group respectively. This happened mainly due to high literacy percentage among small and medium farmers. The share of Government schemes in the total loans constitutes 14.10 and 4.78 per cent respectively while of money-lenders is 16.54 and 20.02 per cent on small and medium holding groups respectively. The percentage of loans taken from friends and relatives comes out 4.89 and 13.83 on the small and medium size of holdings, respectively.

Among landless, marginal, small and medium size of holding groups the per capita burden of debt has been worked out Rs. 1474.63, 1270.90, 814.59 and 655.23, respectively which indicates that the per capita burden of debt is higher among the households falling in category of landless and marginal farmers and lower among the households falling on the small and medium size of holdings.

8.5 IMPLEMENTATION OF POVERTY ALLEVIATION PROGRAMMES

This section deals with the implementation of poverty alleviation programmes. Table 8.4 clearly indicates that all the sample households are included under Poverty Alleviation Programmes irrespective of their size of holdings. But the percentage of households who are satisfied with the benefits received under various programme indicates an increasing tendency with an increase in the size of holdings, which came out 67.59, 70.58, 78.66 and 100.00 per cent among the landless, marginal, small and medium size of holding groups respectively, whereas contrary to it the percentage of households dissatisfied with the distribution of benefits indicates a decreasing tendency with an increase with size of holdings which came out 32.41, 29.42, 21.34 and zero per cent for landless, marginal, small and medium size of holding groups respectively. The percentage of household who consider unfair distribution under Anti-Poverty Programmes has been

TABLE 8.4
Implementation of Anti-Poverty Programmes

Sl. No.	Items	Landless	Marginal Holdings	Small Holdings	Medium Holdings
1.	No. of sample households who have been included under Anti-Poverty Programmes	108 (100.00)	102 (100.00)	75 (100.00)	15 (100.00)
2.	No. of Beneficiary households who are satisfied with the distribution of benefits under the Anti-Poverty Programmes	73 (67.59)	72 (70.58)	59 (78.66)	15 (100.00)
3.	No. of beneficiary households who are not satisfied with the distribution of benefits under Anti-Poverty Programmes	35 (32.41)	30 (29.42)	16 (21.34)	—
4.	No. of beneficiary households who considered unfair distribution under Anti-Poverty Programmes	18 (51.42)	17 (56.66)	10 (62.50)	—
5.	No. of beneficiary households who reported non-matching of benefits to their requirements	17 (48.58)	13 (43.34)	6 (37.50)	—

worked out 51.42, 56.66 and 62.50 per cent for landless, marginal and small size of holding group respectively, whereas 48.58, 43.34 and 37.50 per cent households among landless, marginal and small size of holding group respectively reported non-matching of benefits according to their needs and requirements. It is important to mention here that on the medium size of holdings all the households felt satisfied with the distribution of the benefits according to their needs and requirements. It clearly shows that in general the better-off benefited the most and the least better-off benefited the least under the poverty alleviation programme.

8.6 IMPACT OF POVERTY ALLEVIATION PROGRAMMES ON THE HOUSEHOLD ASSETS, INCOME, EMPLOYMENT AND CONSUMPTION

The per household net change in the value of household assets, income, employment and consumption due to the implementation of Anti-Poverty Programmes has been presented in Table 8.5. This Table clearly indicates that the percentage value of household productive assets, percentage increase in household income, percentage increase in employment opportunities and percentage increase in consumption expenditure indicate an increasing tendency with an increase in the size of holdings. The percentage increase in the value of assets has been worked out 7.28, 8.69, 11.43 and 13.93 per cent among landless, marginal, small and medium-size of holding groups respectively whereas the percentage increase in household income account for 11.42, 17.51, 22.39 and 32.18 per cent on these holdings respectively.

TABLE 8.5
Per Household Average Net Change in the Value of Assets, Income, Employment and Consumption due to the Implementation of Anti-Poverty Programmes

(Value in Rs. Employment in Standard Mandays)

Sl. No.	Items	Landless	Marginal Holdings	Small Holdings	Medium Holdings
	(1)	(2)	(3)	(4)	(5)
A.	**Household Assets* (Rs.)**				
A_1	Value of Assets before the implementation of Poverty Alleviation Programmes	50325	90224.26	129781.4	176656
A_2	Value of assets after the implementation of Poverty Alleviation Programmes	54889.7	98069.83	144616.97	201278.54
A_3	Net Change in the value of household Assets ($A_2 - A_1$)	3664.7 (7.28)	7845.57 (8.69)	15835.57 (11.43)	24622.54 (13.93)
B.	**Household Income** (Rs.)**				
B_1	Household income before the implementation of Anti-Poverty Programme	20304.61	23279.51	33703.15	57313.66
B_2	Household income after the implementation of Anti-Poverty Programmes	22624.04	27355.96	41252.43	75757.97
B_3	Net Change in Household Income ($B_2 - B_1$)	2319.43 (11.42)	4076.45 (17.51)	7549.28 (22.39)	18444.31 (32.18)
C.	**Household Employment*** (Standard Mandays)**				
C_1	No. of mandays employed before the implementation of Poverty Alleviation and employment generating programmes	487.36	564.5	814.26	1001.12

(Contd.)

TABLE 8.5 (Contd.)

(1)	(2)	(3)	(4)	(5)
C_2 No. of mandays employed after the implementation of Poverty Alleviation and employment generating programmes	566.67	685.13	1016.59	1299.16
C_3 Net change in Household employment (C_2–C_1)	79.31 (16.27)	120.63 (21.36)	202.33 (24.84)	298.04 (29.77)
D. Household Consumption expenditure (Rs.)				
D_1 Consumption expenditure on food items before the implementation of Poverty Alleviation Programmes	176.1	194.1	216.9	252.9
D_2 Consumption expenditure on food items after the implementation of Poverty Alleviation Programmes	229	257.9	292.8	345
D_3 Net change in expenditure on food items	52.9 (30.03)	63.8 (32.86)	75.9 (34.99)	92.1 (36.41)
D_4 Consumption expenditure on non-food items before the implementation of Poverty Alleviation Programmes	82.36	99.38	116.68	160.27
D_5 Consumption expenditure on non-food items after the implementation of Poverty Alleviation Programmes	109.77	134.15	164.67	231.48
D_6 Net change in expenditure on non-food items	27.41 (33.28)	34.77 (34.98)	47.9 (41.12)	71.21 (44.43)
D_7 Consumption expenditure on food and non-food items before the implementation of Poverty Alleviation Programmes	258.46	293.48	333.58	413.17
D_8 Consumption expenditure on food and non-food items after the implementation of Poverty Alleviation Programmes	338.77	392.05	457.47	577.48
D_9 Net Change in Expenditure on food and non-food items.	80.31 (31.07)	98.57 (33.58)	123.89 (37.14)	164.31 (39.76)

* Household Assets include livestock, buildings, agricultural implement, machinery, khachar rehra, bughi jhota, tonga etc.

** Household income includes income from agriculture and non agricultural sources.

*** Household employment includes employment provided in both agricultural and non-agricultural activities.

The percentage increase in employment in terms of standard mandays, has been worked out 16.27, 21.36, 24.84 and 29.77 per cent among landless, marginal, small and medium size of holdings groups respectively. Due to the implementation of the Poverty Alleviation Programmes the percentage increase in the household consumption expenditure on food items has been worked out 33.03, 32.86, 34.99 and 36.41 per cent among the landless, marginal, small and medium size of holdings respectively, whereas the percentage increase in household consumption expenditure on non-food items came out 33.28, 34.98, 41.12 and 44.43 among the landless, marginal, small and medium size of holdings respectively.

The percentage increase in the household consumption expenditure on food and non-food items has been worked out 31.07, 33.58, 37.14 and 39.76 among the landless, marginal, small and medium size of holding groups respectively. As evident from the Table 8.5, the better-off households falling on larger size of holding groups on account of high literacy percentage, regular and sound sources of household income have been benefited the most and least better off households falling in the category of landless households and on uneconomic size of holdings benefited the least from the implementation of Anti-Poverty Programmes.

9

Summary and Conclusions

Poverty alleviation has been one of the major objectives of the planning process in India since 1951. Ever since the inception of planning, the strategies and programmes are being designed and redesigned, keeping in view the objectives of poverty alleviation. But in spite of the massive development outlays and impressive increase in production recorded in various sectors, the socio-economic status of a vast majority has deteriorated qualitatively. The landless households, marginal and small farmers, agricultural wage earners and casual workers engaged in non-agricultural activities, constitute the bulk of the rural poor. Small land holdings and their low productivity are the main causes of poverty among households dependent on land-based activities for their livelihood. The lower literacy percentage and lack of other vocational skills also perpetuate poverty. Due to poor physical and social capital base, a large proportion of people is forced to continue in the occupations having extremely low levels of productivity as well as income.

One of the most striking experiences of planned efforts in India has been that economically backward regions and economically backward and socially oppressed people, in both developed and backward regions have gained little. The benefits of successive Five Years Plans have passed more to already developed regions. Even within regions, benefits accrued proportionately more to the already rich and socially privileged sections of the society, perpetuating social inequalities and disparities of income and wealth distribution. The benefits of planning have reached only to selected people, which is undesirable from the view point of distributive justice.

The prosperity of an economy depends on the well-being of its inhabitants. Therefore, the primary objective of the development policies in an economy is to achieve growth targets with 'social justice'. The objectives of rural development include sustained increase in the per capita output and income as well as the expansion of productive employment and greater equality in the distribution of the benefits of growth. This implies reducing poverty and the human misery by increasing profitability of the rural poor and providing them greater access to goods and services and also enabling them to take advantage of the safety nets to be provided by the Government. The rural development aimed at target groups must constitute a major part of the development strategy, if larger segment of the poor are to be benefited.

A large number of empirical studies have been conducted on the impact of Poverty Alleviation Programmes on the socio-economic conditions of weaker sections at the national level but a very few attempts have been made in this direction in the State of Haryana. In the present study an attempt has been made to evaluate the impact of Poverty Alleviation Programmes on the socio-economic conditions of the poor in Haryana.

This study has been undertaken in order to achieve the following objectives : (i) to study the income, employment and consumption pattern of the selected households; (ii) to work out the nature and magnitude of unemployment with the help of 'time', 'income' and 'willingness' criterion among the selected households; (iii) to analyse the extent of absolute poverty during the pre and post-anti-poverty programmes implementation with the help of 'Nutrition Plus Approach; (iv) to work out the nature and extent of saving and indebtedness among the sample households; (v) to evaluate the impact of Poverty Alleviation Programmes on the household assets, income, employment and consumption pattern of the selected households; and, (vi) to evolve a set of suggestions for improving the standard of living of the weaker sections in Haryana.

For the present empirical investigation district Yamunanagar has been selected purposely mainly due to the reasons that the area of this district like that of the State as a whole partly falls in the Shivalik Hills and partly in the plain areas, due to which the farm and non-form activities as well as the socio-economic conditions of the weaker sections in this district are more or less the same to that of the state as a whole.Further the inter district-wise percentage of poor varies between 23 to 43 per cent whereas this percentage in Yamunanagar came out 32 per cent. Therefore, both from the topography as well as from the percentage of poor point of view this selected district can represent the economic activities as well as the living conditions of the poor in the State of Haryana as a whole. The district has six developmental blocks viz. Bilaspur, Chhachharauli, Jagadhri, Radaur, Sadhaura and Mustafabad. With the help of multi-stage random sampling a sample of 300 households has been selected from Bilaspur and Sadhaura development blocks. Out of total 300 sample households, 108 landless, 102 marginal, 75 small and 15 fall in the category of medium size of holdings group. The required information, in order to achieve the objectives of the present study, has been collected from the above selected 300 households with the help of a schedule by conducting personal interviews of the informants during the year 2003-04. In the present study the value of minimum nutritional requirements of 2400 calories per consumer unit per day plus the value of minimum non-food items at 2000-01 prices before and at 2003-04 prices after the implementation of Poverty Alleviation Programmes has been taken to estimate the extent of absolute poverty among the selected households. The extent of unemployment has been worked out with the help of 'Time', 'Income', and 'Willingness' Criterion. In order to avoid the overestimation and/or underestimation of the magnitude of poverty among the sample households, the entire population in the study area by size of holdings have been converted into 'standard consumer units' by applying the 'scale of coefficient' suggested by the Nutrition Experts. Among the sample households the total number of 'standard consumer units' have been worked out 1950.0, out of which 655.3 fall among the landless 633.9 on the marginal size of holdings, 548.6 on the small size of holdings and remaining 121.2 fall on the medium size of holding group (Table 4.2).

The different socio-economic indicators which have a direct bearing on the levels of living of the rural people have been empirically analysed in order to find out variations in the pattern of asset distribution, gainful employment opportunities, income and consumption and thereby variations in the levels of living of the sample households. The empirical findings of the present study indicate the average size of family, percentage of family work force and the literacy percentage indicates an increasing tendency, whereas the percentage of dependents shows a decreasing tendency, (with minor fluctuations in between) with an increase in the size of holdings among sample households. The number of 'standard mandays' (by attaching proper co-efficient of efficiency to male, female, children and old persons) have been worked out 436.0, 417.0 , 353.25 and 80.75 among the landless, marginal, small and medium size of holdings respectively. (Table 4.3)

The per household average operated area has been worked out 0.69, 1.52 and 2.80 hectares among the marginal, small and medium size of holdings respectively. Among all the holdings, together the per household area operated came out 1.67 hectares. The percentage of leased-in land came out 7.24, 9.86 and 14.28 per cent on the marginal, small and medium size of holdings respectively. Among all the holdings together this percentage came out 11.97 per cent. The percentage of leased-out land on marginal size of holdings is zero. This is attributed to the fact that due to very small size of holdings the marginal farmers can not afford to lease out their land and they cultivate the land on their own. The percentage of leased-out land increases with increase in the size of holdings. It increased from 1.97 per cent on small size of holding to 3.21 per cent on medium size of holding. The percentage of uncultivated area decreases with an increase in the size of holdings, which has been worked out 17.39, 15.79 and 13.57 per cent on marginal, small and medium size of holdings respectively. The high percentage of uncultivated area on marginal size of holdings is mainly due to the reason that either their land is barren and uncultivable as there is no source of irrigation or the land is a part of a river. The low percentage of uncultivated land on the small size of holdings is mainly due to the lack of alternative regular sources of household income and further the small and medium farmers with large number of dependents can not afford to keep their land uncultivated.

The distribution pattern of household assets (i.e. both productive and household durables) shows that the percentage value of land to the total value of household assets is the lowest on the marginal size of holdings (i.e. 45.38 %) and it shows an increasing tendency with an increase in the size of holdings, i.e. to 65.87 per cent on small and 71.82 per cent on the medium size of holdings. Among all the holdings together this percentage came out 63.70 per cent. The value of livestock, agricultural implements and machinery is lowest among the landless households and it shows an increasing tendency with an increase in the size of holdings. Land, livestock, agricultural implements and machineries used in household cottage industries and transport equipments used for commercial purposes have been treated as the productive assets in the present study.

The percentage value of these productive assets together has been worked out 8.47, 50.45, 71.04 and 77.55 per cent among landless, marginal, small and medium size of holdings respectively which shows an increasing tendency with an increase in the size of holdings. Among all the holding groups together the percentage value of these productive assets came out 69.27 per cent. The percentage value of household durable i.e. furnishing articles, electrical appliances, utensils and beddings etc. to the total value of household assets varies sharply from one holding group to the other. The percentage value of buildings to the total value of household assets has been worked out 76.04, 40.47, 23.14 and 17.74 per cent among landless, marginal, small and medium size of holdings. The percentage value of buildings shows a decreasing tendency with an increase in the size of holdings. It happened mainly because of the fact that the households falling among the landless category and on smaller holding groups due to their uneconomic size of holding and meagre sources of household income have received loans on subsidized rates under Anti Poverty Programmes for the construction of houses, cowsheds, etc. The houses are used by the sample household is entirely for the residential purposes. The percentage value of household durables together to total value of household assets has been worked out 91.53, 49.55, 28.96 and 22.45 per cent among the landless, marginal, small and medium size of holdings respectively. Though the value of household durables in the percentage terms indicates a decreasing tendency with an increase in the size of holdings, but in absolute terms the value of household durables (i.e. household durables and buildings) indicates an increasing tendency with an increase in the size of holdings which has been worked out Rs. 59,574.55, Rs. 10,7027.06, 148364.32 and 193138.65 among the landless, marginal, small and medium size of holdings respectively. The distribution pattern of household assets shows that there exists an unequal distribution of these assets among the different holding groups. The percentage value of land to the total value of household assets is the highest i.e. 63.70 per cent, among all the sample households. The second major household asset is the buildings which accounts for 24.67 per cent. The percentage value of total productive assets came out 69.27 per cent (which is evident from Table 5.8). The per household total value of productive assets viz. land, livestock, agricultural implements, machineries and vehicles indicate an increasing tendency with an increase in the size of holdings. The per household value of buildings and household durables also shows an increasing tendency with an increase in the size of holdings. The per household value of all the household productive assets as well as of household durables has been worked out Rs. 65089.52, 215976.88, 512287.68 and 860238.19 among the landless, marginal, small and medium size of holdings respectively. Among all the holdings together the per household value of household assets came out Rs. 413398.03. Thus, the per household value of the total household assets, (i.e. both household productive assets and household durables) shows an increasing tendency with an increase in the size of holding which is evident from Table 5.8.

The pattern of household total income (i.e. both from agricultural and non-agricultural sources) shows that the percentage share of farm income is the highest on the medium size of holding i.e. 32.17%) as compared to the small (i.e. 22.30%), marginal, (i.e. 16.36%) and medium size of holdings (i.e. 5.49). Among all the holdings together this percentage came out 23.50. This happened mainly due to the reason that the households falling on the medium and small size of holdings make intensive use of their land which is comparatively more fertile. Contrary to it, the households falling on the marginal size of holdings, on account of their uneconomic size of holdings which is generally unproductive and barren they even after their best possible efforts, can not produce food grains even to meet out their domestic needs.

Among the landless households the percentage share of farm income is the lowest. This is due to the reason that as these households do not possess any land of their own, this income totally comes by way of hiring-out their labour in agricultural sector. The percentage share of income earned from livestock activities has been worked out 5.77, 6.63, 9.10 and 11.51 per cent among the landless, marginal, small and medium size of holdings respectively. The percentage share of income earned from livestock activities shows an increasing tendency with an increase in the size of holdings (Table 5.11). The percentage share of household income earned from livestock activities is the lowest among landless and the marginal size of holdings, mainly due to the reason that on account of their smaller size of holdings and meagre household income, they can not afford to keep more cattle. Moreover, most of the cattle they have kept have been received under 'Anti-Poverty Programmes' which are ill nourished, weak and less productive. The percentage share of household income earned from other agricultural sources (i.e. from poultry, fisheries and forestry etc.) to the total household income shows a decreasing tendency with an increase in the size of holdings. The percentage share of agricultural income to the total household income has been worked out 13.77, 24.31, 32.52 and 44.22 per cent among the landless, marginal, small and medium size of holdings respectively. Among all the holdings together this percentage came out 33.99. The percentage share of agricultural income shows an increasing tendency with an increase in the size of holdings (Table 5.11). The percentage share of non-agricultural income earned from services to the total household income has been worked out 16.34, 17.86, 20.56 and 21.34 per cent among the landless, marginal, small and medium size of holdings respectively. The percentage share of household income from services shows an increasing tendency with increase in the size of holdings. This happened mainly due to the higher literacy percentage among the households falling on the larger size of holdings. The percentage share of household income earned from business activities is the highest on the medium size of holdings (i.e. 11.85%) as compared to the small (i.e. 10.08%), marginal (i.e. 8.65%) and landless (i.e. 8.04%).

The percentage share of household income earned from wage work to the total household income has been worked out 42.74, 34.25, 21.72 and 9.28 per cent among the landless, marginal, small and medium size of holdings respectively. The percentage share of household income from wage work is the highest among the landless and shows a decreasing tendency with an increase in the size of holdings. It happened mainly due to reason that these households due to meagre household income, high dependency percentage and higher burden of debt repayment can not afford to remain unemployed and as a result of it, they lay their hands on wage work irrespective of the nature and type of work as well as the wage rate paid to them. Contrary to it, the households falling on the larger holding groups usually get gainful employment on their own farms throughout the agricultural year and, therefore, do not prefer to work on wage basis which they generally consider below their status.

The percentage share of household income earned from household industries which include mainly tailoring, weaving, shoemaking, ban making, basket making, etc. is comparatively high among the landless households (i.e. 13.02%) followed by the household falling on the marginal size of holdings (8.30%) and it shows a decreasing tendency with an increase in the size of holdings i.e. to 6.92 per cent on small and 4.16 per cent on the medium size of holdings. It happened mainly due to the fact that the landless households and households falling on the smaller holding groups, have received financial assistance and skill formation under the self-employment scheme, with a view to supplement their meagre household income. The percentage share of income derived from pension to the total household income as well as the percentage share of income from spouse shows an increasing tendency with the increase in the size of holdings. Similarly the percentage share of household income earned from other sources i.e. religious work, mason, commercial vehicles etc. shows an increasing tendency with an increase in the size of holdings. The percentage share of non agricultural income to the total household income has been worked out 86.23, 75.67, 67.48, and 55.78 per cent among the landless, marginal, small and medium size of holdings respectively, whereas among all the households together, this percentage come out 66.05 per cent. The percentage share of household non-agricultural income to the total household income shows a decreasing tendency with an increase in the size of holding. It happened mainly due to fertile lands, production of commercial crops like sugarcane, on the larger size of holding whereas the households falling on the smaller size of holdings groups and among landless households due to their uneconomic size of holdings, meagre households income, high dependency ratio and higher burden of debt repayment, generally supplement their meagre household agricultural income mainly by way of wage work and partly through other non agricultural sources of household income.

The pattern of household employment shows that the percentage of mandays spent in crop production to the total mandays utilized in different activities, is the lowest among the landless households (i.e. 7.99%) compared to the marginal size of holdings (i.e. 16.67%), small (i.e. 28.32%) and medium size of holdings (i.e. 39.50%), whereas among all the holdings together this percentage came out 26.02 per cent. The percentage of mandays spent in livestock activities is the highest on marginal size of holdings (i.e. 22.78%) as compared to landless households (i.e. 20.10%), small (i.e. 19.30%) and medium (i.e. 16.34%). This happened mainly due to the reason that the landless households as well as households falling on smaller size of holdings due to their uneconomic size of holdings cannot afford to feed the cattle (which have been received by them mainly under Government schemes) at the cattle shed and therefore, they leave the cattle for grazing for most of the time during the day. Further it is observed that during the busy agricultural periods, less mandays are spent per household in looking after the cattle, whereas during lean agricultural seasons, the farmers spent most of their time in looking after the cattle. The percentage of mandays spent in forestry, fisheries and poultry shows a decreasing tendency with an increase in the size of holdings. The percentage of mandays spent in all agricultural activities came out 29.50, 40.42, 48.21 and 56.25 per cent, among the landless, marginal , small and medium size of holdings respectively. Among all the holdings together this percentage came out 45.93 per cent. The percentage of mandays spent in business activities is the highest on the medium size of holdings (i.e 8.90%) as compared to small (i.e. 6.37%), marginal (3.70%) and landless households (i.e. 2.61%). The percentage of mandays spent in wage work is the highest among the landless households (i.e 29.65%), marginal (22.52%), small (i.e. 15.43%) and medium size of holding (i.e 8.76%). Among all the holdings together this percentage came out 17.22 per cent. The percentage of mandays spent in wage work is the highest among the landless households and it decreases with an increase in the size of holdings. This happened mainly on account of the fact that the smallest being poor, are ready to get work, irrespective of nature of work as well as the wage rate paid to them because of the higher dependency and illiteracy percentage. Due to uneconomic size of the holding and meagre income they cannot afford to remain unemployed, whereas, on the larger size of holdings due to higher percentage of literacy, sound and regular sources of income most of the better-off families consider wage work below status. The percentage of mandays spent in household industries is the highest among the landless households (i.e. 5.50%) and it deceases with an increase in the size of holdings.

This happened mainly due to the reason that smaller holding groups have received loans on subsidized rates, training as well as instruments under Anti Poverty Programmes to start their own household industries i.e. mainly weaving, spinning, ban making and shoe making industries in order to supplement their meagre household income. The percentage of mandays spent in services is lowest among the landless households (i.e. 2.52%) and it increases with an increase in the size of holdings, to 3.44%, 6.62% and 8.45% on marginal, small and medium size of holdings respectively. The percentage of mandays spent in other activities mainly religious work, mason work etc. increases with an increase in the size of holdings. The percentage of mandays spent in all the non-agricultural activities has been worked out 41.52, 35.36, 34.03 and 31.39 per cent among the landless, marginal, small and medium size of holdings respectively. The percentage of mandays spent in family affairs, is the highest among the landless households (i.e. 26.08%) and it decreases with an increase in the size of holdings (Table 6.2). The percentage of mandays spent in social affairs has been worked out 2.90, 3.05, 3.10 and 3.25 per cent among the landless marginal, small and medium size of holdings respectively. The percentage of mandays spent in 'necessary activities' to the total mandays spent in all the activities has been worked out 28.98, 24.22, 17.76 and 12.36 per cent among the landless, marginal, small and medium size of holdings respectively. Thus, the percentage of mandays spent in different activities by the sample households clearly indicates that the major proportion of the family human labour mandays is spent in agricultural activities (Table 6.2). The total number of available mandays per household has been worked out 1209, 1224, 1413 and 1614 among landless, marginal, small and medium size of holdings respectively. Among all the holdings together the total number of available mandays comes out 1365.

The percentage of mandays utilized in all the 'agricultural', 'non-agricultural' and 'necessary activities' (i.ę. in both productive and necessary activities) during the year has been worked out 66.00, 73.87, 87.48 and 91.85 per cent among the landless, marginal, small and medium size of holdings respectively. Hence the percentage of unemployed mandays to the full employment norms i.e. of 8 hours a day, 25 days in a month or 300 days in a year according to 'Time 'Criterion' has been worked out 34.00, 26.13, 12.52 and 8.27 per cent among the landless, marginal, small and medium size of holdings respectively, whereas, among all the households together the percentage of unemployed mandays came out 19.04 (Table 6.3). The percentage of mandays available/willing for additional work to the total available mandays has been worked out 38.42, 28.30, 14.23 and 6.79 per cent among the landless, marginal, small and medium size of holdings respectively, whereas, among all the holdings together the percentage of mandays willing for additional work came out 20.70. The percentage of mandays willing for farm work (casual and/or seasonal farm work) shows a decreasing tendency with an increase in the size of holdings, whereas the percentage of mandays willing for non-farm work (mainly services) shows an increasing tendency with an increase in the size of holdings. As a result of it the percentage of voluntarily unemployed mandays has been worked out 1.35 per cent on medium size of holdings whereas, contrary to it, the percentage of mandays willing for over employment came out 4.41, 2.90 and 1.71 among landless, marginal and small households respectively. This clearly confirms the fact that the smallest suffers the most and the least small suffers the least from involuntary unemployment according to 'Willingness Criterion'. The percentage of under employed workers earning less than the minimum desirable monthly income which has been worked out Rs. 413.01 [Table 7.4(b)] in order to meet out the minimum food and non-food requirement of a worker at 2003-04 prices. The number of underemployed workers who are earning less than minimum desirable income, is the highest among the landless households (i.e. 42.24%) as compared to the marginal size of holdings (i.e. 36.36%) and small size of holdings (i.e. 26.50%). Among all the holdings together the percentage of unemployed workers according to 'Income Criterion' came out 33.29 per cent (Table 6.3).

The pattern of household consumption expenditure before and after the implementation of Poverty Alleviation Programme on both food and non-food items shows that the percentage expenditure on food items is the highest among the landless households (ie 68.13% before and 67.60% after the Poverty Alleviation Programmes) and shows a decreasing tendency with increase in the size of holdings, i.e. to 66.4, 65.02. 61.21 per cent before and 65.78, 64.00 and 59.74 per cent after the implementation of Poverty Alleviation Programmes, whereas, among all the households together this percentage came out 64.69 per cent before and 63.70 per cent after the Poverty Alleviation Programmes. Out of total household consumption expenditure on food items, the percentage amount spent on cereals is the highest which has been worked out 61.84, 56.57,

51.59 and 45.22 before and 61.31, 55.08, 49.51 and 42.80 per cent after the implementation of Poverty Alleviation Programmes among landless, marginal, small and medium size of holdings respectively [Tables 7.1(a) and 7.1 (b)]. The percentage share of expenditure on non-food items to the total household consumption expenditure has been worked out 31.87, 33.86, 34.98 and 38.79 per cent before and 32.40, 34.22, 36.00 and 40.26 per cent after the Poverty Alleviation Programmes among the landless, marginal, small and medium size of holdings respectively, whereas among all the holdings together this percentage came out 35.31 per cent before and 36.30 per cent after the implementation of Poverty Alleviation Programmes. The percentage expenditure on food items to the total household consumption shows a decreasing tendency with an increase in the size of holdings. Contrary to it, the percentage expenditure on non-food items shows an increasing tendency with an increase in the size of holdings. Thus, the empirical results of the present study have supported the 'Engel's law of consumption' which states that as the income increases, the percentage expenditure on food items decreases and the percentage expenditure on non-food items increases [Table 7.3(a) and 7.3 (b)].

The per consumer unit per day consumption of cereals has been worked out 519, 524, 534 and 547 gms before and 526, 532, 543 and 553 gms after the implementation of Poverty Alleviation Programmes among landless, marginal, small and medium size of holdings respectively. Among all the holdings together, the per consumer unit per day consumption of cereals came out 531 gms before and 538 gms after the implementation of Poverty Alleviation Programmes against the recommended quantity of 540 grams.

The per consumer unit per day actual consumption of pulses, vegetables and milk has been worked out 11, 91 and 90 before and 13, 94 and 97 gms after the implementation of Poverty Alleviation Programmes, against the recommended quantity of these items i.e., 12, 99 and 80 gms respectively among all the sample households together. The per consumer unit per day consumption of meat, fish and eggs has been worked out 4 gms before and 4 gms after the poverty programmes against the recommended quantity of 5 gms. The per consumer unit per day consumption of oil and fats has been worked out 14 gms before and 17 gms after the implementation of Poverty Alleviation Programmes against the recommended quantity of 15 grams. The per consumer unit per day consumption of sugar and gur came out 16 gms before and 17 gms after the Poverty Alleviation Programmes against the recommended quantity of 13 grams. The per consumer unit per day actual consumption of fruits has been worked out 5 grams before and 7 grams after the Poverty Alleviation Programmes against the recommended quantity of 5 grams. In the present study the value of recommended average daily diet composition has been worked out at 2000-01 prices before and 2003-04 after the implementation of Poverty Alleviation Programmes which provides 2400 calories per consumer unit per day. The value of this diet at 2000-01 prices has been worked out Rs. 205.20 before and Rs. 263.10 after the implementation of Poverty Alleviation Programmes. The actual quantities of food items consumed by each household during the month preceding the survey, has been divided by the number 'standard consumer units' in order to arrive at the per consumer unit per month consumption of food items. The value of per consumer unit per month consumption basket has been calculated by multiplying the quantities of different food items by their respective prices prevailing in the sample area during the year 2000-01 before and 2003-04 after the implementation of Poverty Alleviation Programmes. The per consumer unit per month actual consumption expenditure on food items has been worked out 176.10, 194.10, 216.90 and 252.92 before and 229.00, 257.90, 292.80 and 345.00 after the Poverty Alleviation Programmes among the landless, marginal, small and medium size of holdings respectively. Among all the households together the value of per consumer unit per month consumption expenditure on food items came out Rs. 210.00 before and Rs. 281.16 after the implementation of programmes. [Tables 7.7 (a) and 7.7 (b)]. Thus according to the Nutrition Approach by adopting the value of poverty index i.e. Rs. 205.20 before and Rs. 263.10 after the programmes per consumer unit per month on food items (i.e. 2400 calories per consumer unit per day) as the dividing line between the poor and not poor, the percentage of poor has been worked out 38.19, 30.11, 28.78 and 7.92 among landless, marginal, small and medium size of holdings before and 36.44, 28.11 and 25.11 among landless, marginal and small size of holding groups respectively after the implementation of Poverty Alleviation Programmes. The overall percentage of poor among all the households together came out 31.07 before and 28.32 per cent after the implementation of Poverty Alleviation Programmes (Tables 7.8 (a) and 7.8 (b)). The minimum food requirement is 'necessary' but not 'sufficient' for the existence of mankind. A certain minimum amount of non-food items is equally important for the survival of mankind. In the present study due consideration has been given to the non-food items such as light, clothing, footwear, health, education etc. No specific norm comparable to minimum calorie requirements has so far been suggested by any institution or individual scholar for non-food items. Therefore, in the present study, in order to find out the value of the poverty index, the value of minimum non-food requirements has been worked out by calculating the ratio of non-food expenditure to the minimum food expenditure which came out 46.76, 51.20, 53.79 and 63.37 per cent before and 47.93, 52.01, 56.23, 67.38 per cent after the implementation of Poverty Alleviation Programmes among landless, marginal small and medium size of holding groups respectively. Among all the households together this percentage came out 54.58 before and 56.98 after the implementation of Poverty Alleviation Programmes. (Table 7.7 (a) and 7.7 (b).)

Therefore, the value of poverty index with the help of 'Nutrition Plus Approach' came out Rs. 317.19 (i.e. Rs. 205.20 on food items and 111.99 on non-food items) before and Rs. 413.01 (i.e. Rs. 263.10 on food and Rs. 149.91 on non-food items) after the implementation of Poverty Alleviation Programmes. Thus, all the households who are spending less than Rs. 317.19 before and Rs. 413.01 after the implementation of Poverty Alleviation, Programmes have been considered 'poor' in the present study according to the 'Nutrition Plus Approach'. Therefore, according to this approach the percentage of poor has been worked out 46.37, 41.52, 31.29 and 11.71 per cent before the Poverty Alleviation Programmes among landless, marginal, small and medium holdings respectively and 42.24, 36.36 and 26.50 per cent after the implementation of Poverty Alleviation Programmes among landless, marginal and small size of holding groups respectively. Among all the households together this percentage came out 38.43 per cent before and 33.29 per cent after the implementation of Poverty Alleviation Programmes [Tables 7.9 (a) and 7.9 (b)]. The magnitude of poverty with the help of 'Nutrition Plus Approach' came out higher both before and after the implementation of Poverty Alleviation Programmes as compared to estimates of poverty worked out with the help of 'Nutrition Approach' [(Tables 7.8, (a) 7.8(b), 7.9 (a) and 7.9 (b)]. The value of poverty index after providing due allowances to non-food items turned out higher as compared to the value of poverty index based on food items alone. Therefore, all those studies conducted on poverty by taking into account the food items alone have underestimated the magnitude of poverty.

In the present study the size of holdings-wise household saving have been estimated with the help of 'Current Account Method (i.e. by deducting household consumption expenditure from the income reported by the households) and 'Balance Sheet Method'. In the Balance Sheet Method, savings have been computed as the difference between changes in physical and financial assets minus changes in liabilities. According to Current Account Method per capita per month income falls short of per capita per month expenditure among the landless and marginal households. And as a result of it, the per capita per month saving turned out negative. The extent of per capita per month negative savings is higher among landless households and lower on marginal size of holdings. The deficit of income over consumption expenditure is met out by these households by way of taking loans from the local money lenders as well as by purchasing day-to-day consumption items on credit basis. On the small and medium size of holdings per capita per month income is higher than the per capita per month consumption expenditure and as a result of it the per capita per month savings turned out positive. The extent of per capita per month savings is higher on medium size of holdings and lower on small size of holdings. According to Balance Sheet Method the household saving among landless and on marginal size of holdings too turned out negative (i.e. Rs. 100.80 and Rs. 60.03). The extent of per capita per month negative savings again according to Balance Sheet Method is higher among landless households and lower on marginal size of holdings, whereas on the small and medium size of holdings the per capita per month savings have been worked out Rs. 179.94 and Rs. 961.29 respectively, which clearly indicates an increasing tendency in the per household per month savings with an increase in the size of holdings (Table 8.2).

The outstanding amount of loans includes both principal amount as well as the interest on it. The main sources of loan among the sample households are banks, co-operative societies, Government schemes, money-lenders and other sources like friends and relatives. Generally the loans taken from money lenders have been used by the debtors mainly for unproductive purposes such as for the treatment of prolonged illness, consumption purposes, celebrations of birth, death and marriage ceremonies and partly for productive purposes such as purchase of cattle, training and education of children. The loans received under Anti-Poverty Programmes have been used mainly for productive purposes such as purchase of livestock, starting self-employment activities like shops, household industries etc. The loans taken from banks and co-operative societies at low rate of interest have been used partly for the construction of cow sheds, repair of residential houses, improvement of land as well as to pay back the outstanding loans of money-lenders. The present analysis clearly indicates that the landless and marginal households have received highest percentage of loans i.e. 66.44 and 52.31 per cent through the Government schemes, under the Anti Poverty Programmes, which is advanced at a low rate of interest along with subsidies and have been used for productive purposes. The second major source of loans is village money-lenders which constitutes 29.35 and 22.62 per cent among the landless households and on marginal size of holdings respectively. The loans taken from money-lenders at a very high rate of interest have been used mainly for unproductive purposes by these households. The percentage of loans taken from banks came out 1.83 and 11.90 per cent among the landless and marginal size of holdings respectively. The percentage of loans taken from the banks and co operative societies is less because the procedure of taking loans from banks and co-operative societies is complicated and time consuming as a result of it landless and marginal households avoid these sources of loans. Loans taken from friends and relatives constitute about 2.20 and 3.45 per cent among landless and marginal holdings respectively. On small and medium size of holding groups co-operative societies, constitute the highest percentage of loans i.e. 35.66 and 36.37 per cent respectively. This is mainly due to the reason that there is a good network of co operative societies in Haryana State which provide loans to farmers against securities of their lands. Banks are the second major source of loans, which constitutes 28.81 and 25.00 per cent on small and medium size of holdings. This is mainly due to high literacy percentage among small and medium households. The share of government schemes in the total loans constitutes 14.10 and 4.78 per cent on the small and medium size of holdings. While the share of money-lenders came out 16.54 and 20.02 per cent among small and medium household percentage respectively. The percentage of loans taken from friends and relatives came out 4.89 and 13.83 per cent on the small and medium size of holdings (Table 8.3). Thus in the present study the loans taken under Government schemes is the major source of borrowing which constitutes 39.74 per cent of the total amount of loans. The money lenders account for 22.98 per cent whereas co-operative societies, banks and other sources account for 17.21, 14.76 and 5.31 per cent respectively. The per capita burden of debt has been worked out Rs. 1474.63, 1270.90, 814.59 and 655.23 among the landless, marginal, small and medium size of holdings respectively. Among all the holdings together the per capita burden of debt came out Rs. 1015.83 (Table 8.3).

The above empirical results clearly establish the inter relationship between the value of household productive assets, gainful employment opportunities, household income and the consumption expenditure. Among the landless and smaller size of holdings due to the lack of sufficient productive assets (i.e. mainly land, livestock and machineries), the family human labour days are either unemployed and/or underemployed, which resulted into meagre household income with the help of which they are not even in a position to meet out their minimum food and non-food requirements. Their households income falls short of their consumption expenditure and the deficit is met out generally by taking loans mainly from the village money lenders at high rate of interest. Whereas, contrary to it, the households falling on the larger size of holdings have sufficient productive assets which provide gainful employment opportunities to the family human labour which ensured regular and sound sources of household income with the help of which they can afford to maintain a good standard of living. The income of these households generally exceeds their household consumption expenditure and this surplus of income over consumption expenditure i.e. households savings are generally invested by these household in more productive activities which further push up the future income of these household.

The Anti Poverty Programmes which have been implemented to improve the levels of living of the poorest among the poor first and the poor later on, have proved contrary to the aims and expectations. The fact has been confirmed by the empirical findings of the present study. The percentage of households who are not satisfied with the distribution of benefits is the highest among the smaller size of holdings and it shows a decreasing tendency with an increase in the size of holdings. Further the majority of households falling among the landless and on the smaller size of holding group have pointed out that whatever benefits have been given to them under the Anti-Poverty Programmes are neither fair nor according to their needs and requirements (Table 8.4). It is important to mention here that although the households falling on the medium size of holding group, are not entitled for any benefit under the Anti Poverty Programmes but in the present study some of the farmers falling on the larger size of holding group through pulls and pressures have received the benefits under the programmes and reported to be fully satisfied (i.e. 100%) with the distribution of the benefits under the programmes (Table 8.4). As a result of the wrong selection of beneficiaries, as well as the faulty distribution of assets under the Poverty Alleviation Programmes in the rural areas, the percentage increase in the value of household productive assets is lowest among the landless i.e. 7.28% and is increasing with the increase in the size of holdings i.e. 8.69, 11.43 and 13.93 per cent on marginal, small and medium size of holdings respectively. The percentage increase in income after the implementation of the Poverty Alleviation Programmes also shows an increasing tendency with an increase in the size of holdings i.e. 11.42, 17.51, 22.39 and 32.18 per cent among landless, marginal, small and medium size of holdings respectively. Similarly the percentage increase in the household employment came out 16.27, 21.36, 24.84 and 29.77 per cent among the landless, marginal, small and medium size of holdings respectively. The percentage increase in the consumption expenditure also shows an increasing tendency with an increase in the size of holding group (i.e. 31.07, 33.58, 37.14 and 39.76 per cent among landless, marginal, small and medium size of holding groups). The above empirical findings clearly reveals that the better-off benefited the most and the worst-off benefited the least under the different Poverty Alleviation Programmes.

Thus, it can be concluded from the present empirical study that there exists a lot of inequalities in the distribution of households assets, income and consumption expenditure among the sample households falling on the different holding groups, which resulted in wide variations in the levels of living of the rural households in district Yamunanagar. The better off households are engaged in the gainful activities on their own farms, whereas, the worst off households are suffering from involuntary unemployment and underemployment, the magnitude of which is very high among the landless households and shows a decreasing tendency with an increase in the size of holdings. The per capita burden of debt is highest among the landless households. The loans borrowed by landless households from the money lenders generally used for the unproductive purposes i.e. mainly to meet out the household consumption as well as to celebrate marriage, birth and death ceremonies for which the moneylenders charge exorbitant rates of interests.

It is true that a poor person is born in debt, lives in debt and dies in debt. The Poverty Alleviation Programmes have fallen short of their expectations in the rural areas of district Yamunanagar, because the empirical results of the present study clearly established the fact that through these programmes the better-off benefited the most and the least better-off benefited the least. Therefore, in order to raise the levels of living as well as to reduce the gap between the rich and the poor, the planners, policy-makers and administrators should implement the Poverty Alleviation Programmes more effectively (by ensuring fair selection of beneficiaries as well as distribution of assets as per needs and requirements of the beneficiaries) in the rural area under study in such a way so that the most poor be benefited the most and the least poor be benefited the least. Thus, in order to reduce the incidence of poverty and to raise the levels of living of the poor households through increased availability of productive assets, skill formation and gainful employment opportunities, the planning strategy for development should be judicious mix of beneficiary oriented programmes, human resource development and infrastructure development. Keeping in view the topography and lack of infrastructural facilities in the area under study the emphasis should be placed on the minor irrigation, soil and water conservation, co-operation, rural road and proper implementation of land reforms in the infrastructural sector, drinking water supply, general education, technical and vocational education and health in the social service sector, horticulture, animal husbandry, dairy development, fisheries and forestry in the agricultural sector and small village and cottage industries in the industrial sector. It is only then that the objective of alleviating poverty and raising the level of living of weaker section can be achieved.

Bibliography

A. Books

Adleman, Irma and Robinson, Sherman (1978), *Income Distribution Policies in Developing Countries—A case study of Korea*, Oxford, p. 191.

Ahuja, Kanta (1991), Agricultural Labour and Rural Employment in M.L. Dantwala (ed.), *Indian Agricultural Development Since Independence*, 11th edition, Oxford & IBH Publishing Company, Pvt., Ltd., Bombay, pp. 367-98.

Ali, Mansoor (1979), *Missing Links in Indian Planning*, Light and Life Publishers, New Delhi, pp. 35-381.

Apte, D.P. (1976), *Fifteen Kolaba Villages-Planning for Tribal Development*, (ed.) Ranjit Gupta, Ankur Publishers, New Delhi, pp. 176-81.

Atkinson, A.B. (1975), *The Economics of Inequality*, Oxford University Press, New York, p. 186.

Bannock, G., Bater, R.F. and Rees, R. (1986), *The Penguin Dictionary of Economics*, Penguin Books Limited, Harmandsworth, Middlesex, England, p. 145.

Bhattacharya, Ranjan Vivek (1982), *New Face of Rural India—March of New Twenty Point Programme*, Metropolitan Book Co Pvt. Ltd. Delhi, p. 443.

Bhatti, I.Z. (1974), *Inequality and Poverty in Rural India*, in Poverty and Income Distribution in India (ed.) T.N. Srinivasan and P.K. Bardhan, Statistical Publishing Society, Calcutta, pp. 252-92.

Chopra, Pravesh, K. (2003), *Political Economy of Rural Poverty Alleviation Measures in India: A Micro Level Study of an Indian State*, Wisdom House Academic Books Pvt. Ltd, Panchkula (Haryana).

Dandekar, V.M. and Rath, Nilakantha, (1971), *Poverty in India*, Indian School of Political Economy, Bombay. p. 2.

Department of Economics and Social Affairs (1975), *Poverty, Unemployment and Development Policy*, A Case Study of Selected Issues with Reference to Kerala, United Nations, New York, p. 7.

Desai, Vasant, (1988), *Rural Development*, Vols. I to VI, Himalaya Publishing House, New Delhi, p. 132 (Vol. II).

Deshpande, Vasant (1982), *Employment Guarantee Scheme: Impact on Poverty, Bondage Among Tribals*, Tilak Maharashtra Vidyapath, Pune, pp. 57-66.

Dusenberry, James S. (1967), *Income, Saving and the Theory of Consumer Behaviour*, Oxford University Press, New York, pp. 22-26.

Ghosh, B.N. (1977), *Disguised Unemployment in Underdeveloped countries with Special Reference to India*, Heritage Publishers, New Delhi, p. 90.

Gopalan, C., Ramashastri, B.V. and Balasubramanian, S.C. (1980), *The Nutritive Value of Indian Foods*, The Indian Council of Medical Research, Hyderabad, pp. 10-41.

Gupta, S.P. (1999), *Three Decades of Haryana—A Descriptive Study*, Esspee Publications, Chandigarh, p. 3.

Jain, L.C., Krishnamurthy, B.V. and Tripathi, P.M. (1985). *Grass Without Roots: Rural Development Under Government Auspices*, Sage Publications, New Delhi, pp. 140-41.

Jaiswal, Km. Tripta (1990), *The Socio Economic Status of Scheduled Caste Population in Kalyanpur Block (Distt Kanpur Urban)—A Sample Study of Jeora Village in Schedule Caste and Schedule Tribes in India* (ed.) Dr. B.P. Chaurasia forwarded by Anand Swaroop Jauhari, Chugh Publications, Allahabad, pp. 179-89.

Jalihal, K.A. & Shivanthi, M. (2003), *Pragmatic Rural Development for Poverty Alleviation—A Pioneering Paradigm*, Concept Publishing Company, New Delhi, p. 37.

Joshi, Sandeep (1999), *IRDP and Poverty Alleviation*, Rawat Publications, Jaipur, pp. 187-94.

Kadekod, Gopal and Gregory, Marry 1979), *Income Distribution, Growth and Basic Needs in India,* Vikas Publishing House, New Delhi, pp. 3-4.

Kurian, C.T. (1978), *Poverty, Planning and Social Transformations,* Allied Publishers, New Delhi, pp. 1-2 and 122.

Kurian, C.T. (1986), *Reconciling Growth and Social Justice: Strategies versus Structure,* in M.L. Dantwala, Ranjit Gupta and Keith C.D'Souza (eds.), Asian seminar on Rural Development—The Indian Experience, New Delhi, p. 382.

Mahajan, R.K. (1991), *Integrated Rural Development Programme: A Study of Problems and Prospects in Punjab,* Concept Publishing Company, New Delhi, p. 172.

Mehta, Prakash and Bhardwaj Rattan Chand (1987), *Integrated Rural Development Programme—A Case Study in Himachal Pradesh,* B.R. Publishing Corporation. Delhi, pp. 63-66.

Minhas, B.S. (1974), *Planning and Poor,* S. Chand and Company, New Delhi, p. 7.

Nambiar, A.C.K. (1992), *Rural Poverty: Problems and Prospects,* Ashish Publishing House, Delhi, pp. 9-124.

Parvathamma, C. (1984), *Scheduled Caste and Tribes: A Socio-economic Survey,* Ashish Publishing House, New Delhi.

Patel, M.L. (1975), *Dilemma of Balanced Regional Development,* Progress Publishers, Bhopal, p. 18.

Reddy, G. Ram and Hargopal, G. (1985), *Public Policy and the Rural Poor in India,* Centre for Economic and Social Studies, Hyderabad, p. 238.

Sen, A.K. (1974), *Poverty, Inequality and Unemployment: Some Conceptual Issues in Measurement in Poverty and Income Distribution in India,* (ed.), T.N. Srinivasan and P.K. Bardhan, Statistical Publishing Society, Calcutta, pp. 67-68.

Sen, Amartya (1973), *On Economic Inequality,* Oxford University Press, London, pp. 37-38.

Shapiro, Edward (1984), *Macro Economic Analysis,* Galgotia Publications, New Delhi, p. 32.

Sharma, S.K. (1986), *Chamar Artisans: Industrialization, Skills and Social Mobility,* B.R. Publishing House, New Delhi, pp. 11-162.

Singh, Sukhdev (1994), *IRDP and District Development Role and Implementation of DRDA Schemes,* Deep and Deep Publications, New Delhi, pp. 71-216.

Sundram, K.V. (1981), *Experience of Area Development Planning in India: Alternative Approaches in Rural development in National Policies and Experience,* (ed.), R.P. Mishra, Maruzen Asia, Nagoya Japan, pp. 158-60.

Thakur, Bimla (1991), *Socio-Economic Analysis of the Weaker Sections : A Rural-Urban Comparative Study in Himachal Pradesh,* Daya Publishing House, Delhi, pp. 77-216.

Thakur, Dalip, S. (1985), *Poverty, Inequality and Unemployment in India: Some Conceptual and Methodological Issues in Measurement,* B.R. Publishing Corporation, New Delhi, pp. 224-41.

Yadav, K.C. (2002), *Modern Haryana—History & Culture, 1803-1966,* Manohar Publishers, Delhi, pp. 15-16.

B. Journals

Ali, Sayed, (1998), Income and Employment Generation Through IRDP: An Analysis, *Kurukshetra,* Vol. 46, No. 10, New Delhi.

Bagchee, Sandeep (1987), Poverty Alleviation Programmes in Seventh Plan, *Economic and Political Weekly,* Vol. XXII, No. 4, Bombay, p. 146.

Bose, S.C. (1986), Planning for Tribal Development: Kerala's experience, *Yojana,* Vol. 30, No. 5, New Delhi, pp. 21-23.

Chandakavate, M.S. (1985), Tardy Implementation of IRDP, *Yojana,* Vol 29, No. 19, New Delhi, p. 14.

Chaturvedi, Y.S., Naidu, K.K. and Sridhar, M.J. (1988), Beneficiaries of IRDP in Gujarat, *Kurukshetra* , Vol. XXXVI, No. 12, New Delhi, p. 27.

Claus, H.R.H., Prince (1991). One World and Many, *Development Journal of the Society for International Development,* Rome, No. 2.

Dasgupta, K.R. (1997), Rural Development Programme in India: Concepts and Strategies, *Kurukshetra,* Vol. XLV, No. 11, New Delhi.

Dogra, Bharat (1986), Victims of Poverty Alleviation, *Economic and Political Weekly,* vol. XXI, No. 28, Bombay, p. 1193.

Gopal, G. Hara, And Bala Ramulu, C.H. (1989), Poverty Alleviation Programme: IRDP in Andhra Pradesh District, *Economic and Political Weekly,* Vol. XXIV, Nos. 35-36, Bombay, p. 2031.

Gupta, Dipankar (1986), Tribal Development in a West Bengal District: Programmes, Structure and Process, *Economic and Political Weekly*, Vol. XXI, No 1, Bombay, pp. 35-45.

Hirway, Indira (1988), Planning for Poverty Eradication in Rural Areas: An Observation, *Kurukshetra*, Vol. XXXVI, No. 7, New Delhi.

Jha, Raghbendra (2000), Growth, Inequality and Poverty in India—Spatial and Temporal Characteristics, *Economic and Political Weekly*, Vol. XXXV, No. 11, Bombay, pp. 921-28.

Jose, A.M. (1989), IRDP and Employment Generation for Women: A Micro Level Study in Kerala, *Man and Development*, Vol. XI, No. 2, Chandigarh, p. 15.

Krishna, Raj (1973), Unemployment in India, *Indian Journal of Agricultural Economics*, Vol. 28, No. 1, Bombay, pp. 1-6.

Kaur, Malkit, Aggarwal Kusum and Kharuta, Sushil (1986), Poverty Alleviation Programmes in Haryana, Need for a New Strategy, *Indian Journal of Agricultural Economics*, Vol. 41, No. 4, Bombay, p. 662.

Khatkar, R.K. (1986), An Impact Study of Integrated Rural Development Programmes in Mahendragarh district of Haryana, *Indian Journal of Agricultural Economics*, Vol. 41, No. 4, Bombay, p. 658.

Kulkarni, G., Batta, Ram Chandra and Kumar, N. Ganesh (1989) Integrated Rural Development in Bijapur—An Evaluation of Dairy Scheme, *Social Change*, Vol. 19, No. 89, New Delhi, p. 78.

Kumar, A.V. (1992), Impact of IRDP on Income Employment: A Case Study, *Yojana*, Vol. 35, No. 24, New Delhi, pp. 17-18.

Malyadri. (1988), Financing Pig Farming: A Study, *Kurukshetra*, Vol. XXXVII, No. 3, New Delhi, p. 22.

Malyadri, P. (1986), Success of IRDP; Myth or Reality, *Khadigramodyog*, Vol. XXXII, No. II, Bombay, pp. 11 and 31.

Mishra, Sibranjan (1986), Rural Development : A Challenge Before IRDP, A Fresh Look, *Indian Journal of Agricultural Economics*, Vol. XLI, No. 4, Bombay, p. 656.

Mundinanani, P.S. (1983), Regional Disparities in India, *Yojana*, Vol. 27, No. 19, New Delhi, pp. 3-4.

Mundra, S.N. and Kothari, Kusum (2002), *Indian Journal of Extension Education*, Vol. XXVIII, Nos. 1 and 2.

Mukherjee, Neela (1990), Lessons of Poverty Alleviation Programmes, *Yojana*, Vol. 34, Nos. 14 & 15, New Delhi, pp. 37-40.

Nayak, V. and Prasad, S. (1984), Levels of Living of Scheduled Caste and Scheduled Tribes, *Economic and Political Weekly*, Vol. 19, No. 30, Bombay, pp. 1205-13.

Noorbasha, Abdul, Dakashinamurthy, D. (1983), Rich Farmers Grab All Benefits Leaves Poor Farmers in the Lurch, *Yojana*, Vol. 27, No. 13, New Delhi, p. 23.

Ojha, P.D. (1970), A Configuration of Indian Poverty: Inequality and Levels of living, *Reserve Bank of India Bulletin*, Vol. 24, Bombay, pp. 16-27.

Paul, Mohinder (1989), Composition and Distribution of Income Among Rural Households in Haryana, *Margin*, Vol. 21, New Delhi, pp. 62-76.

Prasad, Kamta (1986), Planning for Alleviation of Poverty in India: Experience and lessons, *Social Change*, Vol. 16, Nos. 2 and 3, New Delhi, pp. 68-75.

Rajshekharan, M.V. (1989), Does IRDP Need Revamping, *Kurukshetra*, Vol. XXXVIII, No. 2, New Delhi, pp. 13-16.

Rao & Natraja, R. (1988), IRDP Assistance in Andhra Pradesh: an Evaluation, *Kurukshetra*, Vol. XXXVI, No. 6, New Delhi, p. 29.

Rao, S.K. (1983), A Note on Measuring Distances Between Regions in India, *Economic and Political Weekly*, Vol. 8, No. 17, Bombay, p. 793.

Rao, V.M. and Erappa, S. (1987), IRDP and Rural Diversification—A Study in Karnataka, *Economic and Political Weekly*, Vol. 22, No. 52, Bombay, pp. A151-160.

Satyanarayan and Peter, Y.J. (1985), Rural Development: An Appraisal, *Kurukshetra*, Vol. XXXVIII, No. 7, New Delhi, pp. 24-25.

Sharma, M.L, Dak, T.M. and Verma, O.P. (1989), IRDP Retrospect and Prospect, *Kurukshetra*, Vol XXXVIII, No. 2, New Delhi, pp. 18-19.

Sharma, P.N. (1978), Planning for the Poor, *Kurukshetra*, Vol. 26, No. 19, New Delhi, pp. 13-21.

Sinha, Chakradhar and Singh, Jivitesh Kumar (1981), Removal of Poverty and SFDA: A Case Study, *Social Change*, New Delhi, p. 14.

Singh, Jasbir K. and Deb, P.C. (1986), People's participation in integrated Rural Development Programme, *Guru Nanak Journal of Society*, Vol. 6, No. 2, Amritsar, p. 77.

Singh, R.R. (1987), Poverty Alleviation: Problems and Prospects, *Khadigramodyog*, Bombay.

Subbarao, K. (1985), Regional Variations in Impact of Anti-Poverty Programmes—A Review of Evidence, *Economic and Political Weekly*, Vol. XX, No. 43, Bombay, pp. 1830-34.

Tewari, Rajendra N. (1985), Is IRDP Lacking Thrust? *Yojana*, Vol. 29, No. 20, New Delhi, pp. 18-19.

Thippaiah, P. (1986), Tackling Rural Poverty, *Yojana*, Vol. 30, No. 22, New Delhi, p. 15.

Tulsyan, S.L. (1987), Why Poverty Hangs On? *Yojana*, Vol. 31, No. 17, New Delhi, p. 19.

Yadav, Hanumant and Mishra, C.S. (1980), Impact of the Tribal Development Programmes of Employment, Income and Asset Formation in Bastar District of Madhya Pradesh, *Indian Journal of Agricultural Economics*, Vol. XXXV, No. 4, Bombay, pp. 69-73.

Zaidi, Nassem, A. (1985), Has IRDP Alleviated Poverty?, *Yojana*, Vol. 229, No. 18, New Delhi, p. 9.

C. Reports

Agricultural Finance Corporation Limited, (1984), *Concurrent Evaluation and Impact Study of IRDP in Rohtak District (Haryana)*, Bombay.

Bhatti, J.P. (1976), *A Study of Incomes Savings and Investment Pattern in Agriculturally Progressive Areas of Himachal Pradesh, Kangra District*, Agro-Economic Research Centre, Shimla (Mimeo), pp. 93-95.

Desai, Mahendra P. (1974), *Problems of low Income Sections in Rural Areas in Rural Development for Weaker Section*, Seminar Series—XII, Indian Society of Agricultural Economics, Bombay, pp. 58-59.

District Credit Plan, Yamunanagar (2004), Punjab National Bank, Chandigarh, pp. 5-97.

Food and Agricultural Organization (1977), *Population and Agricultural Development*, Rome.

Gupta, A.K. and Aggarwal, B.K. (1980), *Socio-Economic Impact of Marginal Farmers and Agricultural Labourers Agencies and the Rural Poor,* Annual Research Report, 1980-81, Deptt. of Eco-Sociology, PAU, Ludhiana, p. 58.

Haryana, Government of (1966), *Development Committee Report,* p. 46.

Haryana, Government of (1984), *Report on Concurrent Evaluation of IRDP Works—District Bhiwani,* (National Productivity Council), Chandigarh.

Haryana, Government of (1987), Evaluation Study of IRDP in Haryana; (Economic and Statistical Organization), Chandigarh.

Haryana, Government of (2001), (Directorate of Census Operations), *Census of India,* Series 7, Paper -2, Chandigarh, pp. 91-164.

Haryana, Government of (2001), (Directorate of Census Operations), *Census of India,* Series 7, Paper—3, Chandigarh, p. 18.

Haryana, Government of (April, 2002), (Directorate of Industries), *Udyog Yug,* Chandigarh, p. 21.

Haryana, Government of (2004), (Economic and Statistical Organization), *Statistical Abstract of Haryana,* Chandigarh, p. 63.

Haryana, Government of (2005), (Economic and Statistical Organization), *Economic Survey of Haryana,* Chandigarh, pp. 1-112.

Haryana, Government of (2005), (Economic and Statistical Organization), *Statistical Abstract of Haryana,* Chandigarh, pp. 14-772.

Haryana, Government of (2007), (Economic and Statistical Organisation), *Economic Survey of Haryana* (2006-07), Chandigarh, pp. 1-126.

Haryana, Government of (2007), (Economic and Statistical Organization), *Statistical Abstract of Haryana,* Chandigarh.

Himachal Pradesh, Government of (Planning Department), (2002), An Evaluation Study on IRDP in Himachal Pradesh, 1992-97, Shimla, pp. 26-73.

Hisar, *District Gazetteer,* (1915), pp. 16-17.

India, Government of (1970), *Report of the Committee of Experts on Employment Estimates,* (Planning Commission), New Delhi.

India, Government of (2001), (The Ministry of Rural Development), *All India Report on Concurrent Evaluation of Indira Awas Yojana, 1989-1999,* New Delhi.

India, Government of (1953), *First Five Year Plan, (People's edition),* New Delhi, p. 1.

India, Government of (1956), *Second Five Year Plan, 1956-51* (Planning Commission), New Delhi, pp. 22 & 26.

India, Government of (1957) , *Review of First Five Year Plan 1956-61,* (Planning Commission), New Delhi, pp. 1-8.

India, Government of (1961), *Third Five Year Plan, 1961-66,* (Planning Commission), New Delhi, pp. 1 & 2, 10.

India, Government of (1966), *Punjab Boundary Commission Report,* Para 136, Point 3, p. 49.

India, Government of (1969) *Fourth Five Year Plan, 1969-74,* (Planning Commission), New Delhi, pp. 15-17.

India, Government of (1972), *Towards an Approach to Fifth Plan, 1969-74,* (Planning Commission), New Delhi, p. 7

India, Government of (1978), *Draft Five Year Plan, 1978-83,* (Planning Commission), Vol. II. New Delhi, p. 36.

India, Government of (1980), *Sixth Five Year Plan, 1980* (Planning Commission), New Delhi, p. 34.

India, Government of (1980), *Sixth Five Year Plan, 1980-85,* (Planning Commission), New Delhi, p. 51.

India, Government of (1985), *Evaluation Reports on Integrated Rural Development Programme,* (Planning Commission), PEO, New Delhi.

India, Government of (1985), *Seventh Five Year Plan, 1985-90,* (Planning Commission), New Delhi, p. 4.

India, Government of (1987), *An Evaluation Report on Provisions of House Sites-cum-House Construction Assistance to the Rural Landless Labour Households,* (Planning Commission, PEO), New Delhi.

India, Government of (1990), (Ministry of Agriculture, Department of Rural Development), *Concurrent Evaluation of IRDP. The main findings of survey for January 1989-September 1989,* New Delhi, pp. VII to X.

India, Government of (1992), *Eighth Five Year Plan, 1982-87,* (Planning Commission), Volume II, New Delhi, p. 36.

India, Government of (1992), *Jawahar Rozgar Yojana—A Quick study for 1991-92,* (Planning Commission, Programme Evaluation Organization), New Delhi, pp. 3-61.

India, Government of (1993), Planning Commission, *Report of the Expert Group on Estimation of Proportion and Number of Poor.*

India, Government of (1997), *Ninth Five Year Plan, 1997-2000* (Planning Commission), Volume I, New Delhi, p. 29.

India, Government of (1997), *Ninth Five Year Plan, 1997-2002,* (Planning Commission), Volume II, New Delhi, p. 2.

India, Government of (2001), Planning Commission, *National Human Development Report.*

India, Government of (2003), *Tenth Five Year Plan, 2002-07,* (Planning Commission), Vol. I, New Delhi, pp. 294-302.

India, Government of (Ministry of Textile) and Craft Council Haryana, Faridabad (2003), *Craft of Haryana,* New Delhi, p. 1.

India, Government of (2005), *Himachal Pradesh Development Report* (Planning Commission), New Delhi, p. 390.

India, Government of (December 2006), Planning Commission, Towards Faster and More Inclusive Growth, An Approach to the Eleventh Five Year Plan, New Delhi, p. 71.

India, Government of (2007), Planning Commission, *Press Information Bureau Release,* New Delhi.

India, Government of (2007), the United Progressive Alliance, Report to the People, 2004-07, New Delhi, pp. 10-32.

India, Government of (2000), *Evaluation Study on Employment Assurance Scheme,* (Planning Commission, Programme Evaluation Organization), New Delhi, pp. I to XIV.

National Council of Applied Economic Research (1970), p. 1.

Patiala, State Bank of (1987), *Financing under Integrated Rural Development Programme: An Evaluation Study,* Patiala, p. 7.

Punjab Boundary Commission Report (1966), Para 136, Point 3, p. 49.

United Nations, Economic and Social Commission for Asia and Pacific, ESCAP (1985), *The Rural Poor,* Bangkok, pp. 2-3.

Index